PRACTITIONER'S GUIDE TO EMPIRICALLY BASED MEASURES OF SCHOOL BEHAVIOR

AABT CLINICAL ASSESSMENT SERIES

Series Editor

Sharon L. Foster
California School of Professional Psychology, San Diego, California

---

PRACTITIONER'S GUIDE TO EMPIRICALLY BASED MEASURES OF ANXIETY
Edited by Martin M. Antony, Susan M. Orsillo, and Lizabeth Roemer

PRACTITIONER'S GUIDE TO EMPIRICALLY BASED MEASURES OF DEPRESSION
Edited by Arthur M. Nezu, George F. Ronan, Elizabeth A. Meadows, and Kelly S. McClure

PRACTITIONER'S GUIDE TO EMPIRICALLY BASED MEASURES OF SCHOOL BEHAVIOR
Edited by Mary Lou Kelley, George H. Noell, and David Reitman

---

A Continuation Order Plan is available for this series. A continuation order will bring delivery of each new volume immediately upon publication. Volumes are billed only upon actual shipment. For further information please contact the publisher.

PRACTITIONER'S GUIDE TO EMPIRICALLY BASED MEASURES OF SCHOOL BEHAVIOR

Edited by

Mary Lou Kelley
Louisiana State University
Baton Rouge, Louisiana

George H. Noell
Louisiana State University
Baton Rouge, Louisiana

and

David Reitman
Nova Southeastern University
Fort Lauderdale, Florida

Kluwer Academic / Plenum Publishers
New York Boston Dordrecht London Moscow

Library of Congress Cataloging-in-Publication Data

Practitioner's guide to empirically based measures of school behavior/edited by Mary Lou Kelley, David Reitman, George H. Noell.
p. cm. — (AABT clinical assessment series)
Includes bibliographical references and index.
ISBN 0-306-47267-8
I. Clinical child psychology. 2. Developmental psychology. I. Kelley, Mary Lou. II. Noell, George. III. Reitman, David. IV. Series.

RJ503.3 .P735 2002
618.92′89—dc21

2002028274

ISBN 0-306-47267-8

233 Spring Street, New York, New York 10013

http://www.wkap.nl/

10 9 8 7 6 5 4 3 2 1

A C.I.P. record for this book is available from the Library of Congress.

Printed in the United States of America

Contributors

Editors

Mary Lou Kelley • Department of Psychology, Louisiana State University, Baton Rouge, Louisiana 70803

George H. Noell • Department of Psychology, Louisiana State University, Baton Rouge, Louisiana 70803

David Reitman • Center for Psychological Studies, Nova Southeastern University, Fort Lauderdale, Florida 33314

Additional Reviewers

Aaron A. Clendenin • Department of Psychology, Louisiana State University, Baton Rouge, Louisiana 70803

Rebecca Currier • Department of Psychology, Louisiana State University, Baton Rouge, Louisiana 70803

Gary Duhon • School of Applied Health and Educational Psychology, Oklahoma State University, Stillwater, Oklahoma 74078-4042

Kristin A. Gansle • Department of Social Work, Louisiana State University, Baton Rouge, Louisiana 70803

Kellie A. Hilker • Department of Psychology, Louisiana State University, Baton Rouge, Louisiana 70803

Stephen D. A. Hupp • Department of Psychology, Southern Illinois University, Edwardsville, Illinois 62026

Nichole Jurbergs • Department of Psychology, Louisiana State University, Baton Rouge, Louisiana 70803

Nicole Francingues Lanclos • Department of Psychology, Louisiana State University, Baton Rouge, Louisiana 70803

Monique M. LeBlanc • Department of Psychology, Louisiana State University, Baton Rouge, Louisiana 70803

Molly A. Murphy • Department of Psychology, Louisiana State University, Baton Rouge, Louisiana 70803

Patrick M. O'Callaghan • Department of Psychology, Louisiana State University, Baton Rouge, Louisiana 70803

Kathy Ragsdale • Department of Psychology, Louisiana State University, Baton Rouge, Louisiana 70803

Shannon Self-Brown • Department of Psychology, Louisiana State University, Baton Rouge, Louisiana 70803

Sara E. Sytsma • Department of Psychology, Louisiana State University, Baton Rouge, Louisiana 70803

Joy H. Wymer • Department of Psychology, Louisiana State University, Baton Rouge, Louisiana 70803

Preface

Children's display of unacceptable behavior in the school setting, school violence, academic underachievement, and school failure represent a cluster of problems that touches all aspects of society. Children with learning and behavior problems are much more likely to be unemployed, exhibit significant emotional and behavior disorders in adulthood, as well as become incarcerated. For example, by adolescence, children with Attention Deficit Hyperactivity Disorder are more likely to be retained a grade, drop out of school, have contact with the law, or fair worse along a number of dimensions than their unaffected siblings (Barkely, 1998). Identification, assessment, and treatment of children with externalizing behavior problems and learningdisabilities is critical to optimizing development and prevention of relatively intractable behavioral and emotional problems in adulthood. For example, poor interpersonal problem solving and social skills excesses and deficits are strongly associated with poor outcome in adolescence and adulthood. The school is where children learn essential academic, social, and impulse control skills that allow them to function effectively in later years. School is where problems in these areas can be most easily identified and addressed.

The purpose of this book is to provide an overview of assessment practices for evaluating children's externalizing behavior problems exhibited in the school environment. Reviews of approximately 100 assessment devices for measuring children's externalizing problems are included. Instruments include structured interviews, rating scales, and observational methods. As rating scales are the primary assessment type supported by statistical studies, they are emphasized in the portion of the book that reviews measures. To complement this necessary emphasis on rating scales, we are including chapters on functional assessment and curriculum-based assessment, both of which emphasize direct assessment of behavior and the environmental contingencies maintaining behavior. These methods are "state of the art" in school psychology and certainly should be familiar to anyone assessing children's behavior in the school setting. Thus, this volume, is an attempt to present a broad, integrative assessment perspective in which evaluation of children's behavior can take many forms depending on the assessment question; however, our emphasis is on answering the ultimate assessment goal, helping children experience competency in the school setting.

Chapter 1 provides an overview of issues relevant to the assessment of children's externalizing behavior problems in the school environment. These issues include purposes of assessment, methods of assessment including multi-informant/multi-method assessment, laws affecting assessment practices, and reimbursement issues. Chapter 2 presents information on diagnostic issues relevant to children's behavior problems in the classroom. This includes discussion of traditional diagnostic classification using the DSM-IV, as well as utilization of functional assessment methods. Functional assessment methods emphasize identifying the function of the behavior with regard to reinforcement contingencies. Chapter 3 expands upon Chapter 2 by presenting specific methodologies for conducting functional assessments of children's behavior problems in the school setting. Functional Behavioral Assessment (FBA) entails identifying environmental factors that maintain or suppress an individual's behavior and links assessment findings to treatment. Chapter 3 provides legal, ethical, and clinical rationales for utilizing FBA in the school setting. Chapter 4 describes Curriculum-Based Measurement (CBM) which is hallmarked as "best practice" for measuring academic skill level. Curriculum-based assessment (CBM), in contrast, measures the student's rate of correct responding on standardized tasks that are representative of the client's curriculum. CBM assesses the client's skill level with regard to the curriculum in which he is placed and can be used to measure reading, mathematics, and written expression skills by behaviorally oriented school psychologists. CBM serves as an alternative to traditional, norm referenced approaches to academic assessment. Norm-referenced assessment, which is characterized by the majority of the assessment instruments reviewed in the latter portion of this volume, leads to assigning a client a position within a normative distribution. For example, most rating scales provide standard scores and percentile rankings which indicate the degree to which the individual differs from the average person in the standardization sample. CBM more closely leads to treatment and assesses the client from within the environment that learning is to take place. Although our focus in on the assessment of externalizing behavior problems, inadequate academic skill relative to the curriculum in which the child is placed is closely associated with displays of negative behavior and therefore is emphasized in the text.

The final portion of the volume provides reviews of measures for assessing children's behavior problems in the school setting. The potential measures for inclusion far exceeds the allotted space. Therefore, the following guidelines were used:

1. The instrument must focus on behavioral or interpersonal problems evidenced in the school environment. In a few cases, we included measures that appeared to have direct relevance to school behavior problems such as measures of aggression.
2. The most comprehensively covered measures are those with the highest degree of reliability and validity supporting the instrument.
3. Norm reference measures of cognitive or academic functioning are not reviewed. Nor are laboratory measures of attention reviewed given their inconsistent relationship to classroom behavior.
4. All measures reviewed must be available in English and have psychometric studies supporting the reliability and validity of the instrument.

All reviews describe the purpose of the instrument, the population for which it was intended, a description of the instrument and administration, scoring guidelines, psychometric properties of the instrument, and general strengths and limitations. Information for obtaining the instrument is provided as well. The volume ends with a glossary of all major terms used in the volume including those used in this preface.

Mary Lou Kelley
Louisiana State University
Baton, Rouge, LA

Contents

Introduction

Mary Lou Kelley

BACKGROUND

The prevalence of children who manifest behavioral and academic problems in the school setting represent a vast source of referral for mental health and school professionals as well as medical personnel. The assessment and treatment of children with Attention Deficit Hyperactivity Disorder (ADHD), for example, has received tremendous media attention with continued confusion as to what constitutes the diagnosis and how it is best treated. The use of well-normed instruments that assess the presence of symptoms and associated problems across environments and caretakers is clearly the recommended practice (Barkley, 1998; Robin, 1998). The American Academy of Pediatrics has recognized ADHD as a chronic and prevalent condition that must be assessed using standardized instruments that document that the child meets the DSM-IV and associated problems (AAP, 2000). Likewise Oppositional Defiant Disorder and Conduct Disorder are commonly evidenced in school-aged children and the behaviors often are manifested in the classroom setting. Complicating the clinical manifestation of externalizing behavior problems in the school setting, is the common presence of academic skill or performance deficits that must be addressed in the assessment and treatment of children.

The purpose of this book is to provide clinicians and researchers with a compendium of instruments for assessing childrens' and adolescents' externalizing or attentional problems in the school setting. Although the primary focus is on the evaluation of problems manifested in the school setting, many instruments reviewed are multi-informant and intended for the comprehensive assessment of children across settings. The instruments reviewed here primarily assessed children's externalizing behavior problems in the school setting. However, we included some measures that may be related to externalizing behavior such as measures of social skills and self-concept. All measures reviewed have psychometric support and are standardized. We did not include measures of academic or cognitive functioning. Although we made an attempt to obtain all norm based instruments related to the assessment of children's school related behavior problems, sometimes we simply could not get the author or publisher to reply

Mary Lou Kelley • Department of Psychology, Louisiana State University, Baton Rouge, Louisiana 70803 or could not locate the author of the measure. We may have overlooked some measures. Thus, this compilation is comprehensive but not exhaustive.

The contemporary assessment of children's behavior problems has moved away from emphasis on interview and questionnaire data. Instead, the emphasis is on functional assessment of children within the classroom setting. Functional assessment refers to identifying the function of the behavior with regard to reinforcement contingencies. Given the importance of this approach, Dr. George Noell, a leader in the field, has written a chapter on functional assessment methods. He also wrote a chapter on curriculum based assessment which refers to the students' rate of correct responding on standardized tasks that are representative of the clients' curriculum. This chapter was included given the attention this approach to academic assessment is emphasized in the School Psychology literature as best practice. It serves as an alternative to, or augmentation of, norm based academic testing. The chapter was included given the frequency of academic skill deficit in children with externalizing behavior problems displayed in the school setting.

STRUCTURE OF THE BOOK

The book is organized into two sections. The first section presents four chapters on the assessment of children. Following measures are reviewed which are presented in alphabetical order. Measures are summarized in a grid preceding the reviews. The grid presents the title of the measure, general purpose, population for its intended use, respondents (i.e., teacher, parent, student), administration time, norms, and strengths and limitations. Finally, a glossary of terms used throughout the book is presented.

FORMAT OF INSTRUMENT DESCRIPTIONS

All instruments are reviewed in a standard format. The reviews were completed by a variety of individuals with training in measurement. Many times reviews were completed collaboratively with one of the editors and a doctoral student in clinical or school psychology. After presenting the title and reviewer, each instrument was reviewed using the following format.

Purpose

The author's intended purpose is presented.

Population

The age range and gender of students for whom the measure is appropriate.

Description

This section presents a brief overview of the measure including the structure, scales, item type, and response format (e.g., 5 point Likert-type scale). When appropriate, all versions of the scale are described, such as inclusion of a parent and teacher version of the instrument or variations of the instrument for different aged students.

Administration

This section gives the approximate time to complete the measure as well as intended respondent.

Scoring

This section provides a description of the scoring procedures including availability of computerized scoring.

Psychometric Properties

Norms. Described the standardization sample and available norms.

Reliability. Describes studies on the instrument's internal consistency, inter-rater, and test-retest reliability.

Validity. Describes studies on validity (e.g., construct, convergent, predictive, discriminant, and factorial).

Clinical Utility

Rates our estimates of the clinical utility of the instrument from High to Limited. Ratings indicate whether the instrument is frequently used in clinical settings and/or would be appropriate and easily used in clinical work. These ratings are subjective only and based on the reviewer's perceptions of clinical utility.

Authors

The authors of the instrument.

Publication Year

Lists the publication year if available.

Source

Identifies how the measure can be obtained. When the measure is published by a large publishing house, the address, telephone/fax number, and email address are listed.

Fee

Specifies whether or not there is a fee for obtaining the measure.

Part I
Behavior Problems of Children in the School Setting

Chapter 1

Assessment of Children's Behavior in the School Setting

An Overview

Mary Lou Kelley

The assessment of children's behavioral and academic functioning within the school setting has evolved dramatically over the past decade (Franz & Gros, 1998). There is movement away from classification-centered assessment methods toward methods producing data that lead directly to treatment planning. This trend is evidenced in the school psychology literature where direct assessment approaches such as curriculum-based assessment and functional assessment abound. In fact, federal laws governing assessment of children's behavior in the school setting now require the evaluation of behavior within the context in which it occurs. These direct assessment approaches are supplanting the more inferential and indirect approaches traditionally employed in schools, such as intelligence testing and other methods used for classification purposes (Witt, Daly, & Noel, 2000). Unfortunately, research on the reliability and validity of these approaches has not kept up with the clinical uses of ideographic assessment techniques.

This chapter provides an overview of issues pertaining to the assessment of children's behavior in the school setting. Methods and scope of assessment, laws affecting assessment practices, and issues related to reimbursement will be discussed. Although diagnostic and classification decisions remain a standard part of the assessment and treatment process, the emphasis in this chapter is on behavioral assessment procedures used in treatment planning.

Mary Lou Kelley • Department of Psychology, Louisiana State University, Baton, Rouge, Louisiana 70803

PURPOSES OF ASSESSMENT

Assessment methods may vary substantially depending on the purpose of the assessment. Figure 1 shows a modification of the assessment funnel developed by Elliott and Piersel (1982).

The model sequences the various assessment methods according to specificity and purpose. As seen in the figure, at the molar or most general level, assessment may be conducted in order to screen for children's emotional and behavioral problems. Assessment methods used to screen children are likely to be norm-referenced tests and scales that compare the child to a standardization sample. Screening may be conducted with groups of children such as screening for behavior problems in children attending a pediatric clinic. Screening also may

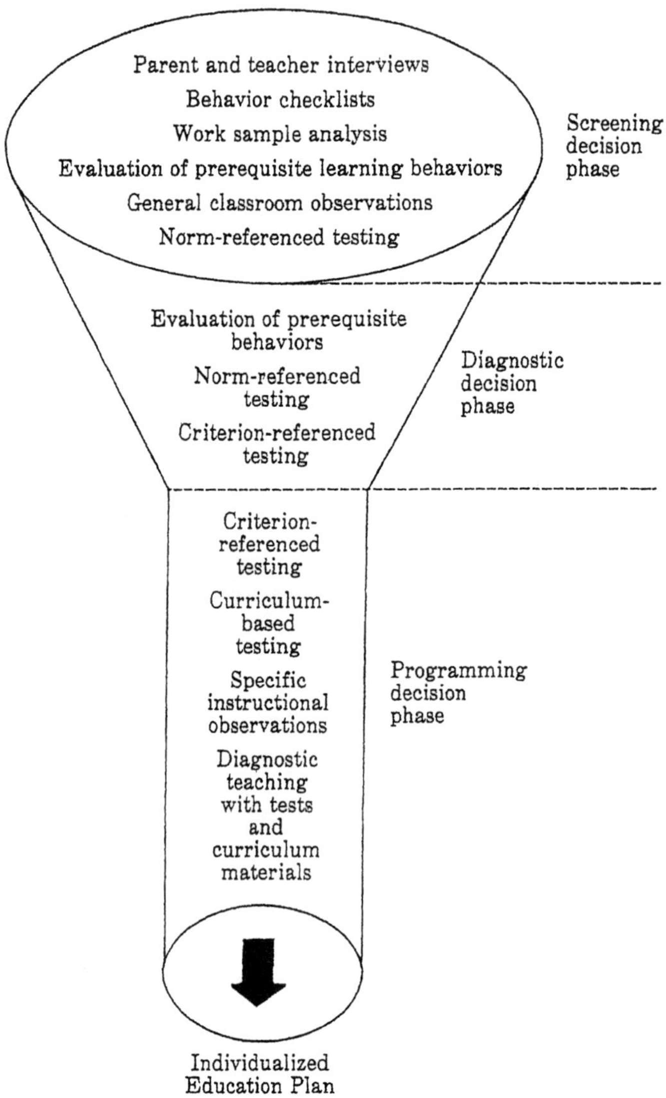

Figure 1.1. The assessment funnel. (From "Direct Assessment of Reading Skills: An Approach Which Links Assessment to Intervention" by S. N. Elliott and W. C. Piersel, 1982, *School Psychology Review, 11*, pp. 267–280. Copyright 1982 by National Association of School Psychologists. Reprinted by permission.)

be conducted with an individual client or student where the evaluator is ruling in or out the presence of a wide range of problems. For example, initial assessment of a client referred for treatment often begins with the completion of comprehensive parent or teacher questionnaires such as the Achenbach Child Behavior Checklist (Achenbach, 1991; Achenbach & Edelbrock, 1987). Although the initial referral may be to improve classroom conduct, the assessment evaluates the presence of a wide array of potential symptoms that could be related to disruptive classroom behavior. These may include affective disturbances due to depression or family stressors, anxiety, obsessive-compulsive behavior, Attention Deficit Hyperactivity Disorder, or learning difficulties.

As seen in the figure, a second assessment purpose is to diagnose or classify a child based on his behavior, cognitive functioning, or academic skills. This typically involves the use of norm referenced instruments; teacher, parent, and child interviews; and classroom observations. For classification purposes, such as diagnosing ADHD, it is recommended that a multi-method, multi-informant assessment approach be taken. In this way, the severity and pervasiveness of symptoms can be assessed and may offer preliminary information on situational variables influencing behavior frequency or severity. For example, measures often used to assess ADHD in children include multi-informant measures such as the Conner's Rating Scales (Conners, 1997), and the Attention Deficit Disorders Evaluation Scales (McCarney, 1995a, 1995b).

A third assessment purpose, and one most closely related to behavioral assessment, is to obtain information for treatment planning and treatment evaluation. Assessment at this level is idiographic, focused on specifying behaviors for treatment and concerned with identifying antecedents and consequences maintaining the behavior. The evaluator also is interested in determining whether the targeted behavior is due to a skill versus a performance deficit; that is, does the student have the skills to perform a targeted, appropriate behavior but lack effective contingencies of reinforcement or does the student lack skills for performing a desired behavior? This third level of assessment typically does not rely on norm-referenced testing but instead employs functional assessment in the form of observational data collection, self-monitoring, or criterion referenced testing. Functional assessment answers the question "why" does the behavior occur and is an important component of assessment for treatment planning and evaluation (Ervin, DuPaul, Kern, & Friman, 1998). Unfortunately, few standardized measures exist for conducting functional assessments. However, the mechanics of conducting functional assessment are delineated in Chapter 3. As seen in Chapter 3, functional assessment involves evaluating behavior and contingencies of reinforcement maintaining the behavior.

The literature consistently indicates a strong relationship between externalizing behavior problems and academic underachievement (Hinshaw, 1992). Directionality has not been identified and the two variables appear to have reciprocal effects. It is very important to be able to determine whether the curriculum is frustrating or instructional for the child as inappropriate curriculum placement can contribute to classroom behavior problems and must be addressed in treatment planning. Curriculum based measurement (CBM) involves evaluating whether the student is performing at the appropriate level for his/her placement in the curriculum. CBM, like functional assessment, has few standardized measures representing the approach. However, as CBM is ideographic and concerned with an individual child's placement in his curriculum and progress in skill acquisition, standardization is less relevant. Given the importance, however, of determining whether a student is appropriately placed in his/her curriculum, the mechanics of conducting CBM are described in Chapter 4.

The assessment funnel is consistent with the successive levels model of assessment that has been widely accepted by school psychologists. The model emphasizes the use of psychometrically sound, norm referenced measures for initial screening, classification, and diagnostic decisions. As the evaluation progresses to treatment planning, other sources of information such as observational and interview data are emphasized.

ETHICAL AND LEGAL ISSUES PERTAINING TO ASSESSMENT

Numerous laws and statutes at both state and federal levels have direct bearing on assessment practices in the school setting. Current laws generally support the use of norm-referenced testing to document severity of problems and symptoms in order to justify legally mandated services. As these laws, statutes, and related ethical guidelines have been described extensively elsewhere, they are briefly summarized here (Latham & Latham, 1993; McEwan, 1995; Witt et al., 1998).

Two laws, in particular, have significantly impacted the assessment and provision of services to children with emotional and behavioral problems evidenced in the school setting. The core issue of all school laws and subsequent litigation is that children are entitled to receive a free and appropriate public education (Witt et al., 1998). In 1975, PL 94–142 established guidelines for assessment and stipulated that children must be provided with the least restrictive educational environment. In 1990, PL 94–142 was modified and renamed the Individuals with Disabilities in Education Act (IDEA). IDEA expanded the scope of the law to include new programs for children with serious emotional disturbance and clear insistence that parental consent must be obtained prior to beginning an assessment. According to Witt et al. (1998), and others (Latham & Latham, 1993) the major provisions of IDEA included:

1. Free and appropriate public education regardless of severity of the disability.
2. Nondiscriminatory assessment that is multi-faceted, and comprehensive.
3. Development of an Individual Education Plan with specific objectives.
4. Due process.
5. Record privacy.
6. Least restrictive educational environment.
7. Support services including psychological services needed to assist the child in benefiting from special education.

IDEA specified that children are eligible if they meet the criteria for one of 13 disabilities: Autism, Deaf-Blind, Deaf, Hearing Impairment, Mental Retardation, Multiple Disabilities, Orthopedic Impairment, Other Health Impaired, and Serious Emotional Disturbance. The disability must significantly impair academic performance in such a way that the child's performance is below that of his classmates.

In 1997, IDEA was amended (U.S. Congress, 1997), and introduced a number of changes. The amendment emphasized using instructionally valid techniques, to service based or needs rather than labels, and focusing on competencies not deficits (See Telzrow, 1999 for a complete review of the changes). As Telzrow (1999) discussed, the use of "serious" in reference to emotional disturbance was dropped and the term "developmentally delayed" can be used in children up to age nine rather than only used through the preschool years. Additionally, students who receive special education services are required to participate in state or district wide testing for increased accountability of service delivery. Changes to educational re-evaluation monitoring and the individual educational plan (IEP) also were mandated to increase accountability (Telzrow, 1999).

Other Health Impaired can include Attention Deficit Hyperactivity Disorder when the symptoms significantly impact learning. Although this was initially questioned, the U.S. Department of Education issued a memorandum (September 16, 1991) that summarized existing legislation pertaining to ADHD and concluded that some ADHD children may qualify as "Other Health Impaired" under some circumstances.

The U.S. Department of Education Memorandum further stated that ADHD children who do not qualify for services under IDEA, may be eligible for services under Section 504 of the Rehabilitation Act of 1973. Section 504 is an anti-discrimination law that provides equal opportunity for children with physically or mentally handicapping conditions in school systems receiving federal funds (Latham & Latham, 1993). Section 504 is much more inclusive and has been used to gain services for children with a variety of DSM- IV diagnoses such as ADHD or Major Depression as well as medical conditions such as HIV (Witt et al., 1998). The U.S. Department of Education Memorandum not only specified that ADHD students are eligible for services either under IDEA or Section 504, but went on to specify examples of accommodations in which they may benefit as students in a regular education classroom. These accommodations included: "repeating and simplifying instructions about in-class and homework assignments; supplementing verbal instructions with visual instructions; using behavioral management techniques; adjusting class schedules; modifying test delivery; using tape recorders, computer aided instruction and, other audio-visual equipment; selecting modified textbooks or workbooks; and, tailoring homework assignments." (U.S. Department of Education Memorandum, September 16, 1991) The memorandum further stated that state and local educational agencies should ensure that teachers are trained to better recognize and address the needs of children with ADHD.

Knowledge of the legislation affecting children who qualify for services either under IDEA or Section 504 is important to assessment at all levels and treatment planning. Clearly, assessment practices and procedures are pivotal to helping children gain access to services and accommodations that they are entitled to under the law. Furthermore, evaluation of the extent to which these services and accommodations result in improved academic performance is mandated in the law and court rulings.

TEST RELIABILITY AND VALIDITY

Given the importance of assessment to the wide range of children's academic and behavioral adjustment, it is imperative that assessment practices be appropriate to the purpose and be conducted by competent individuals. The laws, statutes, and ethical guidelines about testing indicate that tests must be reliable, valid, and appropriate for the assessment purposes. Testing cannot consist only of a standardized battery that is employed with all children.

The tests reviewed in the latter portion of the book are evaluated with regard to the psychometric properties supporting the test. Appendix A, briefly defines the psychometric terms used in the volume.

In addition to meeting psychometric standards in terms of reliability and validity, assessment devices should also be normed on the population to which a child's scores are compared. Well-standardized measures contain normative data with adequate samples of children of varying ages, ethnicities, socioeconomic backgrounds, and geographic locations. Data on the reliability, validity and standardization of a test should be clearly and thoroughly described in the test manual. As will be evident in latter portions of this volume, few instruments have attempted to obtain norms using different ethnic or cultural samples. This is an important flaw as significant differences may and often do exist across varying ethnic groups. For example, African American children receive higher scores than Caucasian children on measures of ADHD symptoms (DuPaul, Anastopoulos, Power, Reid, Ikeda, McGoey, 1998, Gingerich, Turnock, Litfin, & Rosen, 1998; Reid, Riccio, Kessler, DuPaul, 2000) and are much more likely to be diagnosed with Attention Deficit Hyperactivity Disorder than their Caucasian counterparts using standard assessment instruments. Little is known, for example, about the utility of many instruments for accurately diagnosing ADHD in this population. Unfortunately, the brevity of this chapter does not lend itself to a thorough discussion of issues concerning psychometric properties important to the test utility. The reader is encouraged to review more comprehensive sources such as those listed above.

ASSESSMENT METHODS

Interviews

Interview formats vary with assessment purpose. Interviews for diagnostic or classification purposes typically focus on assessing psychological symptoms and situational variables related to their occurrence. Interview methods employed vary in the level of structure. Structured interviews such as the Diagnostic Interview for Children and Adolescents-R (DICA-R; Herjanic & Reich, 1982) or the Diagnostic Interview Schedule for Children-4 (DISC; Costello, Edelbrock, Kalas, Kessler, & Klaric, 1982) required the interviewer to adhere to a protocol leading to a DSM IV diagnoses. Semi-structured interviews are more flexible and often are aimed at assessing problems or behavior across an array of situations. Semi-structured interviews include the Semi-structured Clinical Interview for Children and Adolescents (McConaughy & Achenbach, 1994) and the Child Assessment Schedule (CAS; Hodges, Kline, Stern, Cyrtyn, & McKnew, 1982). The CAS contains both parent and child self-report versions, and has good psychometric properties (Hodges, Cools, & McKnew, 1989). Interviewers probe the domains of school, friends, family activities, self-image, behavior, mood, and thought disorder, as well as the onset and duration of specific behaviors. Use of the measures provide a systematic method for obtaining information and have good reliability and validity (Reich, Shayka, & Taibleson, 1992). The SCICA is intended for use as one component of a multi-method-multi-informant assessment using the Achenbach scales (CBCL, TRF, DOF; Achenbach, 1991; McConaughy & Achenbach, 1994). Structured and semi-structured interviews are advantageous in that they have some psychometric support and information is gathered in a systematic, consistent, and comprehensive manner. However, they can be very time-consuming to administer. As with any assessment instrument, symptom endorsement may be quite different from the parent and child perspective. In general, parents tend to report more problems than do children (e.g., Kotsopoulos, Walker, Copping, Cote, & Stavrakaki, 1994). However, children provide a unique perspective and often provide information on internalizing problems not detected by parents. Generally, as the child becomes older more emphasis is placed on their symptom report, especially with regard to internalizing disorders. However, parent and teacher report is especially important in evaluating externalizing behavior disorders. Another structured or semi-structured interview is the Child Assessment Schedule (CAS; Hodges, Kline, Stern, Cytryn, & McKnew, 1982). The CAS contains both parent and child versions. Interviewers probe the domains of school, friends, family, activities, self-image, behavior, mood, and thought disorder, as well as the onset and duration of specific behaviors. While the CAS requires more clinical judgement than a structured interview, it retains some of the rapport-building qualities of an unstructured interview. Structured interviews have been developed which minimize clinical judgement during the interview at the expense of flexibility and rapport. The Diagnostic Interview Schedule for Children-4 (DISC-4) conforms to the DSM-IV criteria for a wide range of child psychopathology. While more research needs to be conducted to determine the reliability and validity of this instrument, research on previous versions of the interview have reported good psychometric properties (Costello, Edelbrock, Kalas, Kessler, & Klaric, 1982; Jensen, et al., 1995; Piacentini, et al., 1993). Computerized assessment using the DISC-IV is now available, though it cannot yet be self-administered.

Behavioral interviews are an integral component of assessing children's classroom functioning. Behavioral interviews focus on obtaining specific information about behavior frequency and other information pertinent to the functional analysis. The behavioral interview is intended to gather information that will directly lead to problem solving. The behavioral interview format typically used in the school setting is the consultative format developed by Bergan and his colleagues (Bergan & Kratochwill, 1990; Bergin, 1977; Bergan & Tombari, 1975). This model consists of four problem-solving steps applied to interviewing teachers and parents. The steps are problem identification, problem analysis, plan implementation, and problem evaluation.

Problem identification involves interviewing teachers and parents to obtain information on specific problem behaviors and maintaining variables, identifying client strengths, and determining goals and potential reinforcers (Bergan & Kratochwill, 1990; Gresham & Davis, 1988). Problem identification also involves determining methods for collecting data regarding behavioral frequency. Although the problem identification interview certainly could and should involve parents, the majority of the research on behavioral consultation has been conducted with teachers.

The *problem analysis* interview has four objectives and typically is conducted after baseline data collection (Gresham & Davis, 1988). These objectives include validating the existence of a problem by evaluating baseline data, comparing baseline rates to other children in the classroom, analyzing the conditions under which the behavior occurs, designing an intervention, and arranging for subsequent meetings to evaluate treatment progress.

Plan implementation requires the consultant to implement or supervise the implementation of treatment. The consultant monitors treatment progress and treatment integrity.

The overall purposes of problem analysis according to Bergan & Kratochwill (1990) are to identify variables that may be related to solving the problem and to develop an intervention plan. According to Gresham & Davis (1988), baseline data collection consists of making more rigorous recommendations. Gresham and Davis (1988) state that the *problem evaluation* interview involves determining whether established goals have been accomplished, systematically evaluating intervention effectiveness, and deciding whether treatment should be changed, refined, or ended. This interview usually takes place after treatment has had adequate time to begin to work and may consist of several sessions depending on treatment effectiveness. According to Gresham & Davis (1988) and Bergan & Kratochwill (1990), when goals are not obtained, typically the consultant moves back to problem analysis or in some cases the problem identification phase.

Although often overlooked in the assessment process, client rapport during behavioral interviews must be established for effective problem solving to occur. Very often eliciting opinions about problem solving, listening intently, and empathizing with teacher or parent is key to a successful interview and subsequent treatment. For example, in discussing assessment issues with parents and teachers, it is helpful to provide supportive statements regarding past problem solving efforts and commenting on aspects of the situation that are positive or effectively managed. However, supportive, encouraging, and empathetic comments are provided within the context of the interview with problem solving as the ultimate goal.

Although only recently emphasized in the school psychology literature, including parents in the assessment process is critical (Christenson, Rounds, & Gorney, 1992). Parents can provide an important and unique perspective on the conditions under which the child tends to perform and behave best, their perspective on the child's current problems within the school setting, and historical information that only a parent may be able provide but which may prove important to diagnosis and treatment planning. Parents can be very important to skill acquisition and promoting appropriate classroom behavior in that they can provide practice and contingent consequences that are more salient than those available in the classroom. Obtaining input from parents also increases the likelihood that they will support and participate in an intervention program.

Rating Scales

Psychometrically sound questionnaires and checklists comprise the bulk of the instruments reviewed in this book. Paper and pencil instruments are advantageous in a number of ways compared to less formal, more idiographic methods. Advantages include ease of administration and scoring; standardization in method of eliciting information from parents, teachers, and students; and comparability of responses across informants (Reitman, Hummel, Franz, & Gros, 1998). Rating scales allow for parents', teachers', and students' perceptions to be directly compared which can add greatly to a multi-informant, multi-method assessment approach. Furthermore, ratings scales are an efficient method for beginning to obtain some information on the settings in which behavior occurs. In spite of the positive features of rating scales, they are not sufficient in and of themselves to make diagnostic or classification decisions. Nor do they yield adequately specific information for determining variables maintaining behavioral frequency or severity.

Questionnaires vary in their comprehensiveness with some assessing psychopathology or behavior and emotional problems across a wide range of areas. Other scales are more specific and are intended for aiding in the assessment of specific diagnoses or problems. Comprehensive, multi-informant-multi-method scales are useful for screening and include measures such as the Child Behavior Checklist (CBCL; Achenbach, 1991) or the Behavior Assessment System for Children (BASC; Reynolds & Kamphaus, 1992). Both the CBCL and the BASC have teacher, parent, and self-report versions, are well normed, and are psychometrically sound. It is important to include a broad band, comprehensive instrument in an initial assessment protocol. Inclusion of a measure such as the CBCL allows for potential problems to be quickly identified or dismissed with minimal effort or time. Also, from a liability perspective, it can be important to document the presence or absence of suicidal ideation, aggression, or other significantly important or potentially life threatening behaviors. Questionnaire data are one easy way to obtain documentation.

Another important use of rating scales for screening purposes is the use of self-report measures assessing parent psychopathology or environmental stressors. For example, we recommend having parents complete the Beck Depression Inventory (Beck, 1961) or the Parenting Stress Index (Abidin, 1990) when assessing children's behavior problems for a number of reasons. First, parental depression consistently has been associated with poorer treatment outcome when not addressed in the treatment plan (Forehand, 1987). Also, the literature suggests that parents' ratings of their children's behavior is negatively biased by the presence of parental depression (Friedlander, Weiss, & Traylor, 1986; Middlebrook & Forehand, 1985). Thus, both parent perceptions, treatment implementation, and treatment outcome can be negatively impacted by parental depression.

Other measures that often are included in a comprehensive assessment due to their effects on treatment outcome include measures of marital distress, social support, and treatment acceptability (Dadds, 1989; Dadds, Schwartz, & Sanders, 1987). Treatment acceptability measures generally evaluate parents' and teachers' perceptions and acceptance of a variety of interventions (Miltenberger, 1990; Tarnowski, Simoniah, Park, & Bekeny, 1992). This information can be incorporated into treatment planning. For example, depending on parent or teacher preferences, the type of intervention offered could be altered or the therapist might provide explanation on the rationales for using a specific treatment approach. Measures related to parent psychopathology, stress, and treatment acceptability are listed and briefly described in the final section of this volume.

Direct Observation

Direct observation of children's behavior in the setting in it occurs often is essential to treatment planning and treatment evaluation. Numerous authors have recommended direct observation in the classroom as a method of obtaining information on academic performance as well as classroom behavior (Alessi, 1988; Lentz & Shapiro, 1986). Obtaining a direct, objective sample of children's behavior and the environment in which it occurs can yield important information that is not biased by perception or expectations as is often the case with parent and teacher report. As discussed in Chapters 2 and 3, direct observation is essential to functional assessment and answering questions about "why" behavior occurs. Additionally, direct observation of the child in the classroom allows for comparisons of the referred child to other children in the classroom.

A variety of standardized measurement codes for use in the classroom setting are available and reviewed in this volume. For example, Abikoff, Gittelman, and Klein (1980) have developed an observational system that has been shown to be reliable and valid in the observational assessment of ADHD children in the classroom. The Abikoff, et al. (1980) observational system, like many others requires interval coding of behavior. With this system and others like it, the occurrence of operationally defined behavior are recorded when it occurs within a specified time interval such as 10, 15, or 30 seconds. The beginning and ending of intervals are cued thru the use of a stop watch attached to a clip board in close proximity to the recoding sheet or with an audio-tape recording that cues the observer to move to the next interval. Barkley and his colleagues (Barkley, 1990) provide an observational symptom that is useful in the assessment of Attention Deficit Hyperactivity Disorder and associated symptoms. Other direct observation measures include the BASC-SOF (Reynolds & Kamphaus, 1992) and the CBCL Direct Observation Form(DOF; Achenbach, 1986) Both measures are useful in classroom observations.

Generally, observational data are collected on the target child as well as one or more classroom peers that serve as comparison children. Rates of on-task behavior should be included as an important target behavior (Lentz & Shapiro, 1986). Off-task therefore consists of behaviors that compete with or are incompatible with the child's appropriate engagement. Examples of off-task behaviors include talking without permission, looking away from the stimulus materials for a specified amount of time, or playing with objects. Typically, data are recorded in terms of the percentages of intervals observed in which the child was "on-task" for the entire interval. Along with rates of on-task behavior, it is very useful to document the presence of a variety of setting variables such as the type and content of instruction, where the child is seated and seating arrangements. Teacher variables in the form of antecedents and consequences are also important to measure and are included in most observational systems. Direct observation in a laboratory or clinical setting can provide information regarding parent-child interactions or other behaviors. For example, Roberts (1990) evaluated the discriminant validity of the Systematic Observation of Academic and Play Settings (SOAPS). The system correctly classified 88% of hyperactive and non-referred children during a restricted academic period. The importance of collecting observation data for diagnosis, classification, and treatment planning is underscored by a recent assessment that I conducted. The child was referred due to the teacher's concerns that he exhibited significant problems with inattentiveness, talking without permission, and lack of efficient task completion. The child recently was placed in a private school with a very small student-teacher ratio after several years of home schooling. The parents indicated that they have not observed the child's attention span to be problematic and their scores on questionnaires assessing this were well within the average range. However, the teachers' scores on similar measures were highly elevated on factors measuring inattentiveness, impulsivity, and hyperactivity. Observation of the child in the classroom revealed a highly disorganized environment situated between two other classrooms in such a way that traffic passed thru the classroom to get to the other areas. The teacher was instructing one group of children while my client was expected to work independently. Further, in spite of the teacher's complaints that the child talked without permission, she responded to his comments and on several occasions asked for more information when he interrupted and talked without permission. Thus, the environment was very problematic for the majority of the children in the classroom who were no more likely to be off-task that my client.

Direct observation generally is most appropriate when conducted in elementary school settings with younger children. In these situations children usually are in one or two classroom settings for the majority of the day in contrast to the many classroom environments encountered by an older student (Robin, 1998). Also, younger children tend to be less reactive to the presence of an observer and therefore, a more accurate representation of daily behavior is likely to be obtained.

Direct observation may be very useful to evaluating the home environment and a variety of observational methods are available for evaluating children's behavior in this environment although these systems can be rather complex (e.g., Wahler, House, & Stambaugh, 1976). For clinical purposes, simply evaluating rates of compliance to parental instructions and parent provided antecedents and consequences may be sufficient. For the purposes of assessing children's home related school problems such as adherence to a homework routine, other forms of data collection, such as parent or self-monitoring may be more feasible and adequate.

Other Sources of Information

A variety of other sources of information may be useful to the assessment process at each stage. Permanent products such as achievement test scores, school records, report cards, and tests and classwork can be very useful to diagnosis and treatment planning. For example, examining the consistency in which a child responds on mathematics tests provides information on carelessness, direction following, and skill level.

An important but often overlooked source of information is teacher- or parent-collected data on student performance and behavior. Additionally, self-monitoring by students can be useful both from an assessment and treatment perspective. For example, I have often required students to record whether or not they engage in a variety of homework behaviors important to accuracy, thoroughness, and efficiency. Self-monitoring can be a source of important information for gathering students' self-perceptions as well as serve as feedback to the student. Students may monitor such classroom behaviors as class participation or completion of independent seatwork (Nelson, Smith, Young, & Dodd, 1991).

Another important source of information about student behavior as well as a viable treatment method is the use of a school-home note or daily report card. This procedure requires teachers to evaluate students' behavior at various intervals throughout the day. Parents review the information with the child and provide consequences based on the evaluation (Kelley, 1991; Kelley & McCain, 1995). Initially, parents are told to review the information daily in a nonjudgmental manner and one that encourages problem solving regarding instances of negative behavior and praise, encouragement, and reflect upon instances of positive behavior.

As the child begins to bring the note home consistently, new contingencies are established in which improved behavior earns positive consequences. However, data from the note may also be used to assess situations in which the behavior is worse or better and to evaluate the effects of treatments such as medication or changes in setting variables or teacher behavior. An example of a school-home note that we frequently use in our clinical work is shown in Figure 2. As seen in Figure 2, the day is divided into intervals and teachers are encouraged to evaluate behavior at the end of each interval. Behaviors listed may vary depending on the behaviors targeted for a given child. As illustrated Figure 2, we tend to word behaviors positively and always include some index of academic performance. Evaluative data on academic performance is included as research consistently indicates that as academic productivity improves so does rate of on-task behavior. Declines in disruptive behavior often are seen as well.

A final, somewhat controversial method of evaluating students' attention are various laboratory tasks that measure attention, impulsive responding, and persistence. When assessing ADHD the use of laboratory tasks, such as the continuous performance task, offer a source of independent assessment of attention that can be collected in the office. In his review of various laboratory measures, Barkley (1998) concludes that some of the measures, particularly the continuous performance tasks measures, do discriminate between children who have ADHD and normal children. Unfortunately, research has not indicated that performance on these tasks is even moderately correlated with classroom observation data. Nor do the laboratory tasks adequately differentiate ADHD children from those with other disorders (Barkely, 1991, 1998). Furthermore, Barkley insists that laboratory measures be used as only one component of an assessment battery for evaluating ADHD. However, in contrast to Barkley's position that formal classroom observations are not economical, my recommendation would be to opt for a

Name:____________________ Date:________

Reading

Followed Directions	Good Fair No
Used Time Wisely	Good Fair No
Talked Only with Permission	Good Fair No
Comments:	

Reading

Followed Directions	Good Fair No
Used Time Wisely	Good Fair No
Talked Only with Permission	Good Fair No
Comments:	

Language Arts

Followed Directions	Good Fair No
Used Time Wisely	Good Fair No
Talked Only with Permission	Good Fair No
Comments:	

Math

Followed Directions	Good Fair No
Used Time Wisely	Good Fair No
Talked Only with Permission	Good Fair No
Comments:	

Parent Comments or Questions/Consequences Provided:

Figure 1.2. School-Home Note.

classroom observation which directly assesses the behavior of interest rather than administer a laboratory measure of behavior.

SCOPE OF THE ASSESSMENT

Teacher and Classroom Variables

A host of classroom variables may directly impact children's appropriate and inappropriate classroom behavior (McKee & Witt, 1990). First and foremost, classrooms should be adequately structured with set schedules in which activities occur. Rules should be posted, intermittently reviewed, and well familiar to all children in the classroom. Consequences for rule infractions should be clearly delineated and class wide behavior management procedures should be established and consistently applied by the teacher. The referred child's behavior should be evaluated within the context in which the behavior is problematic. Very often, children will be referred for an evaluation when the classroom environment is one in which behavior management methods are generally ineffective. Furthermore, children with impulse control or other self-control problems, or who lack motivation and goal-directed behavior, especially need and require well-structured classroom environments where teachers implement consequences effectively. A series of studies by Dr. Susan O'Leary and her colleagues evaluated the behavior of children with ADHD under various classroom management conditions (Pfiffner, Rosen, & O'Leary, 1985; Pfiffner & O'Leary, 1987; Sullivan & O'Leary, 1990). Overall, these studies found that teachers who are non-emotional and controlled in their delivery of consequences are most effective. They also found that ADHD children do best when positive behavior is reinforced but also negative behavior is followed by a reprimand or negative consequences. All positive methods of managing disruptive behavior, such as the use of praise and tangible rewards, were less effective. Furthermore, other research suggests that reprimands, delivered in a controlled manner, may provide immediate feedback to children with impulse control problems. This has been shown to be an important method of improving behavioral control in children with ADHD. Thus, when evaluating classroom variables it is important to evaluate the structure and predictability of routines, rules, and consequences as well as the use of both positive and negative teacher consequences utilized in a controlled and effective manner. Reavis, et al. (1996) present detailed instructions on a variety of empirically supported child management techniques. Included are easy to read chapters for teachers and professionals on effective reprimands, cooperative learning, time out, and teacher praise.

Other classroom variables important to consider in the diagnosis and treatment planning of children with behavior problems in the school setting include number of students in the classroom and the seating arrangement. Children sitting in close proximity to other children are likely to engage in more interaction which is good for cooperative learning but less conducive to sustained attention during times of independent seat work. Also, assess the placement of the referred child in the classroom environment (McKee & Witt, 1990).

A final, but very important consideration, is the amount of time children spend engaged in academic responding. Increases in academic responding, such as increased drill and practice of newly learned skills, is related to academic achievement which is the ultimate goal for schooling. When parents receive few papers or other products of actual responding and little is known about instructional goals and activities, the situation should be further evaluated. The ideal environment is one in which children are provided with clear instruction and allowed to practice newly learned skills in a group and individual format. Feedback and rehearsal should be evident in the classroom instruction.

Multi-Informant/Multi-Method Assessment

Best practice dictates that the diagnosis of children's behavior problems be conducted in a comprehensive manner. Typically, the assessment of children's behavior problems includes conducting interviews with parents, teachers, and the child. The interview would be conducted for the purposes of diagnosis and treatment planning and thus, would follow the behavioral interviewing methods described above but also solicit information needed for diagnosis and treatment planning. Multi-informant measures are recommended so that information from parents, teachers, and when appropriate the student, can be compared. Multi-informant measures that are well standardized and relatively easy to complete include the Achenbach Child Behavior Checklist (Achenbach, 1991) the Eyberg Child Behavior Inventory (Eyberg & Ross, 1978) and Attention Deficit Disorders Evaluation Scale (McCarney, 1989), Conner's Rating Scales (Conners, 1997) and several others reviewed in this volume. Importantly, assessment should emphasize developmental variables so that judgements and treatment planning are appropriate (Bierman & Montminy, 1993; Franz & Gros, 1998). Although all include scales for parents and teachers, some also have a self-report version for obtaining the students' self-perceptions. In addition, supplementary measures aimed at further assessing or documenting other specific problems such as depression, anxiety, social skills or parent psychopathology are included as appropriate. I would recommend the inclusion of a measure of parent depression. This can be accomplished by using a depression scale, such as the Beck Depression Inventory (1961) or the Parenting Stress Index (1990) or other scales that measure parental behavior shown to effect parents' perceptions of their children's behavior and parenting behavior (Ferguson, Lunskey, & Horwood, 1993; Middlebrook & Forehand, 1985; Webster-Stratton, & Hammond, 1990).

It is strongly recommended to include of observation of the child in the school setting during times when problematic behavior are said to occur. A classroom observation typically is essential to a comprehensive understanding of the variables influencing behavior. Although some of this information could be obtained by interviewing the teacher and the parent, these sources of data are often inaccurate or incomplete which inevitably diminishes treatment effectiveness. Furthermore, classroom observations offer an important opportunity for identifying classroom variables impacting behavior that often are unrecognized by teachers as well as an opportunity for comparing the referred child to other children in the classroom.

REIMBURSEMENT ISSUES

In this era of managed health care, reimbursement for testing is often very problematic. Most managed health care agencies award sessions based on specific CPT codes that exclude testing and assessment. For example, most managed health care agencies with whom I have encountered award one diagnostic interview session (90801) and one or more family (90844) or individual therapy (90806) sessions. Testing sessions must be requested separately which can be very time consuming and may be denied or may be excluded from the policy holders' insurance. Typically, one out of ten cognitive or academic skills testing sessions are covered by insurance. I have addressed this dilemma in a number of ways so that appropriate evaluation methods are employed. First, some agencies have increased the fee for a diagnostic interview so that rating scales can be employed with adequate reimbursement for measurement cost and scoring time. Also, I often obtain reimbursement by requesting testing sessions for evaluations of Attention Deficit Hyperactivity Disorder. Typically, I complete the required forms but attach a summary of the intake interview and a checklist we developed that lists a large number of tests and testing rationales. I simply check which tests and rationales are appropriate for the client.

Included in the list is a brief written report. The intake summary is simply expanded upon when writing the brief report that documents developmental history, current problem behaviors and maintaining variables, diagnosis, and treatment recommendations/classroom accommodations. This information is presented to the parents after the assessment is completed and a copy of the written report provided to the school or child's physician with the parent's consent.

REFERENCES

Abidin, R. R. (1990). *Parenting Stress Index-Short Form Test Manual.* Charlottesville, VA: Pediatric Psychology Press.

Abikoff, H., Gittleman, R., Klein, D. (1980). *Classroom Observation Code for Hyperactive Children: A Replication of Validity.* New Hyde Park, New York: Long Island Jewish-Hillside Medical Center.

Achenbach, T.M. (1986). *Child Behavior Checklist – Direct Observation Form (rev. ed.).* Burlington: University of Vermont. Department of Psychiatry.

Achenbach, T. M. (1991). *Manual for the child behavior checklist/4–18 and 1991 profile.* Burlington, VT: University of Vermont Department of Psychiatry.

Achenbach, T.M., & Edelbrock, C. (1981). Behavioral problems and competencies reported by parents of normal and disturbed children aged four to sixteen. *Monographs of the Society for Research in Child Development,* 46(Serial No. 188).

Achenbach, T. M. & Edelbrock, C. (1987). *Manual for the youth self-report and profile.* Burlington, VT: University of Vermont Department of Psychiatry.

Alessi, G. (1988). Direct observation methods for emotional/behavior problems. In: Edward Shapiro, Ed. & Thomas Kratochwill, Ed; et al. *Behavioral assessment in schools: Conceptual foundations and practical applications.* New York: Guilford.

Barkley, R. A. (1991). The ecological validity of laboratory and analogue methods of ADHD. *Journal of Abnormal Psychology, 19,* 149–178.

Barkley, R. A. (1998). Attention Deficit Hyperactivity Disorder: A handbook for diagnosis and treatment (2nd Edition) New York: Guilford.

Barkley, R. A. (1990). *Attention Deficit Hyperactivity disorder: A Handbook for Diagnosis and Treatment.* New York: Guilford.

Beck, A. T., Ward, C., Mendelson, N. M., Mock, J., Erbaugh, J. (1961). An inventory for measuring depression. *Archives of General Psychiatriy, 4,* 53–63.

Bergan, J. R., & Kratochwill, T. R. (1990). *Behavioral Consultation & Therapy.* New York: Doubleday.

Bergan, J. R. & Tombari, M. L. (1975). The analysis of verbal interactions occurring during consultation. *Journal of School Psychology, 13,* 209–226.

Bergin , J. (1977). *Behavioral Consultation.* Columbus, OH: Charles E. Merrill.

Bierman, K. L., & Montminy, H. P. (1993). Developmental issues in social-skills assessment and intervention with children and adolescents. *Behavior Modification, 17,* 229–254.

Christenson, S. L., Rounds, T., & Gorney, D. (1992). Family factors and student achievement: An avenue to increase students' success. *School Psychology Quarterly, 7,* 178–206.

Conners, C. K. (1997). *Conner's Rating Scales-Revised Technical Manual.* North Tonawanda, NY: Multi-Health Systems, Inc.

Costello, A. J., Edelbrock, C., Kalas, R., Kessler, M. D., & Klaric, S. H. (1982). *The NIMH Diagnostic Interview Schedule for Children (DISC).* Unpublished Interview Schedule, University of Pittsburgh, Department of Psychiatry.

Dadds, M. R. (1989) Child behavior therapy and family contest: Research and clinical practice with maritally distressed families, *Child & Family Behavior Therapy, 11,* 27–43.

Dadds, M. R., Schwartz, S., & Sanders, M. R. (1987). Marital discord and treatment outcome in behavioral treatment of child conduct disorders. *Journal of Consulting and Clinical Psychology, 55,* 396–403.

DuPaul, G. J., Anastopoulos, A. D., Power, T. J., Reid, R., Ikeda, M. J., McGoey, K. E. (1998). Parent ratings of Attention-Deficit/Hyperactivity Disorder Symptoms: Factor Structure and Normative Data, *Journal of Psychopathology and Behavioral Assessment, 20,* 83–102.

D'Zurilla, T. J. & Goldfried, M. R. (1971). Problem solving and behavior modification. *Journal of Abnormal Psychology, 78,* 197–226.

Elliot, S. N. & Piersel, W. C. (1982). Direct assessment of reading skills: An approach which links assessment to intervention. *School Psychology Review, 11,* 257–280.

Ervin, R. A., DuPaul, G. J., Kern, K., & Friman, P. C. (1998). Classroom-based functional and adjunctive assessments: proactive approaches to intervention selection for adolescents with attention deficit hyperactivity disorder. *Journal of Applied Behavior Analysis, 31,* 65–78.

Eyberg, S. M. & Ross, A. W. (1978). Assessment of child behavior problems: The validation of a new inventory. *Journal of Clinical Child Psychology, 7,* 113–116.

Ferguson, D. M., Lynskey, M. T., Horwood, L. J. (1993). The effect of maternal depression on maternal ratings of child behavior. *Journal of Abnormal Child Psychology, 21,* 245–269.

Forehand, R. (1987). Parental roles in childhood psychopathology. In C. L. Frame & J. L. Matson (Eds.), *Handbook of assessment in childhood psychopathology* (pp. 489–507). New York: Plenum Press.

Franz, D., & Gros, A. M. (1998). Assessment of child behavior problems: Externalizing disorders. In: Alan S. Bellack, Ed, *Behavioral assessment: A practical handbook (4th ed.)* Boston, MA: Mic & Bacon, Inc.

Friedlander, S., Weiss, D. S., & Traylor, J. (1986). Assessing the influence of maternal depression on the validity of the Child Behavior Checklist. *Journal of Abnormal Child Psychology, 14,* 123–133.

Gingerich, K. J., Turnock, P., Litfin, J. K., & Rosen, L. A. (1998). Diversify and Attention Deficit Hyperactivity Disorder, *Journal of clinical Psychology, 54,* 415–426.

Gresham, F. M., & Davis, C. J. (1988). Behavioral interviews with teachers and parents. In E. S. Shapiro & T. R. Kratochwill (Eds.), *Behavioral assessment in Schools: Conceptual Foundations and Practical Applications* (pp. 455–493).

Herjanic, B., & Reich, W. (1982). Development of a structured psychiatric interview for children: Agreement between child and parent on individual symptoms. *Journal of Abnormal Child Psychology, 10,* 307–324.

Hinshaw, S. P., (1992). Externalizing behavior problems and academic underachievement in childhood and adolescence: Causal relationships and underlying mechanisms. *Psychological Bulletin, 111,* 127–155.

Hodges, K., Cools, J., & McKnew, D. (1989). Test-retest reliability of a clinical research interview for children: The Child Assessment Schedule. *Psychological Assessment, 1,* 317–322.

Hodges, K., Kline, J., Stern, L., Cytryn, L., & McKnew, D. (1982). The development of a child assessment interview for research and clinical use. *Journal of Abnornal Child Psychology, 10,* 173–189.

Jensen, P., Roper, M., Fisher, P., Piacentini, J., Canino, G., Richters, J., Rubio-Stipec, M., Dulcan, M., Goodman, S., Davies, M., Rae, D., Shaffer, D., Bird, H., Lahey, B., & Schwab-Stone, M. (1995). Test-retest reliability of the Diagnostic Interview Schedule for Children (DISC 2.1): Parent, Child, and combined algorithms. *Archives of General Psychiatry, 52,* 61–71.

Kelley, M. L. (1991). *School-Home Notes: Promoting children's Classroom Success.* New York: Guilford.

Kelley, M. L., & McCain, A. P. (1995). The relative efficacy of school home notes with and without response cost. *Behavior Modification, 19,* 357–375.

Kotsopoulos, S., Walker, S., Copping, W., Cote, A. & Stavrakaki, C. (1994). Parent-rating and self-report measures in the psychiatric assessment of adolescents. *Adolescence, 29,* 653–663.

Kratochwill, T. R. & McGivern, J. E. (1996). Clinical diagnosis, behavioral assessment, and functional analysis:. Examining the connection between assessment and intervention. *School Psychology Review, 24,* 342–355.

Kractochwill, T. R. & Sheridan, S. M. (1990). Advances in behavioral assessment. In T. B. Gutkin & C. R. Reynolds (Eds.), *The Handbook of School Psychology (2nd Ed.;* pp 328–364).

Latham, P. S., & Latham, P. H. (1993). *Learning Disabilities and the Law.* Washington, D.C.: JKL Publications.

Lentz, F. E. & Shapiro, E. S. (1986). Functional assessment of the academic environment. *School Psychology Review, 15,* 346–357.

McCarney, S. B. (1995a). *Attention Deficit Disorders Evaluation Scale: Home Version Technical Manual.* Hawthorne Educational Services, Inc. Columbia, MO.

McCarney, S. B. (1995b). *Attention Deficit Disorders Evaluation Scale: School Version Technical Manual.* Hawthorne Educational Services, Inc. Columbia, MO.

McCarney, S. & Bauer, Angela Marie. (1989). Attention Deficit Disorders Evaluation Scale Hawthorne Educating Services, Inc.

McConaughy, S. H. & Achenbach, T. M. (1994). *Manual for the Semistructured Clinical Interview for Children and Adolescents.* Burlington, VT: University of Vermont Department of Psychiatry.

McConaughy, S. H. & Achenbach, T. M. (1996). Contributions of a child interview to multi method assessment of children with EBD and LD. *School Psychology Review, 1,* 24–39.

McEwan, E. K. (1995). *Attention Deficit Disorder.* Wheaton, IL: Harold Shaw Publishers. Lexington, VT: University of Vermont Department of Psychiatry.

McKee, W. Witt, J. C. (1990). Effective teaching: A review of instructional and environmental variables. In T. B. Gutkin & C. R. Reynolds (Eds.), *The Handbook of School Psychology.* New York: Wiley.

Middlebrook, J. L. & Forehand, R. (1985). Maternal perceptions of deviance in child behavior as a function of stress and clinic versus nonclinic status of the child: An analogue study. *Behavior Therapy, 16,* 494–502.

Miltenberger, R. G. (1990). Assessment of treatment acceptability: A review of the literature. *Topics in early childhood special education, 10,* 24–28.

Nelson, J. R., Smith, D. J., Young, R. K., & Dodd, J. M. (1991, May). A Review of Self-Management Outcome Research Conducted with Students who Exhibit Behavioral Disorders. *Behavioral Disorders,* 169–179.

Pfiffner, L. J. & O'Leary, S. G. (1987). The efficacy of all-positive management as a function of the prior use of negative consequences. *Journal of Applied Behavior Analysis, 20,* 265–271.

Pfiffner, L. J., Rosen, L. A., & O'Leary, S. G. (1985). The efficacy of an all-positive approach to classroom management. *Journal of Applied Behavior Analysis, 18,* 257–261.

Piacentini, J., Shaffer, D., Fisher, P., Schwab-Stone, M., Davies, M., & Giola, P. (1993). The Diagnostic Interview Schedule for Children-Revised Version (DISC-R): III. Concurrent criterion validity. *Journal of the American Academy of Child and Adolescent Psychiatry, 32,* 658–665.

Reavis, H. K., Sweeton, M. T., Jenson, W. R., Morgan, D. P., Andrews, D. J., & Fister, S. B. (1996). *Best Practices: Behavioral and Emotional Strategies for Teachers.* Longmont CO: Sorpis West.

Reich, W., Shayka, J. J., & Taibleson, C. C. (1992). Diagnostic Interview for Children and Adolescents-Revised. St. Louis, MO: Washington University, Division of Child Psychiatry.

Reid, R., Riccio, C. A., Kessler, R. H., DuPaul, G. J., Power, T. J., Anastopoulos, A. D., Rogers-Adkinson, D., & Noll, M. B. (2000). *Journal of Emotional and Behavioral Disorders, 8,* 38–48

Reitman, D., Hummel, R., Franz, D. Z., & Gros, A. M. (1998). A review of methods and instruments for assessing externalizing disorders: Theoretical and practical considerations in rendering a diagnosis. *Clinical Psychology Review, 18,* 555–584.

Reynolds, C. R., & Kamphaus, R. W. (1992). Manual Behavior Assessment System for Children. Circle Pines, NIV. American Guidance Service.

Robin, A. L. (1998). *ADHD in Adolescence.* New York: Guilford.

Sullivan, M. A. & O'Leary, S. G. (1990). Maintenance following reward and cost token programs, *Behavior Therapy, 21,* 139–149.

Tarnowski, K. J., Simoniah, S. J., Park, A., Bekeny, P. (1992). Acceptability of treatments for child behavioral disturbance: Race, socioeconomic status, and multicomponent treatment effects. *Child & Family therapy, 14,* 25–37.

Telzrow, C. F. (1999). IDEA Amendments of 1997: Promise or Pitfall for Special Education Reform? *Journal of School Psychology, 37,* 7–28.

U.S. Congress (1997). *Individuals with disabilities education act amendments of 1997.* Washington, D.C.: U.S. Congress.

Wahler. R. G., House, A. E., & Stambaugh, E. E. (1976). *Ecological assessment of child problem behavior: A clinical package for home, school, and institutional settings.* Elmsford, NY: Pergamon.

Webster-Stratton, C. & Hammond, M. (1990). Predictors of treatment outcome in parent training for families with conduct problem children. *Behavior Therapy, 21,* 319–337.

Witt, J. C., Daly, E., & Noell, G. H. (2000). *Functional assessments: A step-by-step guide to solving academic and behavior problems.* Longmont, CO: Sopris West.

Witt, J., Elliott, S., Daly, E., Gresham, F., & Kramer, J. (1998). *Assessment of at-risk and special needs children.* Boston: McGraw-Hill.

Chapter 2
Behavior Problems in the School Setting

Synthesizing Structural and Functional Assessment

David Reitman and Stephen D. A. Hupp

Traditional approaches to a discussion of disruptive behavior problems in the school environment tend to rely heavily on the Diagnostic and Statistical Manual of Mental Disorders—4th edition (DSM-IV; APA, 1994) or other structural criteria for classifying behavior (Daly, Witt, Martens, & Dool, 1997). Authors typically begin by describing diagnostic criteria and providing case examples of children who display prominent symptoms of the "disorder". To be sure, there are many children in school settings who display behaviors consistent with the diagnostic criteria for Attention Deficit Hyperactivity Disorder (ADHD), Oppositional Defiant Disorder (ODD), and even Conduct Disorder (CD). However, in keeping with the purpose of this text, we wish to introduce a framework for the synthesizing the traditional diagnostic approach with a contemporary behavior analytic approach to assessment and treatment. To accomplish this task, we borrow from conceptual analyses of these issues which have been developed by some of the leading experts on behavioral assessment in the schools (DuPaul & Ervin, 1996; Scotti, Morris, McNeil, & Hawkins, 1996).

Contemporary approaches to the assessment of school based behavior problems recognize the need for both traditional (structural) and behavioral (functional) assessment. The traditional or structural approach is embodied in the DSM and is essentially a description of the "what" of assessment (Scotti et al., 1996). For example, a detailed description of symptoms displayed is highly relevant to determining proper diagnosis. By contrast, functional assessment is intended to provide the clinician with a basis for answering the "what for" or "why" question. In

David Reitman • Center for Psychological Studies, Nova Southeastern University, Fort Lauderdale, Florida 33314
Stephen D. A. Hupp • Department of Psychology, Southern Illinois University, Edwardsville, Illinois 62026

Table 2.1. Revised DSM-IV Axial Format as Suggested by Scotti et al. (1996)

	DSM-IV	Scotti et al. 1996
Axis I	Clinical Disorders	Unchanged
Axis II	Personality Disorders/Mental Retardation	Unchanged
Axis III	General medical conditions that are relevant to the management of the individual's "mental disorder."	Psychosocial and Environmental Strengths and Assets
Axis IV	Psychosocial problems that may affect diagnosis, treatment, or prognosis.	Ideographic case analysis (functional assessment). Also includes biological and general medical factors.
Axis V	Global Assessment of Functioning (Range 1 to 100; 100 indicative of "superior functioning")	Unchanged, but supplemented with rating scale and other data as indicated.

functional assessment, the clinician asks, "What is the function or purpose of this behavior?". Hawkins (1979) earlier described a strategy for combining structural and functional assessment as a "funnel", with structural diagnostic tasks (at the top of the funnel) preceding the task of selecting specific targets for intervention and making treatment decisions. More recently, Scotti et al. (1996) recommended that the existing multi-axial assessment format of the DSM be altered to more explicitly accommodate functional assessment. Such an alteration is consistent with recent legal trends in school settings that have made compulsory functional assessment for school behavior problems a reality (Gresham & Noell, 1998).

As illustrated in Table 2.1, DSM-IV Axes I (clinical disorders), II (personality disorders and mental retardation), and V (global assessment of functioning) would remain unchanged and continue to provide the foundation for a structural assessment; facilitating classification, communication, and financial compensation from third-party providers. By contrast, significant changes would occur in both Axis III and IV. First, Axis III, which presently concerns itself only with general medical conditions, would be expanded to include information about the strengths and/or weakness of the child and family relevant to management of the target behavior. Information about gang membership, special talents or abilities, family history, social support or stressors would all prove relevant at this phase of the assessment. These Axis III factors could be seen as contextual elements that influence the problem behavior on the periphery; including distal or historical influences. By focusing on both positive and negative elements of the child's behavioral repertoire and support network, a greater emphasis is placed upon building skills and replacing or altering destructive behavior through cultivating the individual's strengths.

Axis IV would be significantly altered to permit a more individualized assessment of potentially controllable factors which may be contributing to the target problems (Haynes & O'Brien, 1990). At present, the DSM-IV instructs users of Axis IV to describe psychosocial problems that may affect diagnosis, treatment, or prognosis. Scotti et al. (1996) argue that this role could be vastly expanded to provide more detailed information about the antecedents and consequences of problem behavior; the heart of a functional approach to assessment. In behavioral terms, this means identifying the variables which may lead to effective treatment or conducting a functional assessment (Vollmer & Smith, 1996).

In keeping with the above model, this chapter describes recent work in the traditional assessment arena as it applies to the disruptive behavior disorders (ADHD, ODD, and CD) and follows that review with a description of what a functional assessment would include that might lead to more effective intervention. We also seek to illustrate relative strengths and limitations of structural and functional assessment. In contrast to traditional assessment, functional assessment is founded on the assumption that problem behaviors may be maintained through a relatively small number of functional relationships. That is, problem behaviors across a diverse number of situations (e.g., school and home), and indeed, diagnostic categories, can be seen to satisfy basic needs of the individual. It will become apparent that many poorly understood problem behaviors actually "pay off" for the student. For example, problem school behaviors such as arguing, threatening, and fighting which are characteristic of ODD and CD, may produce teacher or peer attention, highly valued tangibles, access to favored activities, and escape from or avoidance of unrewarding activities (e.g., attending to a boring lecture). Occasionally, a problem behavior like daydreaming (inattention), which may be typical of a child diagnosed with ADHD-inattentive type, may be rewarding in its own right. To illustrate the interplay of structural and functional assessment, we begin by describing salient diagnostic issues and instruments used in a structural assessment of disruptive behavior problems (e.g., ADHD, ODD, and CD), followed by a consideration of the benefits of a functional approach to assessment and a case example of a child diagnosed with ADHD. In the present volume we do not address how mood or anxiety-related problems may be addressed using these strategies, however, these disorders are discussed in some detail in Scotti et al. (1996).

DESCRIPTION OF ADHD

Behaviors associated with ADHD (i.e., inattention, impulsivity, and hyperactivity) often lead to difficulties for children in academic settings (DuPaul & Stoner, 1994). In school-aged children the prevalence of ADHD is commonly accepted to be 3% to 5% and roughly 3 times more prevalent in males than females. However, rates vary based on how ADHD is defined, since target behaviors associated with the disorder occur on a continuum of frequency and severity (Breen & Altepeter, 1990). Children qualifying for a diagnosis must display at least 6 of 9 "inattentive" and/or "hyperactive-impulsive" behaviors to receive a diagnosis, and must demonstrate significant impairments in social, academic, or occupational functioning and "some" impairment in multiple settings. Unfortunately, little guidance is afforded the clinician in determining what constitutes "some impairment", consequently much is left to judgement with respect to identifying symptoms across settings. Parents of ADHD-diagnosed children usually first notice excessive hyperactivity when their children are toddlers, and the disorder is most commonly diagnosed in the elementary school years when demands for independent seatwork increase and academic impairment becomes more noticeable (Barkley, 1990). Though significant hyperactivity generally subsides as the child grows into late adolescence or adulthood, childhood impairment is related to continued problems in adulthood (Weiss & Hechtman, 1986). In particular, children with an ADHD diagnosis who also display significant aggression are thought to be at greater risk for future academic and social problems (see Robin, 1998).

For early conceptualizations of ADHD appearing in the DSM-II (APA, 1968), greater emphasis was placed on hyperactivity, and the disorder was labeled Hyperkinetic Reaction of Childhood Disorder. By the publication of DSM-III (APA, 1980), the cluster of behaviors was renamed Attention Deficit Disorder (ADD), reflecting a greater emphasis on inattention. The DSM-III model of ADD distinguished between inattentive, hyperactive, and impulsive behaviors, suggesting a three-factor model of the disorder. In DSM-III-R (APA, 1987), the three factors were combined into a single diagnostic entity with a modified label, ADHD, and reestablished hyperactivity as a salient feature of the diagnosis. The 4th edition of the manual (DSM-IV, APA, 1994), distinguishes between "predominately inattentive", "predominately hyperactive-impulsive", and "combined" subtypes of ADHD.

Biological conceptualizations of ADHD have received empirical support; however, evidence also suggests environmental influences contribute significantly to the maintenance or exacerbation of inattentive and hyperactive behavior (Barkley, 1990). Twin studies provide support for genetic influence. For example, Levy, Hay, McStephen, Wood, and Waldman (1997) reported that ADHD has high heritability (.91) compared to other behavioral disorders. Interestingly, Levy, Hay, McStephen, Wood, & Waldman (1997) concluded that ADHD is best viewed as the extreme of a continuum of behavior that varies genetically throughout the entire population, rather than as a discrete diagnostic entity. In addition to genetic factors, environmental factors have also been viewed as causally related to ADHD diagnosis. For example, research has demonstrated that hyperactive and inattentive behaviors can be influenced by consequences such as praise and peer attention (Firestone & Douglas, 1975; Northup, Broussard, Jones, George, Vollmer, & Herring, 1995; Willis & Lovaas, 1977) and through parent training (Barkley, 1990).

State-of-the-art methods for evaluating externalizing disorders call for behavioral assessment with multiple methods and informants (Reitman, Hummel, Franz, & Gross, 1998). A thorough assessment of ADHD includes teacher and parent interviews, behavioral rating scales and direct observation of classroom performance. Some also advocate the use of laboratory measures but there is a lack of consensus regarding their utility in ADHD assessment (Barkley, 1998; Robin, 1998). Most of the instruments described in this section are reviewed and described in more detail later in this book.

PARENT AND TEACHER INTERVIEWS

In the parent interview, parents provide information regarding developmental and family history in addition to providing details about the problem behavior itself. Unstructured interviews provide clinicians with flexibility when asking questions; however, they may significantly reduce agreement between interviewers where diagnostic accuracy is a concern. Over the past 10 years or so, semistructured and structured interviews have been developed which attempt to enhance the reliability and validity of the interview format (Reitman et al., 1998).

Although we are unaware of any DSM-oriented teacher interview developed specifically for diagnostic purposes, DuPaul and Stoner (1994) make several recommendations for conducting teacher interviews. The first step of the interview consists of describing the student's difficulties, including antecedents and consequences surrounding specific problem behaviors. In addition to assessing for ADHD, teachers should be asked to consider behaviors indicative of other disorders such as ODD, CD, anxiety, and depression, as well as social and academic functioning. Finally, the teacher interview should focus on attempted behavior management strategies. As noted above, no structured interviews have been developed for teachers. However, one potentially useful tool which has recently been developed is the Functional Assessment Interview (FAI; O'Neill, Horner, Albin, Sprague, Storey, & Newton, 1997). This interview could be classified as semistructured and can be delivered to either teachers or parents. Unlike the CAS and the DISC, the FAI is geared toward obtaining functional assessment data rather than for establishing a diagnosis, and would be useful for assessment of any of the disruptive behavior disorders. Information gleaned from the FAI would be valuable in elaborating Axis III and IV in the revised DSM protocol described by Scotti, Morris, McNeil, & Hawkins (1996) and detailed in Table 2.1.

BEHAVIOR RATING SCALES

Several rating scales have been developed to assist in the assessment of ADHD. Some rating scales measure a wide range of child psychopathology (i.e., broadband scales), and other scales focus more specifically on ADHD or other diagnoses (narrowband scales).

The Conners' Rating Scale-Revised (Conners', 1997) is a broad-band scale that consists of parent, teacher, and child self-report scales, and contains both empirically derived subscales such as Cognitive Problems and Hyperactivity, and subscales based on DSM-IV classifications. Strengths of the CRS-R include distinct Hyperactivity and Inattention subscales. In addition, the scale includes all 18 DSM-IV criteria for ADHD. The CRS-R has corresponding Short Forms approximately half the length of the Long Form, which makes the instrument potentially valuable in as a measure of treatment utility or when used in larger battery of tests. The CRS-R has been shown to be reliable, valid, and useful in evaluating treatment effectiveness (Conners, 1997; McNeil, Clemens-Mowrer, Gurtwitch, & Funderburk, 1994; Mullin, Quigley, & Glanville, 1994).

The ADHD Rating Scale-IV (DuPaul, Anastopolous, Power, Reid, McGoey, & Ikeda, 1998), School Situations Questionnaire-Revised (SSQ-R; DuPaul & Barkley, 1992), and the Home Situations Questionnaire-Revised (HSQ-R; DuPaul & Barkley, 1992) are some of the most commonly used narrow-band instruments developed to assess ADHD. The ADHD Rating Scale-IV consists of the 18 inattentive, hyperactive, and impulsive behaviors derived from the DSM-IV (some were reworded for clarity). Each behavior is evaluated using a 4-point likert scale, representing a continuum of frequency. Teacher and parent ratings on the ADHD Rating Scale-IV have been shown to be reliable and correspond to observations of classroom behavior and the CRS-R (DuPaul et al., 1998). Use of the ADHD Rating Scale-IV is complimented by the SSQ-R and the HSQ-R because these instruments assess specific school and home situations in which inattentive and hyperactive behaviors are displayed. In this sense, the behavior rating scales may yield hypotheses about behavioral function which may be tested in a subsequent functional assessment.

Because children diagnosed with ADHD often experience social difficulties (Landau, Milich, & Diener, 1998), part of a complete evaluation includes an assessment of the child's possible social impairment. The MESSY (Matson, 1990; Matson, Rotatori, & Hesel, 1983) and the SSRS (Gresham & Elliot, 1990) are two relatively brief questionnaires designed to measure social functioning. The two factors of the MESSY on the teacher report scales are Inappropriate Assertiveness and Appropriate Social Skills. A self-report version is also available that contains additional factors related to Jealousy, Overconfidence, and Impulsivity. The psychometric data on the MESSY are limited, and it may be best utilized as a brief screening device. By contrast, the SSRS assesses a wide range of social skills and has forms for teachers, parents, and children, and has been shown to be reliable and valid (Reitman et al., 1998).

DIRECT MEASURES

Although interview and rating scales are important features of any ADHD assessment, direct observation of child behavior, especially for younger children with ADHD, is considered an essential component of the evaluation process. Observations of child behavior can be conducted in the child's classroom or in analogue settings and are useful in both the assessment process and in the evaluation of treatment effectiveness. Moreover, depending upon how they are conducted they can be useful for both structural and functional assessment. The ADHD Behavior Coding System (see Barkley, 1990) has been used to assess off-task behavior, fidgeting, and inappropriate vocalizations, and other behaviors consistent with the diagnostic criteria for ADHD. These behaviors are typically coded during 10 to 30 second intervals for approximately 15 minutes. Peers in the classroom may also be observed as a basis for comparison. The BASC-Student Observation Form (BASC-SOF; Reynolds & Kamphaus, 1992) is another time-sampling observation procedure yielding information such as response to the teacher, peer interaction, on-task behavior, transitional behaviors, hyperactivity, and inattention. The

CBCL Direct Observation Form (DOF; Achenbach, 1986) can also be used during classroom observations. The observer rates the significance of externalizing and internalizing problems using a rating scale comparable to the original CBCL (Achenbach, 1991).

One of the more controversial components of ADHD assessment has been laboratory measurement of inattentive and impulsive behavior (Robin, 1998). Two of the most commonly used laboratory measures for the assessment of ADHD include the Conners' Continuous Performance Test (CPT; Conners & MHS Staff, 1995) and the Gordon Diagnostic System (GDS; Gordon, 1991). The CPT can be obtained on disk and loaded onto a standard personal computer, while the GDS is a self-contained computerized device. In sustained attention tasks such as these, children are required to respond to stimuli on a screen for approximately 9 to 15 minutes. Research supports the ability of the CPT to distinguish ADHD-diagnosed children from age-matched controls (Inoue, Nadaoka, Oiji, Morioka, Totsuka, Kanbayashi, & Hukui, 1998). Unfortunately, other studies suggest that while these laboratory measures typically have a low false-positive rate (i.e., few normal children classified as inattentive), they often have a high false-negative rate (i.e., ADHD children scoring within the normal range) (Barkley & Grodzinksy, 1994; Trommer, Hoeppner, Lorber, & Armstrong, 1988). Because these tests appear to classify more children as "normal" than ought to be the case, they may be better at confirming a diagnosis of ADHD than ruling out the diagnosis (Barkley, 1998). The poor diagnostic utility of these devices may arise from the fact that they poorly simulate the classroom conditions in which ADHD symptoms are typically expressed. For example, the CPT and Gordon systems are administered in relatively quiet, controlled conditions while the symptoms of the diagnosis generally occur under regular classroom conditions with far greater number of distractions present.

DESCRIPTION OF ODD AND CD

In the DSM-IV (APA, 1994), ODD is represented by cluster of behaviors best described as noncompliance, defiance, and hostility to authority figures. Children must demonstrate at least 4 out of 8 defiant behaviors (e.g., loses temper, argues with adults, refuses to comply, blames others, often angry, etc.) for at least 6 months to qualify for a diagnosis. This pattern of behavior must occur more frequently than is typically observed in developmentally matched children. Diagnosis of CD requires that a child demonstrate at least 3 of 15 antisocial behaviors (e.g., aggression, destruction of property, deceitfulness, and serious rule violations) over the past 12 months and at least 1 within the past 6 months. A key element which distinguishes ODD and CD is that in CD, children demonstrate a pattern of behavior that consistently violates the basic rights of others. Many children meeting criteria for CD diagnosis also exhibit behaviors associated with ODD, but ODD diagnosis is not given if the child meets criteria for CD. Prevalence rates of ODD have been estimated to be 2.4% (Angold & Costello, 1996), and approximately 1.5% to 5.5% of children in the general population have been reported to meet criteria for CD (Costello, 1989). Both disorders are considered to be more prevalent in males. To meet criteria for ODD and CD, the behaviors must cause clinically significant impairment in social, academic, or occupational functioning.

Despite a few minor changes in the number and severity of behaviors listed, the diagnosis of ODD has undergone few revisions since its first appearance in the DSM-III, and defiance of authority is still the defining feature of the diagnosis (APA, 1980). On the other hand, CD has undergone more significant theoretical changes in the DSM. In the DSM-III, youths meeting criteria for CD were distinguished on two dimensions: "socialized" versus "undersocialized" and "aggressive" versus "nonaggressive", with four subtypes of the disorder emerging. The socialization dimension distinguished between acts that were committed with groups (i.e., socialized) and acts that were committed alone (i.e., undersocialized). The DSM-III-R (APA, 1987) increased the number of conduct-disordered "symptoms" required for a diagnosis from 1 to 3. Currently, the DSM-IV (APA, 1994) distinguishes between childhood-onset (problems prior to age 10) and adolescent-onset types, and diagnosticians must also rate the severity of the behaviors as mild, moderate or severe. The former distinctions made between subtypes of aggressive and socialized CD are no longer diagnostically relevant.

Oppositional defiant disorder has been shown to precede CD in some children (Biederman, Faraone, Milberger, Jetton, Chen, Mick, Greene, & Russell, 1996), and longitudinal studies have demonstrated that antisocial behavior in childhood corresponds to antisocial behavior in adolescence and adulthood (Farrington, 1991; 1994). Children meeting criteria for CD at an earlier age are at a greater risk for developing more severe forms of antisocial behaviors (Moffit, 1993; Tolan & Thomas, 1995). The frequency of overt acts of antisocial behavior (e.g., fighting) decreases as children grow older; however, covert acts of antisocial behavior (e.g., lying) increase with age (Clarizo, 1997).

Recent models regarding the etiology of ODD and CD focus on the interaction between environment and biology (Hinshaw & Anderson, 1996). Horne and Glaser (1993) presented a conceptual framework regarding the etiology of conduct problems. They suggested that some children have a genetic predisposition that may contribute to conduct problems and low cognitive potential. The conduct problems lead to maladaptive parent-child interactions, and family factors such as poor parenting, parental psychopathology, economic stressors, and marital conflict may contribute to the development or maintenance of conduct problems. Additionally, conduct problems may then lead to academic problems, social competence difficulties, and cognitive distortions (i.e., attributional bias of hostility toward peers) which may in turn exacerbate the conduct problems and promote the acquisition of a deviant peer group (see also Patterson, Reid, & Dishion, 1992).

ASSESSMENT OF ODD AND CD

Many of the assessment strategies employed in the assessment of ADHD are relevant to ODD and CD evaluation (see Frick, 1998 for a review). As with ADHD, semi-structured and structured interviews continue to play an important role in the assessment process. In addition to teacher and parent interviews, information such as school and police records enhance the evaluation of behavior problems (Horne & Glaser, 1993). Forgatch and Patterson (1995) suggest that, ultimately, only school and police records can serve to establish the treatment validity of interventions aimed at serious child mental health problems such as CD.

Broadband rating scales, such as the CRS-R[1], CBCL, and BASC, compliment behavioral interviews. For example, the Oppositionality subscale of the CRS-R could be useful in determining if a given pattern of problem behavior can be regarded as "abnormal" or "severe" enough to qualify for a diagnosis of ODD.

Narrow-band questionnaires which are relevant to the assessment of ODD and CD symptomatology include the Eyberg Child Behavior Inventory (ECBI; Eyberg, 1974) and the Children's Symptom Inventory (CSI-4; Gadow & Sprafkin, 1995). Both measures provide an efficient means of assessing the frequency of behavior problems consistent with ODD/CD

[1]In some respects the CRS-R is both a narrowband and broadband measure. For example, the ADHD Index is a nearly verbatim reproduction of the symptom criteria for ADHD. However, empirically-derived broadband measures are also available (i.e., the Global Index).

diagnoses. The Children's Symptom Inventory (CSI-4; Gadow & Sprafkin, 1995) was designed to closely correspond with behaviors indicative ODD and CD diagnosis. The HSQ-R and the SSQ-R, can be used to assess the setting generalization of child behavior problems.

Direct observation of symptoms of CD and ODD present significant challenges to clinicians and researchers. The most formidable problem is that many symptoms of CD and ODD are low base rate behaviors (e.g., aggression, property destruction, theft, arguing). Consequently, direct observation can be an inefficient means of gathering information about symptom presentation for these disorders. Direct observation is especially unlikely to be profitable for the assessment of Conduct Disorder where research has shown that symptom presentation may be largely covert rather than overt (Frick, 1998). Direct observation of the symptoms of ODD (e.g., noncompliance, blaming and/or annoying others) may be more feasible. For example, classroom observations such as the BASC-SOF and the CBCL-DOF could provide useful information regarding the frequency of noncompliance. However, while both observation systems include a measure of aggression, they may be of limited utility given the low base rate of this behavior, even among children known to hit and tantrum.

A more interesting and potentially fruitful approach to the assessment of low base rate problems may be create an analogue situation or observe during a naturally occurring events that are known to be associated with a greater likelihood of problem behavior. For example, the Compliance Test (Bean & Roberts, 1981) provides a series of standardized commands for the parent to deliver to the child and has been used to assess clinical noncompliance. Systems have also been developed for parents of older children in which families are engaged in problem-solving exercises and communication styles are observed (Foster & Robin, 1988; Robin & Weiss, 1980). In school settings, scatterplot data gathered over many days or weeks by a classroom teacher can be used to determine the most opportune times for conducting observations (Kazdin, 1982; DuPaul & Stoner, 1994).

THE FUNCTIONAL APPROACH TO ADHD, ODD, AND CD

As noted earlier in the chapter, our goal to this point has been to provide the reader with a foundation for understanding the structural assessment of disruptive behavior disorders. By contrast, the functional approach goes beyond traditional assessment and asks not "what" but "why". We now turn our attention to the reasons why a given child may display problem behavior in the school setting. The emphasis on behavioral function rather than form frees the assessor to focus on problem target behaviors rather than diagnostic status. In functional assessment, the purpose of the assessment is not to assign the individual to a diagnostic category or determine eligibility for services, but to discover the variables that influence the display of problem behavior. Consequently, the assessor will need to more comprehensively address the elements of the home or school setting which contribute to classroom problems, including both antecedents (what occurs before) and consequences (what occurs after) of the problem behavior.

There are essentially three types of contingency relations that make up the functional system: escape and avoidance-, attention-, and tangibly-motivated behaviors (Iwata, Dorsey, Slifer, Bauman, & Richman, 1994). The first, escape/avoidance, refers to behaviors which occur to facilitate the termination or delay of activities. For example, a child may request frequent trips to the bathroom during classroom exercises which he finds difficult or frustrating. The second, attention, refers to behavior which occurs because of social rewards such as the laughter of a peer or a teacher's encouragement (see Ellis & Magee, 1999). Finally, tangibly-motivated problem behavior occurs when such action produces tangible (material) outcomes. For example, a child may tantrum when denied an afternoon snack. In the following section we illustrate how common behavior problems observed in school settings can be understood in terms of their function. In an attempt to illustrate the benefits of functional assessment we briefly consider a typical structural assessment for a child diagnosed with ADHD and elaborate on these data using information gleaned from the functional assessment.

The Case of Bobby

Structural Description. Bobby is an 8-year-old boy diagnosed with ADHD, combined type, following a referral from his classroom teacher. The primary complaints identified by his classroom teacher included "does not seem to listen", "extreme fidgeting", "frequently out-of seat", "doesn't wait his turn", and "loud and boisterous behavior." Rating scale data obtained from the Conners' Teacher and Parent rating scales indicated elevations (T scores of 77 and 79, respectively) on the externalizing subscale, Hyperactivity, and seven symptoms endorsed on both the Inattentive and Hyperactive-Impulsive scales comprising the DSM-IV subscale for ADHD. These ratings were confirmed through clinical interview with his mother (DISC-4 [Shaffer et al., 2000]), direct observation utilizing a comparison peer, and a teacher interview as recommended by DuPaul and Stoner (1994). Unfortunately, knowledge that Bobby meets diagnostic criteria for ADHD (e.g., scores above the 98%ile on parent and teacher checklists of behavior problems, direct observation of symptom presentation), provided little information regarding the development of an individualized treatment plan, as required by law. In contrast to structured interviews, rating scales, and other traditional assessment techniques, the behavioral interview (see Gross, 1984; O'Neill et al., 1997) and direct observation methods geared toward functional assessment (see Chapters 3 and 4) provide the most straightforward means of developing hypotheses about behavioral function.

In Table 2.2 we contrast the results of a structural assessment for Bobby using the traditional DSM-IV approach, with the data gathered using a functionally-modified DSM-IV (as suggested by Scotti et al. (1996). In our view, the modified and more detailed information provided on Axis III and IV makes the formulation of a treatment plan more likely to result in successful modification of classroom behavior.

FUNCTIONAL ASSESSMENT

To provide information relevant to a functional assessment (and Scotti et al.'s revised Axis III and IV) both behavioral interview and naturalistic observation were employed. Bobby's Axis III resources included involved and concerned parents, teachers who were willing to work with Bobby, and the absence of significant marital distress or substance abuse in the family. Relevant deficits were Bobby's poor social skills and associated problems in developing age-appropriate friendships. Selection of targets was developed from rating scale and interview data from the structural assessment. On the basis of these sources of information, out-of-seat behavior was selected as a "target" along with seatwork completion (a variable also more amenable to a permanent products evaluation).

The idiographic case analysis recommended by Scotti et al. (1996) for inclusion on Axis IV includes a functional assessment of the chief problem targets. In the present case, a structurally-oriented observation indicated that Bobby was out-of-seat during 60% of recorded intervals versus 23% for a comparison peer. However, behavioral interviews with the teacher and parents and more detailed behavioral observations suggested that Bobby was far more likely to fidget and be out-of-seat during math assignments than English seatwork. Moreover, after many reprimands by the teacher, Bobby became more active and began to shout loudly that he "wasn't going to do it" and sing in a loud voice. Following progressively louder verbalizations Bobby was usually placed in time-out or sent to the office, but not before issuing a variety of

Table 2.2. Contrast of Traditional and Functionally-based DSM Approaches in the Case of Bobby

	Traditional DSM-IV	Functional DSM-IV
Axis I	Attention-Deficit Hyperactivity Disorder-Combined Type (314.01) V62.3 Academic Problem	Unchanged
Axis II	None (V71.09)	Unchanged
Axis III	None	*Strengths*: Strong parental support and skilled, interested teacher, stable family environment. *Weaknesses*: Poor social skill development (no friends), poor math skill repertoire, poor work habits, inappropriate academic instruction (does not promote learning).
Axis IV	Educational Problems	*Antecedents*: Poor math skills and an educational setting in which many children signal an audience for behaviors inconsistent with learning. *Behavior*: Disrupting classroom with shouting and insulting other children, refusal to complete assignments, tantrums. *Consequence*: Classroom disruption often leads to escape from task completion, the provision of assistance from teacher's aide and laughter from other children.
Axis V	GAF: 55-Moderate to serious impairment in academic and social functioning at school	Unchanged, but well validated measures (e.g., the CBCL) and permanent products (homework, grades) are used to evaluate the effectiveness of interventions.

threats and accusations to peers and teachers (many of which elicited laughter from students and occasionally, even adults who were present). After a period of time, generally 30 to 45 minutes, he returned to the classroom and was often given a second opportunity to complete the assignment. On the rare occasion when he completed the seatwork, it was usually with a great deal of assistance from a teacher's aide whom Bobby favored. This scenario had apparently been played out many times and was obviously highly disruptive to other students in the classroom.

The results of the functional assessment suggested that problem behaviors that Bobby displayed in the classroom could be related to a variety of elements present in the classroom environment. First, it was observed that Bobby was most disruptive during Math seatwork, suggesting that his misbehavior at these times could be negatively reinforced. That is, the misbehavior often produced near immediate escape from (potentially) difficult or aversive tasks via the administration of a time out and a visit to the principal's office. Positive reinforcement for problem behavior was apparent in the subsequent delivery of one-on-one instruction from a favored teacher after time-out or referral to the office. Following these observations it was recommended that Bobby receive an evaluation to determine his instructional level in Math, which turned out to be far below (2 grades below) the difficulty of his present Math seatwork. However, even after the administration of Math seatwork at his instructional level, Bobby continued to display attentional problems, though not as seriously as before.

A second recommendation based on data gathered during the functional assessment required Bobby to finish assignments on his own whenever possible. When it was not possible for him to complete the work independently, he was to receive extra assistance from his non-preferred teacher, rather than the teacher's assistant whom he appeared to be able to manipulate into completing his assignments. Teachers were also to attend only minimally to out-of-seat behaviors and instead to focus on the accurate completion of seatwork (see Daly et al., 1997 for an excellent discussion of functional assessment and academic problems). Correct seatwork was rewarded with extra recess time and special one-on-one tutoring sessions with his preferred teacher (in order to bring his seatwork up to grade level). Social skills training was also pursued in an attempt to reduce the social isolation, and potentially, the reinforcer salience of peer attention contingent on disruptive behavior.

Summary of Bobby's Case

Although structural assessment provides a good starting point in the assessment of a school-related behavior problem, descriptors such as ADHD, learning disability, or severely emotionally disturbed (all of which might have been considered in the present case) provide little guidance about how to intervene effectively in the classroom setting. Importantly, the functional assessment procedures and behavioral interviewing techniques described here are practical and have been shown to be effective in a variety of settings with a variety of children of vastly different ages, ethnicities, and educational backgrounds (see. Daly et al., 1997; Ellis & Magee, 1999; Kratchowill & McGiven, 1996; Northup, Wacker, Sasso, Cigrand, Cook, & DeRaad, 1991; Northup, Wacker, Berg, Kelly, Sasso, & DeRaad, 1994; Vollmer & Northup, 1996).

For example, Piazza et al. (1997) utilized a functional analysis procedure to assess severely destructive classroom behavior for a 9-year-old boy. Results of the analysis suggested that his destructive behavior was maintained by escape from self-care tasks and an extinction procedure (in which destructive behavior did not result in the cessation of self-care activity) was successful in reducing the frequency of destructive acts. Similarly, Broussard and Northup (1995) reported the use of brief functional analyses to identify escape from academic tasks as a factor in classroom behavior problems. Still another benefit of the functional assessment approach is that it requires more direct contact between the clinician, teacher, and other support staff. Therefore, treatments derived functionally may facilitate establishing the rapport between the therapist and school personnel that is vital to the success of the assessment and intervention effort. Indeed, functional assessment seems to dictate that the evaluation yield "solutions" rather than global recommendations that appear all-to-common in traditional approaches to assessment.

Perhaps most relevant to the present discussion, Ervin, DuPaul, Kern, and Friman, (1998) described a teacher consultation model in which functional analysis was used to guide the development of curricular modifications for two boys dually-diagnosed with ADHD and ODD. The functionally-derived assessment results for one child's escape-motivated avoidance of writing resulted in the introduction of teacher-student "brainstorming" sessions and the opportunity to write some assignments using a computer. For the other child, peer attention was hypothesized to interfere with on-task behavior and the teacher was given several options for influencing the provision of peer attention in the classroom. The teacher ultimately chose to have the student self-monitor on-task behavior and provided contingencies for other children who negatively influenced the child by providing attention for off-task behavior in the classroom. The intervention was successful in reducing off-task behavior in the classroom and was notable in several ways. First, it was conducted with adolescents rather than children, suggesting the even older children who have been unsuccessfully treated via other measures may benefit from functionally-based interventions (a general contingency management intervention was unsuccessful in promoting increased on-task behavior). Second, the intervention was regarded by both students and teachers as practical and successful. Lastly, the intervention featured curricular or "antecedent" modifications of the classroom environment (including peer and teacher behavior), which reduce the stigma associated with "diagnosis" and serve to promote problem resolution rather than passive reliance on pharmacological interventions. Such interventions are important because many interventions prove insufficient for children diagnosed with externalizing behavior problems and may produce quite limited long-term benefits (Pelham, Wheeler, & Chronis, 1998).

The remaining chapters in this book describe in greater detail the tools and technical know-how necessary for conducting effective structural and functional assessments of behavior problems that arise in school settings. While blending these two approaches may prove challenging, it is our expectation that this is the most practical course to follow and that many children stand to benefit from the changes in assessment recommended within this text.

REFERENCES

Achenbach, T. M. (1986). *Child Behavior Checklist—Direct Observation Form (rev. ed.).* Burlington: University of Vermont.

Achenbach, T. M. (1991). *Manual for the Child Behavior Checklist/4–18 and 1991 Profile.* Burlington: University of Vermont, Department of Psychiatry.

Angold, A., & Costello, J. (1996). Toward establishing an empirical basis for the diagnosis of oppositional defiant disorder. *Journal of the American Academy of Child and Adolescent Psychiatry, 35(9),* 1205–1212.

American Psychiatric Association (1994). *Diagnostic and statistical manual of mental disorders (4th Edition).* Washington, DC: Author.

American Psychiatric Association (1987). *Diagnostic and statistical manual of mental disorders (3rd Edition-Revised).* Washington, DC: Author.

American Psychiatric Association (1980). *Diagnostic and statistical manual of mental disorders (3rd Edition).* Washington, DC: Author.

American Psychiatric Association (1968). *Diagnostic and statistical manual of mental disorders (2nd Edition).* Washington, DC: Author.

Barkley, R. A. (1990). *Attention Deficit Hyperactivity Disorder: A handbook for diagnosis and treatment.* New York: Guilford.

Barkley, R. A. (1998). *Attention Deficit Hyperactivity Disorder: A handbook for diagnosis and treatment (2nd Edition).* New York: Guilford.

Barkley, R. A., & Grodzinsky, G. (1994). Are tests of frontal lobe functions useful in the diagnosis of attention deficit disorders? *Clinical Neuropsychologist, 8,* 121–139.

Bean, A. W., & Roberts, M. W. (1981). The effect of time-out release contingencies on changes in child compliance. *Journal of Abnormal Child Psychology, 9,* 95–105.

Biederman, J., Faraone, S. V., Milberger, S., Jetton, J. G., Chen, L., Mick, E., Greene, R. W., & Russell, R. L. (1996). Is Oppositional Defiant Disorder a precursor to adolescent Conduct Disorder? Findings from a four-year follow-up study of children with ADHD. *Journal of the American Academy of Child and Adolescent Psychiatry, 35,* 1193–1204.

Breen, M. J. & Altepeter, T. S. (1990). *Disruptive behavior disorders in children.* New York: Guilford Press.

Broussard, C. D., & Northup, J. (1995). An approach to assessment and analysis of disruptive behavior in regular education classrooms. *School Psychology Quarterly, 10,* 151–164.

Clarizio, H. F. (1997). Conduct Disorder: Developmental considerations. *Psychology in the Schools, 34,* 253–265.

Conners, C. K. (1997). *Conners' Rating Scales-Revised Technical Manual.* North Tonawanda, NY: Multi-Health Systems.

Conners, C. K., & MHS Staff. (1995). *Conners' Continuous Performance Test computer program 3.0 user's manual.* North Tonawanda, NY: Multi-Health Systems.

Costello, E. (1989). Developments in child psychiatric epidemiology. *Journal of the American Academy of Child and Adolescent Psychiatry, 28,* 836–841.

Daly, E. J., Witt, J. C., Martens, B. K., & Dool, E. J. (1997). A model of conducting a functional analysis of academic performance problems. *School Psychology Review, 26,* 554–574.

DuPaul, G. J., & Barkley, R. A. (1992). Situational variability of attention problems: Psychometric properties of the Revised Home and School Situations Questionnaires. *Journal of Clinical Child Psychology, 21,* 178–188.

DuPaul, G. J., Anastopolous, A. D., Power, T. J., Reid, R., McGoey, K. E., & Ikeda, M. J. (1998). Parent ratings of ADHD symptoms: Factor structure, normative data, and psychometric properties. *Journal of Psychopathology and Behavioral Assessment, 20,* 83–102.

DuPaul, G. J., & Ervin, R. A. (1996). Functional assessment of behaviors related to attention-deficit/hyperactivity disorder: Linking assessment to intervention design. *Behavior Therapy, 27,* 601–622.

DuPaul, G. J., & Stoner, G. (1994). *ADHD in the schools: Assessment and intervention strategies.* New York: Guilford.

Ellis, J., & Magee, S. K. (1999). Determination of environmental correlates of disruptive classroom behavior: Integration of functional analysis into public school assessment process. *Education and Treatment of Children, 22,* 291–316.

Ervin, R. A., DuPaul, G. J., Kern, L., & Friman, P. C. (1998). Classroom-based functional and adjunctive assessments: Proactive approaches to intervention selection for adolescents with attention deficit disorder. *Journal of Applied Behavior Analysis, 31,* 65–78.

Eyberg, S. M. (1974). *Eyberg Child Behavior Inventory.* (Available from Sheila Eyberg, Department of Clinical and Health Psychology, Box 100165 HSC, University of Florida, Gainesville, Fl 32610.)

Farrington, D. (1991). Antisocial personality from childhood to adulthood. *The Psychologist, 4,* 389–394.

Farrington, D. (1994). Child, adolescent, and adult features of violent males. In L. Huessmann (Ed.), *Aggressive behavior: Current perspectives* (pp. 215–240). New York: Plenum.

Firestone, P. & Douglas, V. (1975). The effects of reward and punishment on the reaction times and autonomic activity in hyperactive and normal children. *Journal of Abnormal Child Psychology, 3,* 201–216.

Forgatch, M., & Patterson, G. R. (1995). Predicting future clinical adjustment from treatment outcome and process variables. *Psychological Assessment, 7,* 275–285.

Foster, S. L., & Robin, A. L. (1988). Family conflict and communication in adolescence. In E. J. Mash & L. G. Terdel (Eds.), *Behavioral assessment of childhood disorders* (2nd edition, unabridged, pp. 717–775). New York: Guilford.

Frick, P. J. (1998) *Conduct disorders and severe antisocial behavior.* New York: Plenum.

Gadow, K., & Sprafkin, J. (1995). *Manual for the Child Symptom Inventory (4th ed.).* Stony Brook, NY: Checkmate Plus.

Gordon, M. (1991). *Instruction manual for the Gordon Diagnostic System, Model III-R.* DeWitt, NY: Gordon Systems.

Gresham, F. M., & Elliot, S. N. (1990). *Social Skills Rating System: Manual.* Circle Pines, MN: American Guidance Systems.

Gresham, F. M., & Noell, G. H. (1998). Functional analysis assessment as a cornerstone for noncategorical special education. In D. J. Reschly, W. D. Tilly, & J. P. Grimes (Eds.), *Functional and noncategorical identification and intervention in special education.* Iowa Department of Education.

Gross, A. M. (1984). Behavioral interviewing. In T. H. Ollendick & M. Hersen (Eds.), *Child behavior assessment: Principles and procedures* (pp. 61–79). New York: Pergamon.

Hawkins, R. P. (1979). The functions of assessment: Implications for selection and development of devices for assessing repertoires in clinical, educational, and other settings. *Journal of Applied Behavior Analysis, 12,* 501–516.

Haynes, S. N., & O'Brien, W. H. (1990). Functional analysis in behavior therapy. *Clinical Psychology Review, 10,* 649–668.

Hinshaw, S. P., & Anderson, C. A. (1996). Conduct and oppositional defiant disorders. In E. J. Mash, & R. A. Barkley (Eds.), *Child psychopathology* (113–149). New York: Guilford.

Horne, A. M., & Glaser, B. A. (1993). Conduct disorders. In R. T. Ammerman, C. G. Last, & M. Hersen (Eds.), *Handbook of prescriptive treatments for children and adolescents* (pp. 85–101). Boston: Allyn and Bacon.

Inoue, K., Nadaoka, T., Oiji, A., Morioka, Y., Totsuka, S., Kanbayashi, Y., & Hukui, T. (1998). Clinical evaluation of Attention-Deficit Hyperactivity Disorder by objective quantitative measures. *Child Psychiatry and Human Development, 28,* 179–188.

Iwata, B. A., Dorsey, M. F., Slifer, K. J., Bauman, K., & Richman, G. S. (1994). Toward a functional analysis of self-injury. *Journal of Applied Behavior Analysis, 27,* 197–209.

Kazdin, A. E. (1982). *Single-case research designs.* New York: Oxford University Press.

Kratchowill, T. R., & McGiven, J. E. (1996). Clinical diagnosis, behavioral assessment, and functional analysis: Examining the connection between assessment and intervention. *School Psychology Review, 25,* 342–355.

Levy, F., Hay, D. A., McStephen, M., Wood, C., & Waldman, I. (1997). Attention-Deficit Hyperactivity Disorder: A category or a continuum? Genetic analysis of a large-scale twin study. *Journal of the American Academy of Child and Adolescent Psychiatry, 36,* 737–744.

Landau, S., Milich, R., & Diener, M. B. (1998). Peer relations of children with Attention-Deficit Hyperactivity Disorder. *Reading and Writing Quarterly: Overcoming Learning Difficulties, 14,* 83–105.

Matson, J. L. (1990). *The Matson Evaluation of Social Skills with Youngsters (MESSY): Manual.* Orland Park, IL: International Diagnostic Systems.

Matson, J. L., Rotatori, A. F., & Hesel, W. J. (1983). Development of a rating scale to measure social skills in children: The Matson Evaluation of Social Skills in Youngsters (MESSY). *Behavior Research and Therapy, 21,* 335–340.

McNeil, C. B., Clemens-Mowrer, L., Gurwitch, R. H., & Funderburk, B. W. (1994). Assessment of a new procedure to prevent timeout escape in preschoolers. *Child and Family Behavior Therapy, 16,* 27–35.

Moffit, T. E. (1993). Adolescence-limited and life-course persistent antisocial behavior: A developmental taxonomy. *Psychological Review, 100,* 674–701.

Mullin, E., Quigley, K., & Glanville, B. (1994). A controlled evaluation of the impact of a parent training program on child behavior and mothers' general well-being. *Counseling Psychology Quarterly, 7,* 167–180.

Northup, J., Wacker, D., Sasso, G., Steege, M., Cigrand, K., Cook, J., & DeRaad, A. (1991). A brief functional analysis of aggressive and alternative behavior in an out-patient clinic setting. *Journal of Applied Behavior Analysis, 24,* 504–522.

Northup, J., Wacker, D., Berg, W. K., Kelly, L., Sasso, G., & DeRaad, A. (1994). The treatment of severe behavior problems in school settings using a technical assistance model. *Journal of Applied Behavior Analysis, 27,* 33–47.

Northup, J., Broussard, C., Jones, K., George, T., Vollmer, T. R., & Herring, M. (1995). The differential effects of teacher and peer attention on the disruptive classroom behavior of three children with a diagnosis of Attention Deficit Hyperactivity Disorder. *Journal of Applied Behavior Analysis, 28,* 227–228.

O'Neill, R., Horner, R., Albin, R., Sprague, R., Storey, K., & Newton, L. (1997). *Functional assessment of problem behavior: A practical assessment guide (2nd ed.)* Pacific Grove, CA: Brooks/Cole.

Patterson, G. R., Reid, J. B., Dishion, T. J. (1992). *Antisocial boys.* Eugene, OR: Castalia.

Pelham, W. E., Wheeler, T., & Chronis, A. (1998). Empirically-supported psychosocial treatments for Attention Deficit Hyperactivity Disorder, *Journal of Clinical Child Psychology, 27,* 190–205.

Piazza, C. C., Fisher, W. W., Hanley, G. P., Remick, M. L., Contrucci, S. A., & Aitken, T. L. (1997). The use of positive and negative reinforcement in the treatment of escape-maintained destructive behavior, *Journal of Applied Behavior Analysis, 30,* 279–298.

Reitman, D., Hummel, R., Franz, D. Z., & Gross, A. M. (1998). A review of methods and instruments for assessing externalizing disorders: Theoretical and practical considerations in rendering a diagnosis. *Clinical Psychology Review, 18,* 555–584.

Reynolds, C. R., & Kamphaus, R. W. (1992). *Manual: Behavior Assessment System for Children.* Circle Pines, MN: American Guidance Service.

Robin, A. L. (1998). Training families with ADHD adolescents. In R. A. Barkley (1998). *Attention-Deficit Hyperactivity Disorder: A handbook for diagnosis and treatment (2nd ed.)* (pp. 413–457). New York: Guilford.

Robin, A. L., & Weiss, J. G. (1980). Criterion-related validity of behavioral and self-report measures of problem solving communications skills in distressed and nondistressed parent-adolescent dyads. *Behavioral Assessment, 2,* 339–352.

Scotti, J. R., Morris, T. L., McNeil, C. B., & Hawkins, R. P. (1996). DSM-IV and disorders of childhood and adolescence: Can structural criteria be functional? *Journal of Consulting and Clinical Psychology, 64,* 1177–1191.

Shaffer, D., Fisher, P., Lucas, C. P., Dulcan, M. K., & Schawabstone, M. E. (2000). NIMH Diagnostic Interview Schedule for Children, Version IV (NIMH, DISC-IV): Description, differences from previous version, and reliability of some common diagnoses. *Journal of the American Academy of Child & Adolescent Psychiatry, 34,* 28–38.

Tolan, P. H., & Thomas, P. (1995). The implications of age of onset for delinquency risk, II: Longitudinal data. *Journal of Abnormal Child Psychology, 23,* 157–181.

Trommer, B. L., Hoeppner, J. B., Lorber, R., & Armstrong, K. (1988). Pitfalls in the use of a continuous performance test as a diagnostic tool in attention deficit disorder. *Developmental and Behavioral Pediatrics, 9,* 339–346.

Vollmer, T. R., & Northup, J. (1996). Some implications of functional analysis for school psychology. *School Psychology Quarterly, 11,* 76–92.

Vollmer, T. R., & Smith, R. G. (1996). Some current themes in functional analysis research. *Research in Developmental Disabilities, 17,* 229–249.

Weiss, G., & Hechtman, L. (1986). *Hyperactive children grown up.* New York: Guilford.

Willis, T. J. & Lovaas, I. (1977). A behavioral approach to treating hyperactive children: The parent's role. In J. B. Millichap (Ed.), *Learning disabilities and related disorders* (pp. 119–140). Chicago: Year Book Medical.

Chapter 3
Functional Assessment of School-Based Concerns

George H. Noell

Functional assessment is a relatively well-established model for identifying environmental factors that maintain or suppress an individual's behavior and linking assessment findings to treatment. The development of functional assessment has legal and ethical implications for clinical practice with children. At the legal level, a Functional Behavioral Assessment (FBA) has been codified as a civil rights and/or due process protection for children protected by the Individuals with Disabilities Education Act (IDEA; 1997). Specifically, children who are identified as disabled under IDEA and who are subjected to disciplinary sanctions such as suspension are entitled to a FBA. The results of the FBA are then to guide revision of the student's Individualized Education Plan so that it more effectively addresses his or her current educational needs. Given that children receiving clinical services may be disabled under IDEA and may also be at risk for suspension or expulsion, it is crucially important for clinicians to understand the protections afforded to children under IDEA.

The legal mandates for functional assessment apply to schools rather clinicians. The clinician's primary role in cases where functional assessment is legally mandated is likely to be advocating for the client's civil rights and collaborating with educators to ensure that a complete and informative assessment is completed. However, ethical and practical considerations suggest a broader use of functional assessment in clinical practice with children beyond those instances in which it is statutorily required. The single most important consideration is that functional assessment is the *most* strongly empirically supported method of developing

George H. Noell • Department of Psychology, Louisiana State University, Baton Rouge, Louisiana 70803 treatments for problematic behaviors (Kratochwill & McGivern, 1996). Additionally, function based treatments have been found to be more effective than those that are not in the few comparative studies available to date (Carr & Durand, 1985; Taylor & Miller, 1997). Where it is applicable, functional assessment is entirely consistent with clients' proposed rights to pretreatment assessment, effective treatment, and ongoing evaluation (see Van Houten et al., 1988). The appropriate use of functional assessment is also consistent with the American Psychological Association's (1992) ethical code's emphasis on the use of scientifically and professionally derived knowledge as the basis for making decisions.

Functional assessment is a conceptual model that was derived from operant principles of learning and behavior. Within this general framework, data can be drawn from sources that are indirect, descriptive, and experimental (Horner, 1994). Indirect assessment is the gathering of information through interviews and/or rating scales from informants who have witnessed the behavior. A descriptive assessment is completed by directly observing in the natural context, recording the behavior, its antecedents, and its consequences (Bijou, Peterson, & Ault, 1968; Lerman & Iwata, 1993; Sasso et al., 1992). A functional analysis (i.e., an experimental assessment) is conducted by implementing a series of planned test conditions within a single subject experimental design. Functional analysis is the most powerful and widely researched functional assessment tool.

DISTINGUISHING BETWEEN FUNCTIONAL ASSESSMENT AND FUNCTIONAL ANALYSIS

When discussing function based clinical tools it is useful to clarify the distinction between the general application of functional analysis and the narrower use of functional analysis within functional assessment. Clarity in definition reduces the risk of miscommunication. Functional analysis is the experimental examination of the effect of an independent variable on a dependent variable (Johnston & Pennypacker, 1993; Skinner, 1953). In this general usage any experimentally controlled evaluation of the effect of one variable upon another is a functional analysis. An immense functional analysis literature exists, but most of these studies are not functional assessments as the term typically is used.

Most published functional analyses are evaluations of a treatment. Even though evaluating treatment is the most important application of functional analysis, it is not synonymous with functional assessment. Functional assessment attempts to identify the antecedents and consequences that maintain or suppress a behavior *prior to intervention* (Repp, 1994). Functional assessment is used to identify the naturally occurring factors that set the occasion for and maintain the target concern. In contrast, functional analysis is a general case experimental approach that can be used to evaluate the function of variables that do not occur naturally (e.g., a self-monitoring treatment package) as well as potential maintaining variables. As the behavior modification and psychopharmacology literatures readily demonstrate, an independent variable need be not be derived from a naturally occurring maintaining variable to change behavior.

Functional assessment provides a means of developing interventions that have an increased probability of success, act on naturally occurring contingencies, and have an increased probability of fitting into the environmental context (Iwata, Vollmer, & Zarcone, 1990). The development of internally valid procedures for evaluating environment – behavior relationships is the most important technical contribution to a function-based model of assessment and treatment. Functional analysis is relatively unique in its extensive history of application as both a basic research procedure and as a model for assessment and treatment (Baer, Wolf, &

Risley, 1968; Vollmer & Northup, 1996). For example, Taylor and Miller (1997) evaluated both the function of students' behavior and the efficacy of a timeout procedure using a functional approach.

The ability to evaluate intervention effects at an individual level is useful for disciplines such as education and psychology in which the target of referrals and services are typically individuals. Traditional group designs create a mismatch between the unit of analysis, the behavior of groups, and the typical target of referrals: an individual. It is simply irrelevant to an individual child exhibiting aggressive behavior that a time out procedure works for most of the children in some group or population. The important question is whether or not the procedures are effective for an individual child. When the function of an individual client's behavior is considered, time out may be an indicated or a contraindicated treatment (Vollmer & Northup, 1996).

PURPOSE OF THIS CHAPTER

This chapter describes critical considerations in the design and use of functional assessment. The primary focus is on four crucial elements of functional assessment: the variables that may be assessed, the methods that may be used to assess them, the contexts in which assessment may be conducted, and the linkage to treatment. Ideally, functional assessment will be an ongoing element of the treatment process whose focus will adapt as the client's needs change (Horner, 1994; Taylor & Miller, 1997). This chapter is also designed to provide a clear linkage between functional assessment as a clinical activity and the research base from which it derived. In this regard, functional assessment is a scientifically derived clinical practice and an educational best practice.

The intent of the authors is to provide the reader with a fundamental conceptual description of functional assessment. This description is intended to facilitate experienced clinicians integrating elements of functional assessment into their ongoing professional activities. The broader focus of this volume and space limitations preclude a step-by-step procedural description of functional assessment. Readers interested in a more detailed description should consider O'Neill, Horner, Albin, Sprague, Storey, and Newton (1997), Witt, Daly, and Noell, (2000) and/or Sturmey (1996). These volumes are devoted exclusively to functional assessment in either educational contexts or clinical practice. As a result they provide detailed and procedural descriptions of functional assessment tools.

FUNCTIONAL ASSESSMENT OF SCHOOL-BASED CONCERNS

Functional assessment emphasizes the identification of the learned functions of problematic behaviors (Iwata et al., 1990). A primary purpose of assessment is the identification of the consequences that maintain problematic behavior. The consequences that typically have been examined are positive reinforcement, negative reinforcement, and automatic (e.g., sensory) reinforcement. Positive reinforcement in the form of attention or access to tangible items contingent on problematic behavior has been extensively examined within the functional assessment literature. For example, every time a client disrupts the classroom her teacher may reprimand her. This provides the client with attention that may positively reinforce disruption.

Similarly, numerous studies have demonstrated that problematic behavior can be negatively reinforced by escape from demands. A client who behaves belligerently may be sent to the school's office. The termination of the academic demands in the classroom may inadvertently reinforce belligerent behavior. Negative reinforcement (escape from demands) has been demonstrated to reinforce a variety of behaviors for specific individuals (e.g., classroom disruption, Umbreit, 1995, and aggression, O'Reilly, 1995). Finally, some functional analyses have indicated that the behavior examined persists independent of environmental events. These behaviors have been described as automatically reinforced, indicating that the behavior itself may produce reinforcement (e.g., pleasurable stimulation) independent of social mediation (Iwata et al., 1990). For example, a client may engage repetitive behavior because they enjoy the stimulation it produces or because it alleviates some discomfort.

Functional assessment is based on the assumption that understanding the function of a behavior is more useful in changing the behavior than is a description of the behavior's topography (Carr, 1993; Sturmey, 1996; Vollmer & Northup, 1996). Stated differently, it is more useful to identify controlling environmental events than to simply describe the behavior. A particular behavior, such as tantrumming may be maintained by differing consequences for different children. One child may tantrum to gain teacher attention and another child's tantrums may function to access preferred items. Functional assessment permits matching treatment to the identified function of behavior. Sometimes, several behaviors (e.g, tantrums, out-of-seat, and talking-out) may occur as a function of a single consequence such as attention. In this case the behaviors would form a functional response class (Sprague & Horner, 1992; Johnston & Pennypacker, 1993). It may then be possible to derive a single functionally relevant treatment for all three behaviors, rather than having to develop a unique treatment for each behavior.

The seminal work in the development of functional assessment began with Iwata and colleagues' (1982) work with individuals with developmental disabilities. The early functional assessment work can be characterized as employing a relatively standard set of conditions to analyze the self-injurious and destructive behavior of individuals with developmental disabilities. As functional assessment has been extended to an increasingly broad range of behaviors and populations there has been an increasing diversity and complexity of variables examined (Iwata, 1994). In addition to extending functional assessment to an increasingly diverse range of populations, behaviors, and stimuli, clinicians and researchers have developed variations in basic assessment methods. This section will consider selected issues as they relate to the design of functional assessment for school related concerns for children. The intent is to introduce and highlight particularly important issues related to the use of functional assessment.

WHAT IS ASSESSED: ANTECEDENTS, BEHAVIORS, AND CONSEQUENCES

Antecedents

The variables examined within functional assessment reflect the operant description of behavior from which functional assessment was developed. Functional assessment is based on the three-term contingency, antecedent-behavior-consequence sequence (A-B-C), that has been analyzed extensively in operant investigations of behavior. Although functional assessment has historically emphasized identification of contingent consequences that maintain behavior (Neef & Iwata, 1994; Vollmer & Northup, 1996), an increasing number of investigations have focused on the role antecedent variables play in the occurrence of behavior. One challenge confronting clinicians attempting to examine antecedents in a functional assessment is the varying conceptualizations of antecedents and their effect on behavior provided in the professional literature (Smith & Iwata, 1997). This section describes published work that has included discriminative stimuli, setting events, establishing operations, and variations in task demands in functional assessments.

A discriminative stimulus is a stimulus in whose presence responses are reinforced (Skinner, 1953). Given sufficient exposure to a differential reinforcement contingency associated with a discriminative stimulus, individuals will emit the relevant behavior more frequently in the presence of the discriminative stimulus. So a child may become more likely to complain of worries and anxiety to his father if the father provides reinforcing attention for these complaints. Although the concept of a discriminative stimulus is old, discriminative stimuli have not been extensively evaluated in functional assessments. However, functional assessments have led to identification of antecedent stimuli associated with increased behavior that have been hypothesized to serve a discriminative function (e.g., Taylor, Sisson, McKelvey, & Trefelner, 1993). Based on data from descriptive and functional assessments, Taylor and colleagues hypothesized that an adult talking to the adolescent girl's teacher functioned as a discriminative stimulus for aggression that was maintained by adult attention.

Setting events are environmental events that alter the subsequent probability of behavior without changing the probability of reinforcer delivery (Michael, 1982; Wahler & Fox, 1981). For example, arguments with parents or siblings may be followed by an increased occurrence of aggressive or argumentative behavior at school. Although data exist demonstrating that setting events can alter the rate of behavior (Chandler, Fowler, Lubeck, 1992; Wahler & Fox, 1981), no conceptually systematic account of how setting events alter behavior has been developed (Iwata, 1994; Smith & Iwata, 1997). Chandler and colleagues (1992) reported a functional analysis of setting events on the social behavior of preschool children with delayed social behavior. The authors identified the absence of the teacher from the activity, a limited number of materials, and the presence of a socially skilled partner as the optimal arrangement for promoting peer interaction and reducing adult-child interaction. Kennedy and Itkonen (1993) examined the effects of setting events that were relatively distant in time and location from the context of interest. Kennedy and Itkonen identified a setting event for each of the two participants that was correlated with subsequent increased rates of self-injury at school. The setting event for one participant was late awakening in the morning and for the other, transportation to school by a route requiring many stops. Subsequent treatment eliminating these setting events was successful in substantially reducing the participants' self-injury.

An emerging theme in the functional assessment literature has been the examination of establishing operations (Keller & Schoenfeld, 1950; Michael, 1982). An establishing operation is a variable that temporarily alters the effectiveness of a stimulus to act as a reinforcer (Keller & Schoenfeld, 1950; Michael, 1982). Deprivation and satiation provide two intuitively obvious establishing operations. An extended period during which a child is ignored can enhance the reinforcing effect of attention and prior access to attention can reduce its reinforcing effect. Prior events such as previous classroom attention for aggression and sleep deprivation have been shown to change the effectiveness of reinforcers such as escape from demands (O'Reilly, 1995; O'Reilly & Carey, 1996). O'Reilly and colleagues found that prior attention for aggression and sleep deprivation both were associated with higher levels of aggression under an escape contingency, but not when aggression led to attention. This indicated that a prior condition, such as sleep deprivation, can make escape from aversive tasks more reinforcing.

Instructional and curricular variables are potential targets for functional assessment. The analysis of these variables has the broadest applicability to high incidence concerns in education. Because of their pervasive importance to children, Chapter 4 of this volume is devoted entirely to academic assessment. Several studies have identified relationships between how and/or what students were taught and increased desirable outcomes (task-engagement) and decreased undesirable outcomes (disruptive behavior). For example, providing clients choice regarding academic tasks can decrease problematic behaviors (Vaughn & Horner, 1997). Assessment procedures examining the effects of instructional variables hold great promise for providing broadly applicable functional assessments because of the ubiquitous nature of instructional demands in schools (Dunlap, White, Vera, Wilson, & Panacek, 1996).

Cooper and colleagues (1992) examined the effects of task preference, task difficulty, and adult attention in experiments conducted in a brief outpatient clinic assessment and a special education classroom. During the brief outpatient evaluation, participants responded differently to differing combinations of materials and attention. Four of the participants demonstrated substantially improved behavior during conditions associated with a particular combination of materials in the absence of a manipulation of contingencies. The remaining four participants exhibited increased appropriate behavior as the result of contingent adult attention. The second part of the study successfully applied the same general conceptual procedures to extended assessment and treatment of two students in a special education classroom (Cooper et al., 1992).

Task preference and the ability to choose between tasks have been found to effect the occurrence of problematic behaviors (Vaughn & Horner, 1997). Students with moderate to severe intellectual disabilities in special education classrooms exhibited higher rates of problem behaviors when presented with low preference academic demands than when they were presented preferred tasks. For some students, being allowed to choose between two low preference tasks resulted in lower rates of problem behavior. When presented with two preferred tasks, problematic behaviors were reduced whether the teacher chose or the student chose. Increasing children's access to choice and preferred academic activities is a potentially effective means of decreasing disruptive behavior.

Functional assessments can integrate a number of assessment procedures (described below) to develop functional hypotheses relevant to antecedents and consequences (e.g., Dunlap et al., 1996). Dunlap and colleagues assessed and treated the task engagement and problematic behavior of three elementary school students who had previously been identified as severely emotionally disturbed (SED) by school district personnel. A functional assessment was conducted for each student that included a review of records, teacher interview, child interview, interview of principal caregiver, and observation of the student in the classroom. From these assessment activities, hypotheses were developed that related student behavior to an observable aspect of the classroom. For example, the size of print on assignments, difficulty level of assignments, and the length of assignments were all examined. Two to three hypotheses per student were incorporated into a treatment package based on modification of the students' assignments. For example, one student's assignments were broken up into smaller tasks to shorten work periods and cues provided to reduce the reading difficulty level of instructions. The effect of treatment, modified assignments, was then evaluated in the classroom using a reversal design. The treatment package developed through the functional assessment resulted in dramatic improvements in student behavior for all children (Dunlap et al., 1996).

The empirically demonstrated relationship between antecedent variables and behavior creates a considerable challenge and opportunity for the integration of functional assessment into clinical practice. Examination of antecedents increases the range of variables that can be modified to improve clients' functioning. Antecedent-based intervention also may provide unique benefits as compared to consequence-based intervention. Antecedent-based treatments are proactive (Gettinger, 1988) and can allow clinicians, parents, and educators to prevent problematic behaviors rather than being limited to developing contingencies for responding to problematic behaviors.

Although determining how antecedents influence behavior is a powerful and productive clinical practice, it also is quite challenging. The brief discussion above includes assessment of variables that occurred long before the target behavior occurred in school (preceding night's sleep, O'Reilly, 1995) to variables that were present at the time the target behavior occurred (presence of a competent peer, Chandler et al., 1992). Although the array of antecedent stimuli that potentially can be manipulated and assessed initially may appear unmanageable, three general principles can be used to guide the assessment of antecedent variables (Witt et al., 2000). First, begin by assessing observable antecedents that are present when the behavior of interest occurs (e.g., Chandler et al., 1992; Dunlap et al., 1996). Second, begin assessment with those variables that are most easily modified and progress to more difficult variables only when this is necessary to obtain positive results (Cooper et al., 1992). Finally, incorporate antecedent events that occur well before the target behavior when the pattern of student behavior indicates that important determinants of behavior are unknown and the pattern is not correlated with stimuli that are present when the behavior occurs (e.g., Kennedy & Itkonen, 1993).

Behavior

An essential goal of functional assessment is to specify how combinations of antecedents and consequences affect behavior. Functional assessment has been extended to an increasing range of school based concerns such as aggression, classroom disruption (Taylor & Miller, 1997), and on-task behavior (Dunlap et al., 1996; Lewis & Sugai, 1996). This increasing diversity of behaviors is necessary for the extension of functional assessment to clinical practice. To state the obvious: practitioners are confronted by an incredibly diverse range of referral concerns. In order for any assessment method to be successfully and broadly integrated into clinical practice, it must be applicable to, and effective with, a diverse array of referral concerns. In a similar vein, the variability in presenting problems confronting clinicians is so great that no assessment and treatment model will produce published studies or guides to address every possible variation. However, functional assessment does provide a conceptual model that can be adapted to a wide range of concerns.

Consequences

The identification of reinforcing consequences is a corner stone of functional assessment (Iwata et al., 1982; Neef & Iwata, 1994; Vollmer & Northup, 1996). Although a variety of potential maintaining consequences have been examined, socially mediated positive and negative reinforcement have been examined most extensively. The functional assessment literature repeatedly has supported the idiosyncratic function of consequences in maintaining specific responses. Attention from teachers will reinforce defiance from some children, but not for others. Although the contingencies that maintain behaviors are specific to individuals, attention and escape have been demonstrated to have a reinforcing effect across a range of populations and for a range of referral concerns. For assessment purposes, attention often has been delivered in the form of reprimands or expressions of concern regarding problematic behaviors and escape has consisted of the withdrawal of demands contingent on challenging behavior. Positive reinforcement, in the form of attention, and negative reinforcement, in the form of escape from demand, might be described as a "standard" functional assessment of contingencies, additional contingencies can and have been examined.

A crucial challenge for conducting a functional assessment is the selection of the contingencies that are to be assessed. This selection raises the issue of whether or not it is necessary to assess differing forms of the same consequence. For example, the idiosyncratic reinforcing effect of attention may include many forms of attention as effective reinforcers or it may be highly specific such that only attention from preferred peers may change behavior. Recent reports have demonstrated that the reinforcing effect of attention is influenced by who delivers attention

(Cooper et al., 1992; Lewis & Sugai, 1996, Northup et al., 1995), the duration of attention (Fisher, Piazza, & Chiang, 1996), and the content of the attention (Fisher, Ninness, Piazza, & Owen-DeSchryver, 1996).

Both logically and in light of the findings listed above, attention is a multidimensional stimulus whose reinforcing effect can depend upon specific dimensions of attention. The same conceptual logic can be readily extended to tangible items and escape. Access to a peer's electronic toy contingent on aggression may function as a reinforcer, but access to his schools supplies may be irrelevant. Similarly, escape in the form of leaving the classroom may function to reinforce cursing and the withdrawal of task demands in the classroom may not reinforce cursing.

As the preceding discussion illustrates, the use of one standard set of assessment conditions will not be consistently effective across referrals. However, the extreme opposite position of including an exhaustive examination of all possible forms of the potential reinforcers examined under the full range of potential contingencies is a practical impossibility. The conflict between an exhaustive assessment and a practical assessment raises different issues for the design of indirect, descriptive, and experimental assessments (described below). Indirect assessments can readily consider a wide range of potential reinforcers because they are based on the reports of persons who are present when the behavior occurs. The primary challenge for indirect assessments is to ensure that a range of possibilities are included in interviews or reporting forms.

Descriptive assessments can potentially examine all relevant consequences if an adequate sample of behavior is obtained. The primary challenges for descriptive assessment are differentiating functionally relevant from functionally irrelevant variables and ensuring that the observational codes are sufficiently detailed that the obtained data can contribute to this differentiation. The difficulty of differentiating functionally relevant stimuli from stimuli that are correlated with behavior but are functionally irrelevant is the primary limitation of descriptive assessment (Lerman & Iwata, 1993; Mace & Lalli, 1991; Noell, VanDerHeyden, Gatti, & Whitmarsh, 2001) and will be considered in greater detail in the assessment methods section below.

In a functional analysis, consequences are delivered contingent on the target behavior and their effect on behavior is evaluated as part of the assessment strategy. The consequences evaluated should include those that occur in the natural environment. For example, if the target behavior was supported by peer attention (e.g., Northup et al., 1995), but the analysis had only assessed adult attention the analysis would be incomplete. A similar issue could arise if behavior was maintained by attention from a particular peer and that peer's attention was not included in the assessment.

A general method for designing conditions within a functional analysis to ensure accurate representation of the environment has not been developed. However, the functional analysis literature does include descriptions of procedures designed to increase the applicability of functional assessment results to the natural environment. Prior to initiating functional analyses, evaluators frequently conduct interviews, informal observations, and/or descriptive observations to identify variables that warrant experimental examination. These data can be used to exclude variables that do not occur in the relevant environment. Nonexperimental data also can be used to identify variables occurring in the natural environment that have the potential to be functionally relevant (Iwata et al., 1982). Similarly, identification of the specific dimensions of potential maintaining variables such as the sources and forms of attention that are delivered in the relevant environment can contribute to assessment design.

In some regards, the need for clinical services and functional assessments is created in part by the same factors: the great diversity of children served by schools and their idiosyncratic responding to environmental events. However, this diversity and idiosyncracy also increases the difficulty of specifying what dimensions of what consequences warrant functional assessment.

Table 3.1. Common Problem Behaviors and Some Usual Suspects for Functional Antecedents and Consequences

	Antecedents	Behaviors	Consequences
Grades K-2	Teacher demand Task difficulty Lack of supervision Lack of classroom rules Little structure No planned consequences Transitions	Talking Making noises Moving around Attention seeking Fighting Crying Taking other's things	Teacher attention Peer attention Escape from work Tangibles
Grades 3–5	Teacher demand Confrontation Task difficulty Lack of supervision Lack of classroom rules Little structure No planned consequences Transitions	Talking Making noises Moving around Attention seeking Non-compliance Fighting	Teacher attention Peer attention Escape from work
Grades 6–12	Teacher demand Confrontation Task Difficulty Lack of Supervision Lack of classroom rules Little structure No planned consequences Transitions	Disrespect of authority Talking Moving Around Attention Seeking Non-compliance Fighting Leaving school	Escape from school Escape from tasks Peer attention Status among peers Teacher attention Access to tobacco Access to drugs

Table note: Adapted from Witt, Daly, & Noell (2000) *Functional assessments: A step-by-step guide to solving academic and behavior problems*. Copyright 2000 Sopris West, Longmont, CO, adapted by permission.

Compounding this difficulty is the diversity of educational settings which can contribute to the idiosyncratic nature of person-environment interactions. The preceding discussion regarding the multiple and multidimensional nature of potential sources of reinforcement could be interpreted as a recommendation that functional assessments should test for all possible variations in the sources of reinforcement. However, many functional analyses have obtained clear results by assessing contingencies that could be described as obvious suspects given the context and behavior. Table 3.1 provides a summary of some common "usual suspects" across varying levels of education.

Broussard and Northup (1997) completed an assessment of what might be described as "the usual suspects" in many general education classrooms: adult attention, peer attention, and escape from instruction. The authors completed an assessment condition in which disruptive behavior lead to either time out (i.e., escape), adult redirection, or peer redirection across a series of 10 minute observations in the children's classrooms. For all of the boys participating in this study their disruptive behavior during the assessment was worst when it lead to redirection from a peer (i.e., peer attention). A treatment plan based on providing attention for appropriate behavior and withholding it for inappropriate behavior was subsequently developed, evaluated, and found to be effective.

In summarizing some of his own work Iwata (1994) reported "contingencies presented in a straightforward manner account for much behavior and their influence is not difficult to detect" (p. 413). Frequently schools will have readily apparent straightforward contingencies that are likely to maintain targeted behaviors. It is important to remember that the contingencies may not be influencing behavior in the manner that teachers or parents intended. Reprimands that were intended to punish a behavior may actually reinforce it. A reasonable approach to the selection of consequences for assessment is to begin with the simple form of obvious consequences and progress to the more obscure or differentiated consequences only when students' assessment results are indeterminate. Systematic progression from simple and obvious consequences to more differentiated consequences can greatly increase the practicality of functional assessment.

ASSESSMENT METHODS

The data collection methods used to identify variables maintaining or suppressing behavior fall into three general categories: indirect, descriptive, and analytic (experimental). These data gathering methods also characterize traditional educational and psychological practice and research. What distinguishes functional assessment from more traditional approaches is the conceptual basis for the selection of variables to measure and the inferences that are drawn from the data. This distinction also can be characterized as a difference in epistemology.

Within a traditional, nomothetic approach to assessment, data are evaluated through comparison of an individual's scores to a group's distribution of scores or norm (Cone, 1988). In contrast, in an ideographic-behavioral approach, such as functional assessment, data are evaluated by comparing an individual's behavior across assessment conditions or potentially across settings (Ciminero, 1986). Within a traditional, nomothetic approach, causal inferences or targets of assessment are typically traits that are inferred rather than observed. In contrast, functional assessment is designed to identify the environmental determinants of behavior. Traditional latent trait based approaches to assessment are predicated on a very high level of inference, while behavioral approaches to assessment such as functional assessment are based on a very low level of inference (Cone, 1988). The differing controlling variables assessed (trait versus environmental) and levels of inference (high versus low) also have contributed to differing treatment utility of the two approaches. Although traditional psychometric approaches to assessment are not sufficiently sensitive to have much treatment utility (Cone, 1988; Kratochwill & McGivern, 1996), functional assessment was developed specifically to contribute to intervention development.

The extreme ideographic nature of functional assessment has also led to a rather minimal consideration of cultural and ethnic differences. Since normative constructs are not employed, traditional definitions of bias based on the regression model or item-response theory simply are not relevant. At a more global conceptual level, a detailed accurate and useful ideographic assessment should include recognition of individual differences whether their origin is cultural or otherwise. The broader issues related to rapport, clinician perceptual bias, and preconceptions of how others may function are equally relevant to functional assessment as they are to any clinical interview or observation. Space limitations preclude a detailed examination of these issues other than to acknowledge their importance.

The differing levels of inference employed by traditional psychometric assessment and functional assessment also have contributed to emphasis on different data collection methods. Verbal reports about behavior have been employed extensively as primary data within traditional assessment, but functional assessment has been based on the direct measurement of behavior. Although verbal reports about behavior, naturalistic observations of behavior, and observation under controlled conditions all have contributed to the development of functional assessment, they vary a great deal in the amount of inference required to generate functional hypotheses. In keeping with its historical and epistemological emphasis on what individuals "can be brought to do rather than what can be brought to say" (Baer et al., 1968, p. 93), functional assessment places primary emphasis on the direct measurement of behavior under known conditions.

Indirect Methods

Indirect assessment is the gathering of information through interviews and/or rating scales from informants who have witnessed the behavior. Three features of oral and written reports contribute to their use in functional assessment: simplicity, time, and practicality. Asking someone who may have witnessed the behavior is the simplest way of collecting data. Unfortunately, this data collection method requires the assessor to make difficult judgements about the accuracy of the report. The limitations of human attention and memory can readily result in inaccurate reports.

The potential brevity and cost-efficiency of functional assessment based on interviews and rating scales possesses a logical attraction for researchers and practitioners alike. However, the appeal of indirect assessment is based on the assumption or hope that interviews and rating scales can consistently produce an accurate functional assessment. An inaccurate assessment practice cannot be efficient because it lacks a benefit to offset its costs (Noell & Gresham, 1993; Yates, 1985). Data regarding the efficacy of indirect measures as replacements for more direct assessment could be described as mixed. Although the original validation data reported by the authors of rating scales has supported their efficacy (e.g., Durand & Crimmins, 1988; Kearney & Silverman, 1991), replication of these findings independent of the scale's authors has either been absent or substantially less supportive of the scale's validity (Sturmey, 1996). Considering the potential limitations of verbal reports and rating scales, they are not an adequate *alternative* to direct assessment (Iwata et al., 1990). However, numerous studies report the use of informant reports as a precursor to more direct assessment. A detailed review of indirect measures and their empirical support is available in Sturmey (1996).

Although verbal reports about behavior are not a viable alternative to direct assessment, verbal reports can play an important role in functional assessment. The requests for assistance that may ultimately lead to a formal functional assessment will typically begin with verbal descriptions of behavior. Initial data collected through interviews and paper and pencil instruments will almost inevitably serve as a basis for selecting target behaviors and identifying the relevant environments. The utility of verbal reports in initially focusing assessment and its weakness as an alternative to direct assessment is similar to the assessment of other educational concerns (Shapiro, 1996).

Descriptive Methods

Descriptive assessment consists of the direct observation of the behavior in the criterion environment(s). Evaluating data obtained through descriptive observation requires a much lower level of inference regarding behavior and environmental events than indirect measures. Observational data do not require that the assessor infer that verbal reports accurately reflect environmental events because these events were measured directly. Within the bounds of measurement error, the occurrence and nonoccurrence of environmental events is known.

Observational data do not require inference about the occurrence of environmental events, but inference is required in order for functional conclusions to be made. Functional relationships may reasonably be hypothesized based on observational data. However, observation of naturally occurring events will not necessarily reveal functional relationships (Carr, 1994; Iwata, 1994). Environmental events that are strongly correlated with behavior may be functionally irrelevant and events with low or modest correlations may actually be the environmental determinants of behavior. Suppose for the purpose of illustration, that a particular student's disruptive verbalizations in class are maintained by peers' laughter. Observation of the student's disruptive verbalizations may reveal they produce teacher attention in the form of correction and redirection on nearly every occasion. However, because the relevant peer attention schedule of reinforcement is intermittent (e.g., peers laugh following approximately one disruptive statement in 10) the correlation between peer laughter and disruptive statements may appear unimportant. Based on the observational record alone a reasonable assessor might infer that the student's behavior was maintained by teacher attention, when in fact it was maintained by his peers.

Although data based on descriptive methods alone may be misleading in some circumstances, they have been successfully used to develop treatment plans for educational concerns (e.g., Dunlap et al., 1996; Umbreit, 1995). In fact one of the seminal sources in the area of descriptive assessment was conducted in a preschool (Bijou et al., 1968). Bijou and colleagues (1968) described and demonstrated an observational assessment that began with narrative observation and then progressed to systematic interval based observation to describe the occurrence of behavior and environmental events. The interval recording of antecedents, behaviors, and consequences can be used to empirically specify the relationship between specific antecedents and/or consequences and behavior. This description can form the basis for the development of functional hypotheses that can then be tested through environmental manipulation (Bijou et al., 1968).

The scatter plot (Touchette, MacDonald, & Langer, 1984) provides a more molar descriptive assessment strategy and has contributed to successful intervention design. To implement a scatter plot, a time grid is constructed that divides the day into units for purposes of recording behavior. Figure 3.1 provides an example of a scatter-plot. In order to collect data the target behavior definition would be recorded and relevant time periods would be recorded under time. For example the day might be broken into time blocks (e.g., each half hour) or activity based blocks (e.g., reading, language arts, recess, etc.). The occurrence of behavior throughout the day is recorded on the time grid over several days. This record can be used to identify time periods in which the behavior is more and less likely to occur.

The scatter plot is particularly useful in educational settings in which schedules permit the identification of behavior patterns relative to specific activities. This can permit the generation of functional hypotheses by comparison of activities in which the behavior occurs with those in which it does not. The scatter plot is a particularly valuable tool for the outpatient clinician. It is sufficiently simple in design that teachers and parents can readily be taught to be primary data collectors.

Witt and colleagues (2000) describe an alternative assessment tool, the daily behavioral diary, that can be completed by parents and teachers. This assessment tool consists of a recording form on which care givers (e.g., parents or teachers) record the occurrence of target behaviors, the context in which the behavior occurred, and salient antecedents and consequences. Figure 3.2 provides an example of a behavior diary that could be provided to parents or teachers. The record is then summarized to in order to detect covariation in settings, antecedents, and/or consequences associated with the behavior. The behavior diary is similar to the scatter plot in that it can be a practical approach to data collection when care providers are willing and able to collect data. Witt and colleagues caution that this form of data collection is only appropriate when the behavior occurs at moderate to low rates. It will not be possible for teachers to teach

Child:________________

Week of: ___________

Please record a check mark in the appropriate each time the student:

Behavior Definition:____

____

Time	Mon.	Tues.	Weds.	Thurs.	Fri

Figure 3.1. Scatter Plot.

or parents to care for their children if the behavior occurs so frequently that they are constantly completing the diary.

The research literature has produced mixed results regarding the utility of descriptive assessment tools. Sasso and colleagues (1992) examined the correspondence between descriptive and functional analyses of the aggression and inappropriate language exhibited by two elementary school children who had been diagnosed with autism. Both descriptive and experimental analyses identified escape as the controlling variable. Treatment derived from the escape hypothesis was successful for both students. In contrast to Sasso and colleagues (1992), other studies have resulted in only moderate agreement between descriptive and experimental assessments (Lerman & Iwata, 1993; Mace & Lalli, 1991). Descriptive assessment does provide an empirical basis for generating functional hypotheses, but can require a substantial amount of data and may not correspond with analytic approaches.

Child: ______________

Day: ______________

Unusual Events (Health, Sleep, Food, Visitors)	

Key behaviors to record	1. ______ 2. ______ 3. ______ 4. ______

Problem Behavior

Time	Place	Adults present	Activity	Behavior	Consequence

Special Notes: ______________________________

____

Figure 3.2. Behavior Diary.

Analytic/Experimental Methods

A functional analysis is completed by repeatedly implementing test conditions within a single subject experimental design. If similar changes in behavior occur with each implementation of the test condition a functional relationship is suggested. This has typically been accomplished through a multielement single subject experimental designs. Test conditions are typically presented in random or alternating order so that each condition is presented two or more times. The conditions in which the target behavior occurs at the highest level are typically interpreted as suggesting a functional relationship between the antecedents and consequences that are a part of that condition and the target concern. This general model for assessment has been replicated across a wide range of individuals, settings, behaviors, and independent variables.

A functional analysis can be developed to test a specific variable based on prior indirect or descriptive data (Carr, Newsom, & Binkoff, 1980) or may begin with a test of a more standard set of test conditions (Iwata et al., 1982). Carr and colleagues (1980) examined how escape from demands influenced participants' aggression. The authors demonstrated that participants' aggression and self-injury increased when it was followed by escape. In the seminal study in this area, Iwata and colleagues (1982) assessed the sensitivity of self-injury to attention, escape from demand, a barren environment, and an enriched control environment. The analysis was designed to test for the possibility that self-injurious behavior was maintained by positive reinforcement (attention), negative reinforcement (escape), and automatic reinforcement (occurrence in the absence of contingencies).

The development of the brief functional analysis (Northup et al., 1991) provides an approach that permits the rapid completion of a functional analysis. The brief analysis is particularly promising because it permits assessment at lowered time cost and is more practical in the context of clinical practice. The analysis consisted of a modified functional analysis in which each phase consisted of a single data point. To enhance the demonstration of control the contingency that was associated with the highest level of aberrant behavior was reversed such that the consequence was delivered for a desirable behavior. If for example adult attention lead to increased aggression, a test condition would be conducted in which aggression did not lead to attention, but a desirable behavior did.

Variants of a brief functional analysis have been extended to educational environments (Umbreit, 1995) and high frequency educational concerns in an outpatient clinic (Cooper et al., 1992). Umbreit (1995) tested the impact of adult attention and escape in the classroom in a brief analysis similar to the extended assessment completed by Broussard and Northup (1997; described above). Cooper and colleagues (1992) conducted their brief analyses in an outpatient clinic and examined how assignment preference, assignment difficulty, and adult attention influenced their clients' behavior.

Limitations of Analytic/Experimental Methods (Functional Analysis)

A number of limitations of functional analysis have been identified. The length of time needed, the complexity of implementing test conditions, and resources needed to measure behavior may pose significant barriers to implementing functional analyses (Durand & Crimmins, 1988). However, treatment is very likely to include the modification of the environment and measurement of behavior. If it is not possible to implement these procedures as part of the assessment the prospects for treatment implementation may be bleak. An additional limitation is that it will not be possible to analyze all possible variants of all environmental variables that may be functionally related to the problem behavior. The use of descriptive and indirect data to focus assessment and select conditions may be useful in this regard. Behavior may also acquire a new function as a result of exposure to assessment conditions. For example, a child's verbal aggression can acquire an escape function as a result of exposure to this contingency in the assessment in addition to the attention function it had initially. The use of briefest possible conditions needed to demonstrate control can help reduce the risk of this type of learning (Iwata et al., 1990). Additionally, the use of descriptive data to exclude antecedents and consequences that are not naturally occurring can also be useful in preventing this negative outcome.

A final limitation of functional analysis is that it may not be applicable to some problem behaviors exhibited by children and youth. For example, high intensity but very low rate behaviors such as setting fires, bringing weapons to school, and severe physical aggression toward others cannot be subjected to a functional analysis for two reasons. First, behaviors that occur at very low rates (e.g., twice a month or once in a school year) are unlikely to be amenable to a functional analysis. Second, it would be unethical to construct a test condition designed to elicit a dangerous behavior such as selling drugs or attaching a teacher with a weapon. However, the use of the broader range of functional assessment tools (i.e., interviews, record reviews, behavioral diaries) may be especially critical to the treatment of these types of problems.

A large number of educationally relevant concerns do occur at moderate to high rates and lack the dire consequences of weapons use. For the range of higher frequency less dangerous behavior functional analysis will be possible in at least some cases. Despite its limitations, functional analysis is the most powerful procedure within a functional assessment paradigm. It is the only assessment procedure that permits the demonstration of a functional relation, rather than the inference of functional relations based on correlational evidence.

THE CONTEXT AND COORDINATION OF FUNCTIONAL ASSESSMENT

The context in which a functional assessment is conducted will be a crucial concern for clinicians working in outpatient settings. If functional assessments must always be conducted in the home or at the school they will be less practical. Beginning with the obvious, context is not an important concern for indirect assessment methods. Care providers can be interviewed in an outpatient office and questionnaires completed by care providers can be reviewed in any convenient setting. Unfortunately, these assessment methods require the highest level of inference, are the most subject to measurement error, and have the weakest empirical support (Iwata, 1994). Descriptive assessment is as inflexible regarding the context of assessment as indirect methods are flexible. Descriptive assessment can only be conducted in the relevant context. A trained observer must collect observational data in the context in which the behavior occurs at the time the behavior is occurring.

Functional analyses can potentially be conducted across a variety of settings. Planned observational test conditions have been used in classrooms, analogue settings, and outpatient clinics. A number of studies completed by Wacker and colleagues at the University of Iowa illustrate the possibility of completing brief functional analyses or assessments in an outpatient clinic. These studies have demonstrated the successful use of test conditions within an outpatient clinic to examine a range of behaviors (e.g., aggression and academic engagement) with individuals exhibiting relatively mild to severe disabilities and have successfully integrated parents into the analysis (Cooper et al., 1992; McComas, Wacker, Cooper, Asmus, Richman, & Stoner, 1996; Northup et al., 1991).

Although encouraging results have been obtained for the use of outpatient observational tests, a number of concerns remain relevant. Some children and youth will react so strongly to the novel context that their behavior at the clinic will bare no meaningful resemblance to their behavior at school or at home (Lewis & Sugai, 1996). Unfortunately no method has been developed to identify those children whose behavior can be accurately assessed in an outpatient clinic. It is intuitively appealing to assume that older more behaviorally sophisticated youth are likely to respond so strongly to a novel assessment context that their data are not likely to represent their typical functioning.

For some practitioners drawing the conclusion that a clinically useful functional assessment for many clients will require that data be collected at the relevant settings may make functional assessment appear to be impractical. However, for school related concerns it may be possible to collaborate with other professionals to obtain the needed data. All schools should have access to consulting support professionals such as school psychologists and special educators. It may possible to work with these professionals to complete a clinically useful functional assessment. Additionally, it is an obvious reality that for most children the most effective treatment plan is going to be coordinated with and potentially integrated into their general or special education placement.

A potential means of facilitating this integration is to include school staff in the assessment and treatment planning from the beginning. Through effective collaboration and coordination it may be possible to obtain observational data from the natural setting from educators and school based specialists. These data can potentially include planned observational tests to check the accuracy of functional hypotheses or the utility of treatment options (Witt et al., 2000). The authors acknowledge that coordinating treatment planning with a school is not free of time costs itself. However, it is a means of tapping into an additional set of resources that are available to the client at no cost and assuring that a consistent integrated approach is developed to meet the client's needs.

ASSESSMENT TO TREATMENT LINKAGES

A primary reason that functional assessment was developed was to provide an assessment model that reliably identifies effective treatments for individuals. The detailed ideographic analysis of changeable environmental variables has contributed to the treatment utility of functional assessment. In keeping with the three-term contingency (A-B-C) that forms the basis for functional assessment, treatments have been developed based on modification of either antecedent or consequent events. These modifications have included changes in the antecedents or consequences that were identified in the functional assessment and the use of contingencies to change the effect of antecedents and the use of antecedents to modify the effect of contingencies.

Treatments that manipulate antecedent variables often have been based on the direct approach of eliminating or modifying antecedents identified as problematic in the functional assessment. For example, Kennedy and Itkonen (1993) identified late awakening and a particular route of travel to school as setting events associated with increased self-injurious behavior. Although it was unclear how these setting events and the problematic behavior were related, successful treatment was achieved by eliminating the setting events. Vaughn and Horner (1997) demonstrated that the rate of problem behavior changed as a function of assignment preference and that even permitting the student to choose between tasks that the student did not prefer decreased problematic behaviors. An alternative example would include discovering that aggression at school occurred on days the client had been beaten up at the bus stop. An obvious treatment approach would be to change transportation routines so the client was no longer assaulted.

Dunlap and colleagues (1996) described another example of successful treatment by manipulation of antecedents. Problematic dimensions of classroom assignments were identified based on descriptive assessment and treatment consisted of modification of these antecedents. The modifications were logically derived and could be described as somewhat intuitive (described above). Dunlap and colleagues work highlights a limitation of treatments derived from the identification of functional antecedents. The absence of a conceptually systematic and complete description of how the antecedents are related to the occurrence of behavior can potentially reduce treatment based on antecedents to unsystematic experimentation with modification of antecedents whose effect is unreliable. Alternatively, treatment based on the elimination of the antecedent is the intuitively obvious solution; however, this is not a viable treatment option in many circumstances such as when the antecedent is needed instruction.

One of the interesting elements of non-contingent reinforcement (NCR) as treatment for problem behaviors is that it has both antecedent and consequent elements. NCR is the non-contingent time based delivery of a known reinforcer (Vollmer, Iwata, Zarcone, Smith, & Mazaleski, 1993). NCR has been shown to decrease problematic behaviors that were originally found to be a function of access to that reinforcer in prior functional analyses (Hagopian, Fischer & Legacy, 1994; Vollmer et al., 1993). The application of NCR has been based on the identification of functional consequences, but the conceptual explanations of its effects have included both antecedent and consequent dimensions. One potential element of the effectiveness of NCR is as an establishing operation that reduces or eliminates the effectiveness of the reinforcer. If the client already has adult attention, he or she is unlikely to behave aggressively to get adult attention. NCR may also decrease behavior through extinction by disrupting the contingency between the behavior and consequence that has previously maintained it.

Perhaps the most intuitively obvious treatment derived from the functional analysis literature is the use of extinction. If the child's disruptive behavior is maintained by escape from work demands, then the work demands are maintained even when the child misbehaves. Withholding the reinforcer identified through a functional analysis has been demonstrated to be effective in decreasing problematic behavior across a number of studies (e.g., Lalli, Casey, Goh, & Merlino, 1994). Differential reinforcement based on functional analysis results has also been demonstrated to be effective (Carr & Durand, 1985). In these procedures the reinforcer is withheld for occurrences of the target behavior and is delivered contingent on occurrence of an alternative or incompatible behavior. The reinforcer may also be delivered based solely on the absence of the behavior for specified lengths of time. Mazaleski, Iwata, Vollmer, Zarcone, and Smith (1993) examined the relative contribution of the extinction and the reinforcement delivery component of differential reinforcement in the treatment of self-injurious behaviors. Based on their analyses Mazaleski and colleagues (1993) identified extinction as the critical component of functionally relevant treatment employing differential schedules of reinforcement.

Functional communication training (FCT) is an effective form of differential reinforcement for persons for whom problematic behaviors serve a communicative function (Carr & Durand, 1985). FCT begins with a functional analysis in which the maintaining contingency is identified. This is followed by a training phase based on differential reinforcement during which the reinforced response is an appropriate communicative response in the individual's repertoire. For example, a client who exhibited profanity because it lead to escape from difficult assignments (e.g., getting kicked out of class) could be taught to seek help as a way of reducing the task's aversive qualities and to obtain breaks through appropriate requests. FCT has been found to produce greater maintenance of treatment effects than time out from functionally relevant reinforcement (Durand & Carr, 1992).

This section was intended to introduce the reader to some fundamental treatments derived from functional assessment whose efficacy is well established. Examination of recent issues of various journals in psychology and education will reveal that the technologies for linking functional assessment and intervention are expanding rapidly. Once a number of viable treatments are identified based on the functional assessment the practicality of the various effective treatments is likely to be a central consideration.

FOLLOWING UP ON TREATMENT IMPLEMENTATION AND EFFICACY

Functional assessment is primarily focused on identifying environmental events that may influence the occurrence of problematic behaviors. This information is then used to develop a treatment that directly acts on the environmental factors maintaining the problem or changing the client's response to those environmental factors. In practice, functional assessment is not an end, but a means to achieve an end. The goal is to provide clients with effective services that meet their needs. Despite assessment's occasional indirect benefits (e.g., increased understanding may lead to increased tolerance), the most accurate and complete functional assessment has little merit if it does not lead to an effective treatment that improves a client's functioning.

Obviously, treatment design is the beginning rather than the end of service delivery. The implementation of the treatment and evaluation of its effectiveness are at the core of treatment. Fortunately, functional assessment provides tools that can be used for initial assessment and treatment evaluation. Case studies that include continuous measurement of behavior during treatment (Kazdin, 1982) are practical methods of evaluating treatment when practical realities preclude a true experimental evaluation. Evaluation of intervention effectiveness is equally important for interventions derived through functional assessment as those developed through other assessment procedures.

The use of functional analysis and case studies employing continuous measurement to evaluate treatment outcomes is potentially the most important use of functional assessment. Even if treatments are selected haphazardly the systematic evaluation of outcomes can lead to positive outcomes. Treatment can be found to be ineffective and changes made until an effective treatment is stumbled upon. Although this type of process may ultimately lead to effective interventions for many children it has the potential to waste a great deal of time and resources. A haphazard treatment selection process is obviously undesirable when technologies are available for matching treatments to student needs.

The preceding description of treatment evaluation through functional analysis assumed that the treatment was implemented as planned. However in the absence of the assessment of treatment implementation, evaluation of treatment effects is problematic (Noell & Gresham, 1993; Taylor & Miller, 1997). If a positive treatment effect is not obtained and treatment implementation data are also not obtained at least two conclusions are equally tenable (Gresham, 1989). The treatment may be ineffective or its implementation may be inadequate. In absence of treatment integrity data appropriate revision of the treatment is a matter of conjecture.

CASE ILLUSTRATION OF FUNCTION-BASED TREATMENT OF A SCHOOL-BASED REFERRAL

Table 3.2 summarizes phases and activities of a function-based approach to the treatment of school-based referrals. The initial stages, defining and prioritizing problems, are not unique

Table 3.2. Phases and Activities of a Function-Based Treatment Approach

Phase	Activities
1. Define problematic behaviors	Interviews Observations
2. Prioritize assessment and treatment needs	Interview Review of data
3. Develop functional hypothesis	Indirect assessment Descriptive assessment Analytic assessment Review data
4. Develop treatment plan	Link treatment plan to assessment data
5. Evaluate treatment plan	Ensure accurate plan implementation Collect outcome data Review data

to functional assessment. These ubiquitous clinical activities have been described in detail in other sources (Bergan & Kratochwill, 1990; Cooper, Heron, & Heward, 1987; Sulzer-Azaroff & Mayer, 1991). The crucial concerns for these stages are ensuring clear specific definitions of behaviors, selecting a manageable set for treatment, and assuring that the most important concerns are addressed first.

The third stage of the treatment process, developing functional hypotheses, is the core of functional assessment and is the phase to which the bulk of this chapter has been devoted. Functional hypotheses are developed based on the review and integration of assessment data. For the most part, the same data collection methods are used in functional assessment as in other areas of behavioral assessment: interviews, naturalistic observation, and observational tests using controlled conditions. However, the assessment process within functional assessment is specifically focused on developing testable statements regarding how environmental factors influence the client's behavior.

Within functional assessment the link between assessment and treatment is frequently intuitive. If a client uses excessive complaining to escape demands an obvious initial element of treatment would be to stop providing escape from demands when he complains. Additionally, it may be beneficial to program socially acceptable ways for the client to get breaks from instructional demands. As discussed above, functional assessment can lead to a range of treatment options dependent upon the assessment outcome, individual's needs, and the relevant environment. The final stage of the treatment process is easily the most important and challenging: implementing and evaluating the treatment plan. As with the initial assessment activities this stage is ubiquitous to the treatment of children's concerns.

The Case of Jeremy

The case of Jeremy provides an example of a rather common referral from whom a functional assessment was completed that conforms to the series of phases described in Table 3.2[1]. Jeremy was a kindergarten student who was referred for psychological services due to a range of behavioral concerns. Early in the year he had been frequently absent, occasionally late to school, making numerous physical complaints, and was described by his teacher as passively non-compliant. After trips to the pediatrician indicated no organic problems, Jeremy's mother and father independently decided to be "strict about going to school". His attendance at school improved significantly after this parentally derived intervention.

Phase 1: Defining Problematic Behaviors

At the point of referral Jeremy was described as over active, inattentive, and too easily provoked. Classroom focused concerns included low intensity high frequency disruptive behaviors (e.g., out of seat, talking out, touching others), infrequent completion of assignments, and noncompliance with teacher directions. Jeremy's disruptive behavior in the classroom had been sufficiently severe on a few occasions that his teacher sent him to the principal's office to "settle down". Jeremy's teacher's concerns in low structure settings (e.g., hallways, cafeteria, etc.) included disruptive behaviors and occasional peer conflicts. Peer conflicts included arguing, pushing, and had included hitting. During a brief classroom visit the behavioral concerns described by the teacher were observed. No home-based concerns were reported at the point of referral.

[1]The case materials for Jeremy have been adapted to ensure his anonymity.

Phase 2: Prioritizing Concerns

During the initial interview with Jeremy's teacher she described his in-class behaviors as her top concern. She felt that Jeremy's behavior was interfering with Jeremy's learning, that of his peers, and was creating a "tense" climate in the classroom. She acknowledged that Jeremy's number and intensity of peer conflicts was not terribly dissimilar to other kindergarten boys; they were simply more salient because he was frequently in trouble. The initial behaviors that were targeted for treatment were task engagement and disruptive behavior. Task engagement consisted of following teacher directions and working on academic tasks. Disruptive behavior included talking out, making loud noises, being out of seat without permission, touching others, and taking peers' materials.

Phase 3: Functional Assessment and Hypothesis Development

Both Jeremy's teacher and parents expressed concern that he was "hyperactive". Jeremy's parents were concerned about their son's behavioral difficulties, but were rather mystified by them because they had not had equivalent difficulties at home. Both his parents and teacher described him as out going and liking adult attention. Jeremy's teacher was not confident that she understood how consequences influenced his problematic behavior. She indicated that his behavior might be influenced by peer attention, her attention, and getting out of work.

A classroom observation of Jeremy's behavior and its consequences was conducted using partial interval recording. Jeremy was off task the bulk of the observation and engaged in one form of disruptive behavior or another for approximately half the observation. Jeremy's disruptive behavior produced a range of consequences that included teacher attention, peer attention, and escape from his work. Although no clear pattern was of consequences was evident for disruption, anecdotally Jeremy appeared to solicit interaction with peers and his teacher. Additionally, during the observation Jeremy never received attention when he was on-task or compliant. A structured observation was arranged to examine the effect of adult attention and to check Jeremy's skills in the types of activities that were presented in his classroom.

Jeremy was asked to sit at a desk away from his peers and work on a selection of materials that his teacher had recently assigned. Jeremy completed very little work, fidgeted a great deal, and was out of his seat within a few minutes. Jeremy was redirected to his work, but returned to it only briefly. At this point the consulting psychologist sat with Jeremy and redirected him to his work. As Jeremy worked the psychologist praised his work and interacted with him in an encouraging fashion. As long as Jeremy had this dense schedule of adult attention he worked diligently and produced work that was evaluated as average to above average by his teacher.

At least three elements of the assessment data suggested that Jeremy's disruptive behavior may have been maintained by attention. First, Jeremy appeared to solicit peer and adult attention in the course of his disruptive behavior in class. Second, he received attention when he acted out, but not when he was compliant. Third, when he was provided constant adult attention he worked on assignments and demonstrated age appropriate skills. Based on these data (gathered in two visits to the school) the hypothesis was developed that Jeremy's disruptive behavior was maintained by attention. This hypothesis was tentative because a formal functional analysis was not conducted. Also, the relative importance of peer versus adult attention was not examined because adult attention appeared to be effective, the attention of kindergarten students can be difficult to manipulate, and time constraints. The possibility was held open of examining peer attention more closely if the initial treatment was ineffective.

Phase 4: Developing a Treatment Plan

Based on the tentative attention hypothesis, a treatment plan was developed to increase attention for on-task/compliant behavior and to decrease attention for disruptive behavior. Jeremy's teacher indicated that simply ignoring misbehavior and praising compliance did not seem practical to her. She noted that Jeremy was a kindergarten student and that she felt that it was imperative that she provides corrective feedback to help him learn appropriate school social skills. Additionally, Jeremy's parents supported developing a treatment that dealt with his teacher's concerns and was based on the assessment data.

Based on the assessment data and input from Jeremy's teacher and parents the following treatment plan was developed. A "signal card" was prepared with a green circle on one side and a red circle on the other. Whenever Jeremy was behaving appropriately the signal card would be on his desk with the green side up. When Jeremy engaged in disruptive behavior the card would be turned to the red side. If Jeremy did not begin behaving appropriately within 2 minutes the card would be removed from his desk. When his teacher removed the card from his desk he was required to stand in timeout outside the door to his classroom. In addition, Jeremy's teacher attempted to ensure that she frequently acknowledged Jeremy's compliance and work. She did not talk with Jeremy when the signal card was on red or when he was in timeout. Additionally, Jeremy could earn small activities with a peer, his teacher, or one of his parents by meeting specific and increasingly challenging behavioral goals relevant to the signal card.

Phase 5: Implement and Evaluate Treatment

The consulting psychologist worked with Jeremy, his teacher, and his parents to ensure that everyone understood their roles in the treatment plan. Jeremy and his teacher were observed practicing using the signal card and subsequently using it in class. The primary outcome data collected were then number of timeouts per day. These data were evaluated for trend and against a goal of no more than one timeout per day. Additionally, observational data were collected during two brief classroom visits. Initially Jeremy received several timeouts per day, but the frequency of timeouts trended steadily downward such that he had no timeouts during the third week of treatment. Additionally, he was consistently complaint and on-task during both follow-up class visits. No disruptive behaviors were observed. Jeremy's teacher and parents reported a high degree of satisfaction with his progress. As Jeremy continued to progress the monitoring strategy and his behavioral goals shifted to the number of times the signal card was turned to red (time outs remained very infrequent).

CONCLUSION

Functional assessment is a conceptual model for clinical assessment rather than a specific set of activities. A clinician can conduct an interview or observation as part of a functional assessment or may engage in those same activities to achieve different clinical goals. The goal of functional assessment is to develop an ideographic understanding of the client's interactions with their environment and how these interactions influence the referral concerns. Functional assessment emphasizes examination of changeable environmental variables such as schoolwork demands, attention, and escape from work. Although the bulk of the functional assessment research has been conducted with individuals with low incidence disabilities who exhibit severe challenging behavior (Nelson, Roberts, Mathur, & Rutherford, 1999), an increasing number of functional assessment studies have been published examining milder high incidence problems (e.g., Cooper et al., 1990).

At its most basic level the professional literature relevant to functional assessment and analysis have a rather simple and intuitively obvious message. Measuring an individual's behavior over a series of environmental conditions can contribute to decisions regarding how to improve that individual's functioning. That contribution may be facilitating the design of an effective intervention or it may be the evaluation and modification of an existing treatment. The challenge for clinicians will frequently be identifying and obtaining adequate data upon which to base decisions.

REFERENCES

American Psychological Association Ethics Committee (1992). Ethical Principles of Psychologists and Code of Conduct. *American Psychologist, 47,* 1597–1611.

Baer, D. M., Wolf, M. M., & Risley, T. R. (1968). Some current dimensions of applied behavior analysis. *Journal of Applied Behavior Analysis, 1,* 91–97.

Bergan, J. R., & Kratochwill, T. R. (1990). *Behavioral consultation and therapy.* New York: Plenum.

Bijou, S. W., Peterson, R. F., & Ault, M. H. (1968). A method to integrate descriptive and experimental field studies at the level of data and empirical concepts. *Journal of Applied Behavior Analysis, 1,* 175–191.

Broussard, C. & Northup, J. (1997). The use of functional analysis to develop peer interventions for disruptive classroom behavior. *School Psychology Quarterly, 12,* 65–76.

Carr, E. G. (1993). Behavior analysis is not ultimately about behavior. *The Behavior Analyst, 16,* 47–49.

Carr, E. G. (1994). Emerging themes in the functional analysis of problem behavior. *Journal of Applied Behavior Analysis, 27,* 393–399.

Carr, E. G., & Durand, V. M. (1985). Reducing behavior problems through functional communication training. *Journal of Applied Behavior Analysis, 18,* 111–126.

Carr, E. G., Newsom, C. D., & Binkoff, J. A. (1980). Escape as a factor in the aggressive behavior of two retarded children. *Journal of Applied Behavior Analysis, 13,* 101–117.

Chandler, L. K., Lubeck, R. C., & Fowler, S. A. (1992). Generalization and maintenance of preschool children's social skills: A critical review and analysis. *Journal of Applied Behavior Analysis, 25,* 415–428.

Ciminero, A. R. (1986). Behavioral assessment: An overview. In A. R. Ciminero, K. S. Calhoun, & H. E. Adams (Eds.), *Handbook of behavioral assessment* (2nd ed., pp 3–11). New York: Wiley.

Cone, J. D. (1988). Psychometric considerations and the multiple models of behavioral consultation. In A. S. Bellack & M. Hersen (Eds.), *Behavioral assessment: A practical handbook* (3rd ed., pp. 42–66). New York: Pergamon.

Cooper, J. O., Heron, T. E., & Heward, W. L. (1987). *Applied Behavior Analysis.* Upper Saddle River, NJ: Prentice Hall.

Cooper, L. J., Wacker, D. P., Thursby, D., Plagmann, L. A., Harding, J., Millard, T., & Derby, M. (1992). Analysis of the effects of task preferences, task demands, and adult attention on child behavior in outpatient and classroom settings. *Journal of Applied Behavior Analysis, 25,* 823–840.

Durand, V. M. & Carr, E. G. (1992). An analysis of maintenance following functional communication training. *Journal of Applied Behavior Analysis, 25,* 777–794.

Durand, V. M. & Crimmins, D. B. (1988). Identifying the variables maintaining self-injurious behavior. *Journal of Autism and Developmental Disorders, 18,* 99–117.

Dunlap, G., White, R., Vera, A., Wilson, D., & Panacek, L. (1996). The effects of multi-component, assessment-based curricular modifications on the classroom behavior of children with emotional and behavioral disorders. *Journal of Behavioral Education, 4,* 481–500.

Fisher, W. W., Ninness, H. A. C., Piazza, C. C., & Owen-DeSchryver, J. S. (1996). On the reinforcing effects of the content of verbal attention. *Journal of Applied Behavior Analysis, 29,* 235–238.

Fisher, W. W., Piazza, C. C., & Chaing, C. L. (1996). Effects of equal and unequal reinforcer duration during functional analysis. *Journal of Applied Behavior Analysis, 29,* 117–120.

Gettinger, M. (1988). Methods of proactive classroom management. *School Psychology Review, 17,* 227–242.

Gresham, F. M. (1989). Assessment of treatment integrity in school consultation and prereferral intervention. *School Psychology Quarterly, 18,* 37–50.

Hagopian, L. P., Fisher, W. W., & Legacy, S. M. (1994). Schedule effects of noncontingent reinforcement on attention-maintained destructive behavior in identical quadruplets. *Journal of Applied Behavior Analysis, 27,* 317–325.

Horner, R. H. (1994). Functional assessment: Contributions and future directions. *Journal of Applied Behavior Analysis, 27,* 401–404.

Individuals with Disabilities Education Act Amendments of 1997, (Pub L No. 105–17). 20 U.S.C. ' 1400 *et seq.*

Iwata, B. A. (1994). Functional analysis methodology: Some closing comments. *Journal of Applied Behavior Analysis, 27,* 413–418.

Iwata, B. A., Dorsey, M., Silfer, K., Bauman, K., & Richman, G. (1982). Toward a functional analysis of self-injury. *Analysis and intervention in developmental disabilities, 2,* 3–20.

Iwata, B. A., Vollmer, T. R., & Zarcone, J. R. (1990). The experimental (functional) analysis of behavior disorders: Methodology, applications, and limitations. In A. C. Repp & N. N. Singh (Eds.), *Perspectives on the use of nonaversive and aversive interventions for persons with developmental disabilities* (pp. 301–330). Sycamore, IL: Sycamore Publishing Co.

Johnston, J. M., & Pennypacker, H. S. (1993). *Strategies and tactics of behavioral research.* Hillsdale, NJ: Lawrence Erlbaum Associates.

Kazdin, A. E. (1982). *Single-case research designs: Methods for clinical and applied settings.* New York: Oxford University Press.

Kearney, C. A. & Silverman, W. K. (1990). A preliminary analysis of a functional model of assessment and treatment for school refusal behavior. *Behavior Modification, 14,* 340–366.

Keller, F. S. & Schonfeld, W. N. (1950). *Principles of psychology: A systematic text in the science of behavior.* New York: Appleton-Century-Crofts.

Kennedy, C. H., & Itkonen, T. (1993). Effects of setting events on the problem behavior of students with severe disabilities. *Journal of Applied Behavior Analysis, 26,* 321–327.

Kratochwill, T. R., & McGivern, J. E. (1996). Clinical diagnosis, behavioral assessment, and functional analysis: Examining the connection between assessment and intervention. *School Psychology Review, 25,* 342–355.

Lalli, J. S., Casey, S., Goh, H., & Merlino, J. (1994). Treatment of escape-maintained aberrant behavior with escape extinction and predictable routines. *Journal of Applied Behavior Analysis, 27,* 705–714.

Lewis, T. J. & Sugai, G. (1996). Functional assessment of problem behavior: A pilot investigation of the comparative and interactive effects of teacher and peer social attention on students in general education. *School Psychology Quarterly, 11,* 1–19.

Lerman, D. C., & Iwata, B. A. (1993). Descriptive and experimental analysis of variables maintaining self-injurious behavior. *Journal of Applied Behavior Analysis, 26,* 293–319.

Mace, F. C., & Lalli, J. S. (1991). Linking descriptive and experimental analysis in the treatment of bizarre speech. *Journal of Applied Behavior Analysis, 24,* 553–562.

Mazaleski, J. L., Iwata, B. A., Vollmer, T. R., Zarcone, J. R., & Smith, R. G. (1993). Analysis of the reinforcement and extinction components in DRO contingencies with self-injury. *Journal of Applied Behavior Analysis, 26,* 143–156.

McComas, J. J., Wacker, D. P., Cooper, L. J., Asmus, J. M., Richman, D., & Stoner, B. (1991). A brief experimental analysis of stimulus prompts for accurate responding on academic tasks in an outpatient clinic. *Journal of Applied Behavior Analysis, 29,* 397–401.

Michael, J. (1982). Distinguishing between discriminative and motivational functions of stimuli. *Journal of the Experimental Analysis of Behavior, 37,* 149–155.

Nelson, J. R., Roberts, M., Mathur, S., & Rutherford, R. (1999). Has public policy exceeded our knowledge base?: A review of the functional behavioral assessment literature. *Behavioral Disorders, 24,* 169–179.

Neef, N. A., & Iwata, B. A. (1994). Current research on functional analysis methodologies: An introduction. *Journal of Applied Behavior Analysis, 27,* 211–214.

Noell, G. H., & Gresham, F. M. (1993). Functional outcome analysis: Do the benefits of consultation and prereferral intervention justify the costs? *School Psychology Quarterly, 8,* 200–226.

Noell, G. H., VanDerHeyden, A. M., Gatti, S. L., & Whitmarsh, E. L. (2001). Functional assessment of the effects of escape and attention on students' compliance during instruction. *School Psychology Quarterly, 16,* 253–269.

Northup, J., Broussard, C., Jones, K., George, T., Vollmer, T. R., & Herring, M. (1995). The differential effects of teacher and peer attention on the disruptive classroom behavior of three children with a diagnosis of attention deficit hyperactivity disorder. *Journal of Applied Behavior Analysis, 28,* 227–228.

Northup, J., Wacker, D., Sasso, G., Steege, M., Cigrand, K., Cook, J., & DeRaad, A. (1991). A brief functional analysis of aggressive and alternative behavior in an outclinic setting. *Journal of Applied Behavior Analysis, 24,* 509–522.

O'Neill, R. E., Horner, R. H., Albin, R. W., Sprague, J. R., Storey, K., & Newton, J. S. (1997). *Functional assessment and program development for problem behavior: A practical handbook* (2nd ed.). Pacific Grove, CA: Brooks/Cole.

O'Reilly, M. F. (1995). Functional analysis and treatment of escape-maintained aggression correlated with sleep deprivation. *Journal of Applied Behavior Analysis, 28,* 225–226.

O'Reilly, M. F., & Carey, Y. (1996). A preliminary analysis of the effects of prior classroom conditions on performance under analogue analysis conditions. *Journal of Applied Behavior Analysis, 29,* 581–584.

Repp, A. (1994). Comments on functional analysis procedures for school-based behavior problems. *Journal of Applied Behavior Analysis, 27,* 409–411.

Sasso, G. M., Reimers, T. M., Cooper, L. J., Wacker, D., Berg, W., Steege, M., Kelly, L., & Allaire, A. (1992). Use of descriptive and experimental analysis to identify the functional properties of aberrant behavior in school settings. *Journal of Applied Behavior Analysis, 25,* 809–821.

Shapiro, E. S. (1996). *Academic skills problems: Direct assessment and intervention* (2nd ed.). New York: Guilford.

Skinner, B. F. (1953). *Science and human behavior.* New York: Macmillian.

Smith, R. G., & Iwata, B. A. (1997). Antecedent influences on behavior disorders. *Journal of Applied Behavior Analysis, 30,* 343–375.

Sprague, J. R., & Horner, R. H. (1992). Covariation within functional response classes: Implications for treatment of severe problem behavior. *Journal of Applied Behavior Analysis, 25,* 735–745.

Sturmey, P. (1996). *Functional analysis in clinical psychology.* New York: Wiley.

Sulzer-Azaroff, B., & Mayer, G. R. (1991). *Behavior analysis for lasting change.* Chicago: Holt, Rinehart, & Winston, Inc.

Taylor, J. & Miller, M. (1997). When timeout works some of the time: The importance of treatment integrity and functional assessment. *School Psychology Quarterly, 12,* 4–22.

Taylor, J. C., Sisson, L. A., Mc Kelvey, J. L., & Trefelner, M. F. (1993). Situation specificity in attention-seeking problem behavior. *Behavior Modification, 17,* 474–497.

Touchette, P. E., MacDonald, R. F., & Langer, S. N. (1985). A scatter plot for identifying stimulus control of problem behavior. *Journal of Applied Behavior Analysis, 18,* 343–351.

Umbreit, J. (1995). Functional assessment and intervention in a regular classroom setting for the disruptive behavior of a student with attention deficit hyperactivity disorder. *Behavioral Disorders, 20,* 267–278.

Van Houten, R. Axelrod, S., Bailey, J. S., Favell, J. E., Foxx, R. M., Iwata, B. A., & Lovaas, O. I. (1988). The right to effective behavioral treatment. *Journal of Applied Behavior Analysis, 21,* 381–384.

Vaughn, B. J., & Horner, R. H. (1997). Identifying instructional tasks that occasion problem behaviors and assessing the effects of student versus teacher choice among these tasks. *Journal of Applied Behavior Analysis, 30,* 299–312.

Vollmer, T. R., Iwata, B. A., Zarcone, J. R., Smith, R. G., & Mazaleski, J. L. (1993). The role of attention in the treatment of attention-maintained self-injurious behavior: Noncontingent reinforcement and differential reinforcement of other behavior. *Journal of Applied Behavior Analysis, 26,* 9–21.

Vollmer, T. R., & Northup, J. (1996). Some implications of functional analysis for school psychology. *School Psychology Quarterly, 11,* 76–92.

Wahler, R. G., & Fox, J. J. (1981). Setting events in applied behavior analysis: Toward a conceptual and methodological expansion. *Journal of Applied Behavior Analysis, 14,* 327–338.

Witt, J. C., Daly, E., & Noell, G. H. (2000). *Functional assessments: A step-by-step guide to solving academic and behavior problems.* Longmont, CO: Sopris West.

Yates, B. T. (1985). Cost-effectiveness analysis and cost-benefit analysis: An introduction. *Behavioral Assessment, 7,* 207–234.

Chapter 4
Direct Assessment of Clients' Instructional Needs

Improving Academic, Social, and Emotional Outcomes

George H. Noell

For many children, a referral for psychological services may have its genesis in or be maintained by a mismatch between their educational needs and their instructional program. As a result, the most important element of a comprehensive psychological assessment for many children is the assessment of their instructional needs. A case encountered by one of the authors (GN) illustrates this point. A third grader was referred for psychological services due to his disruptive and disobedient behaviors in the classroom. The problematic behaviors occurred frequently, were relatively chronic, and did not have a promising prognosis. A curriculum-based assessment was conducted in preparation for a series of treatment probes that were planned to identify an effective treatment for his disruption and defiance. Based on this academic assessment the young man was provided instructional materials that were matched to his current educational needs and skills. When the student was provided materials in which he could complete his assignments with a moderate degree of success the problematic behavior *disappeared.*

The curricular modification resulted in the young man following his teacher's directions, sitting quietly at his seat, doing his work, and making use of an opportunity to learn. The more elaborate treatment that was being developed to address his problematic social behavior proved completely unnecessary. Effective treatment was achieved by arranging instructional materials that provided the student the opportunity to learn and succeed at school. It is also important

George H. Noell • Department of Psychology, Louisiana State University, Baton Rouge, Louisiana 70803

Table 4.1. Concerns that Can Be Addressed through Academic Assessment of Clinical Child Referrals

1. Chronic failure and the negative feedback it engenders is an undesirable developmental condition for any child.
2. Chronic academic failure that can set the occasion for problematic behaviors, negative affective states, and a negative self-perception.
3. Chronic academic failure can exacerbate other clinical concerns.
4. Other persons or professionals working with the child may assume that academic failure is the result of emotional or behavioral concerns. As a result, they may not seriously examine the child's academic needs.
5. Learning and academic performance are central expectations of children in schools. Successful treatment should allow a child to meet these expectations.

to recognize that it may have been possible to develop an environmental or pharmacological treatment sufficiently powerful to suppress his antagonizing behaviors without modifying his instructional program. When the referral was initiated the young man's teacher was focused on his disruptive and defiant behavior. Her conception of the referral was consistent with how many parents and teachers approach challenging behavior: the problematic behavior interferes with the client's learning and that of his peers. She did not express any concern that his problematic behavior was the result of a mismatch between his needs and the instructional programming provided to him. Parents and teachers will frequently fail to consider the possibility that a child's problematic emotional state or social behavior is the result of a habitually frustrating and confusing educational context.

The routine examination of clients' academic skills and educational needs can strengthen clinical practice and improve treatment outcomes in several ways (see Table 4.1). First, chronic academic failure sets up a pattern of habitual negative feedback to children from parents and teachers. Habitual feedback that he or she is a failure is an undesirable developmental outcome for any child irrespective of its additional developmental and clinical effects. Second, clinical concerns may originate in a mismatch between the child's needs and instructional program. Antisocial behavior, negative affect, and academic failure are three clinical concerns that are frequently co-morbid (Patterson, 1993). Additionally, for some clients a successful treatment can be achieved through appropriate modification of instruction (e.g., Kern, Childs, Dunlap, Clarke, & Falk, 1994). Third, even if the current referral did not originate with instructional problems, repeated failure and frustration five days a week at school are likely to exacerbate clinical concerns such as anxiety, depression, or antisocial behaviors. Fourth, other professionals working with the child may assume that academic failure is the result of emotional or behavioral problems and may not seriously examine the child's academic needs (Witt, Daly, & Noell, 2000). If the clinician does not ensure that the child's instructional needs are systematically assessed the accuracy of this assumption will remain unknown. Finally, learning and academic performance are central expectations of children in schools. Any treatment that resolves the initial clinical concern, but does not contribute to the child's ultimate academic success is a Pyrrhic victory. Long-term developmental success for children includes academic success.

PURPOSE OF THIS CHAPTER

This chapter is based on the assumption that assessing a child's instructional needs is an important element of the clinical assessment of school-based concerns for children and youth. This chapter describes some fundamental considerations in the assessment of instructional concerns and describes some contemporary approaches to academic assessment. The approaches that have the greatest utility for designing educational programs are emphasized and the limitations of traditional assessment practices for developing instructional programs are considered.

This chapter is intended to be useful to clinicians who may be consumers of academic assessment reports as well as those who may conduct academic assessments themselves. In many cases a clinician working in an outpatient setting may not be in the best position to complete a systematic assessment of the child's instructional needs. School based professionals may be in a better position to conduct an informative academic assessment due to their ready access to curricular information, educational assessment tools, and the relevant classroom. In these instances, the clinician is more likely to be a consumer of reports completed by educators than the individual conducting an academic assessment. Coordinated action by the clinician, family, and school frequently will be an important element of successful treatment. The appropriate interpretation of educational assessment reports is a specialized skill that warrants careful consideration. This is a particularly important issue given that research has shown that some historic interpretations of assessment devices are *invalid*. This chapter addresses some fundamental issues in the design and interpretation of educational assessments.

The authors also acknowledge that clinicians may reasonably choose to forgo an academic assessment in some cases. For example, when teachers, the child, and parents express no instructional concerns *and* the focus of the referral is behaviors that occur outside of the instructional context, an assessment of instructional needs may not be the most appropriate expenditure of resources. However, for a great many children referred for psychological services, academic failure, academic frustration, and/or problematic behavior in the instructional context are a significant element of the referral concern.

TRADITIONAL APPROACHES TO ACADEMIC ASSESSMENT

Standardized norm-referenced ability and achievement tests have been used extensively as assessment tools in educational and clinical assessment. Unfortunately, these assessment tools have little utility in developing effective instructional plans for children. The interpretive guidelines that have been developed for norm-referenced ability tests make instructional recommendations based on an aptitude-by-treatment interaction (ATI) model. An ATI assumes that the test is measuring some underlying aptitude (e.g., being an auditory learner) and that matching instruction to this aptitude to will improve the instructional outcome. Unfortunately, the available literature does not support this intuitively appealing assumption (Braden & Kratochwill, 1997; Macmann & Barnett, 1997). Currently available ability assessment has not been shown to have treatment utility (Braden & Kratochwill, 1997; Macmann & Barnett, 1997).

Further, recent research has called into question the entire enterprise of attempting to identify individual aptitudes through ipsative profile analysis based on currently available instruments. Macmann and Barnett (1997) have demonstrated that ipsative profiles (i.e., subtest scatter analysis) that have been used to identify individual strengths and weaknesses based on the Wechsler Intelligence Scale for Children-III (WISC-III; Wechsler, 1991) are insufficiently reliable to be valid. This is a particularly important finding given the broad use of the WISC-III and the ready availability of interpretative guides (e.g., Kaufman, 1994) that link WISC-III subtest scatter to instructional recommendations.

Standardized achievement tests provide a logical alternative to ability tests for developing educational programs. The major standardized achievement tests are readily available, reliable, and have evidence for their validity (Sattler, 1988). Unfortunately, a number of fundamental considerations limit the utility of the standardized achievement test as a guide to educational programming. First, derived scores are not typically instructionally useful because they are too global and do not describe specific skills. Additionally, derived scores suggest instructional readiness when it is inappropriate to interpret them in this way. Second, standardized achievement tests are poor choices for monitoring clients' progress because they are insensitive to change. Third, scores on achievement tests can be strongly influenced by the extent to which they overlap or fail to overlap with the local curriculum (Bell, Lentz, & Graden, 1992). Fourth, the selection type responses employed in some achievement tests are at odds with typical teaching practices which emphasize production responses. Finally, standardized achievement tests are poorly equipped to consider how the client's environment influences their academic functioning.

In summary, standardized norm-referenced ability and achievement tests were developed within a trait-based nomothetic measurement model. They are designed to assign a position within a normative distribution to individuals and are frequently used to assign group membership to individuals (e.g., mentally retarded). However, they do not provide an adequate basis for making educational programming recommendations. The treatment of utility of ATIs and ability tests remains unsupported by the professional literature. Typical achievement tests are insufficiently specific and give insufficient consideration to the role of the instructional context to serve as a primary basis for developing educational interventions (Shapiro, 1996). The authors encourage clinicians to regard with considerable skepticism any educational programming recommendations that are based primarily on standardized testing.

CURRICULUM-BASED MEASUREMENT

Curriculum-based measurement (CBM) is a collection of standardized measurement procedures that were developed to improve upon and supplement traditional norm-referenced assessment practices. In particular, CBM was developed to provide educators powerful and practical formative evaluation tools. Formative evaluation tools contribute to the identification of problems, specification of current functioning, design of intervention, and evaluation of intervention effectiveness. As a result CBM has been used extensively to identify clients' instructional needs as well as to develop, evaluate, and refine instructional programs (Deno, 1985; Fuchs & Deno, 1991; Shinn, 1989). CBM has emphasized the development of tools that are brief, sensitive, reliable, valid, and for which parallel forms can readily be developed. These characteristics are crucial for a measurement tool that can be used for formative evaluation. The technical and procedural characteristics that have contributed to CBM's utility for educators can also contribute to the incorporation of CBM within clinical practice. The potential utility of CBM for clinical practitioners will be considered after describing critical characteristics of CBM.

CBM measures emphasize the client's rate of correct responding on standardized tasks that are representative of the client's curriculum. As a result, CBM measures are very sensitive to client progress and assess the development of fluency as well as skill acquistion (Shinn, 1989). The development of fluency (i.e., sustained, fast-paced, accurate responding) is a critical academic outcome that prepares clients to apply basic tool skills across a range of tasks. For example, students who can read words fluently are more likely to comprehend what they have read (Deno et al., 1982). CBM procedures were developed such that they can be adapted to a range of assessment needs. For example, alternative parallel forms can readily be developed from available curricular materials. Additionally, standardized CBM materials are also available from sources such as Children's Educational Services, Inc. (Minneapolis, MN). Adaptations of CBM have been developed to identify crucial instructional targets and to identify effective instructional interventions (e.g., Daly, Martens, Dool, & Hintz, 1998).

A relatively extensive research base supports the technical adequacy of CBM as well as its treatment utility. Across a number of studies CBM measures have been found to be reliable (Marston, 1989). Additionally, CBM measures have been found to have moderate to strong validity coefficients when correlated with traditional tests of academic achievement (Marston, 1989). For example, CBM oral reading rates have been found to be strongly correlated to tests of reading comprehension (e.g., $r = .82$; Deno, Mirkin, & Chiang, 1982). Additionally, CBM has been found to have treatment utility. Research supports the treatment utility of CBM both as a tool for developing treatment plans and as a procedure for monitoring their efficacy once they are implemented (Hintze, Daly, & Shapiro, 1998).

The CBM procedures described herein are most relevant to the assessment of basic tool skills such as reading decoding, computation, and basic writing skills. They are the typical assessment targets for elementary school students. For middle school and high school students basic tool skills often are an important concern. The authors have worked with a number of clients at higher grade levels whose academic failure resulted from poor reading skills. CBM is therefore relevant to the assessment of basic tool skills regardless of the age or grade level of the client. Some referred high school students possess basic tool skills, but still struggle with academic demands. These types of referrals may reflect a failure to successfully integrate tool skills or another breakdown in instruction. The five question heuristic for academic assessment described following the CBM section, can readily be used to address concerns appearing in older clients. Readers interested in specific issues and methods that adapt CBM to secondary students should consult Espin and Tindal (1998).

As a result of their shared purpose, CBM measures share several procedural characteristics. Each CBM test, called a probe, is brief. Typical CBM probes require from one to three minutes to administer (Shapiro, 1996). Single brief CBM probes do not provide a sufficient basis for making substantive decisions. Rather, the brevity of each probe permits collection of a substantial number of data points within a time series analysis. As a result CBM measures can be used to continuously evaluate client progress and test clients' responses to a variety of instructional manipulations.

CURRICULUM-BASED MEASUREMENT PROCEDURES

Standard CBM procedures have been developed for reading, written expression, mathematics, and spelling. Extended and detailed descriptions of materials preparation, administration, scoring, and interpretation of CBM probes are provided in Shinn (1989) and Shapiro (1996). The following sections describe primary considerations in developing, administering, scoring, and interpreting CBM probes for the core content tool skills.

Reading

CBM reading probes are constructed by selecting reading passages from the client's curricular materials. Ideally CBM reading passages are drawn from the basal reader that the client is using at school. Basal readers typically carefully control content to insure a consistent level of difficulty within the reader and a consistent progression of difficulty through out the texts. However, increasing numbers of schools have adopted literature-based reading texts. These anthologies typically include a diverse range of literature that may vary widely in the reading difficulty of stories. Wide variations in readability across passages will confound a CBM assessment. For clients who are instructed in a literature-based series, it is frequently more informative to use materials drawn from a basal reader. Ideally the basal reader will be as similar as possible to the client's literature-based series.

Stories or passages that include poetry, extensive use of novel vocabulary (e.g., foreign language names), or extensive dialogue are excluded from CBM probes. Typically, one passage is randomly selected from the beginning, the middle, and the ending sections of the client's reading book. Two copies of the passage are then prepared, one for the examiner and one for the client. When the client's curricular materials are unavailable or are widely variable in readability, standardized reading materials such as *Standardized Reading Passages* (1987) can be substituted. Although standardized materials will not assess the client's reading skills in his or her reading materials they will provide a useful estimate of the client's instructional readiness for materials at varying levels of difficulty. These materials have the advantage of providing carefully controlled content and being developed specifically for the purpose of assessing clients' reading skills. Standardized materials also reduce preparation time.

CBM reading passages are typically administered in a quiet room with few distractions. The examiner is seated across from the client and follows along on his or her copy of the passage as the client reads aloud. The client is asked to attempt each word in the passage and to do his or her best reading. The client then reads aloud for one minute while the examiner follows along on his or her copy. As the client reads the examiner marks oral reading errors committed by the client. Oral reading errors are mispronounced words, substituted words, omitted words, and words that are not read correctly within three seconds of completing the previous word (Shinn, 1989). Additionally, self-corrections of mispronunciations, substitutions, and omissions within three seconds are not counted as errors. If the client hesitates for three seconds on a particular word the examiner provides the client the word and marks it as an error.

A single oral reading probe session will consist of three one-minute timed readings from three different passages. The median oral reading rate and error rate for the three reading passages are used as the primary data for the probe session. The median is used to increase the stability of CBM reading measures and to reduce the influence of any particular reading passage. The primary uses of oral reading rates within CBM have been to monitor student progress through curricular materials and to develop recommendations for placement in instructional level reading materials. Routine progress monitoring data can be taken to ensure that the client is progressing at an appropriate rate and that he or she is on track to reach educationally significant goals. Research has found an average increase in oral reading fluency in grades one through four of approximately one to two words correct per minute per week (Fuchs, Fuchs, Heamlett, Walz, & Germann, 1993).

Several authors have also developed instructional placement recommendations based on CBM reading data. For example, Fuchs and Deno (1982) identified the instructional range for first and second grade materials as falling between 40 and 60 words correct per minute with fewer than five errors. Based on this recommendation, a child who read fewer than 40 words correct per minute would fall within a frustrational range and would need instruction in lower level materials. A child who read in excess of 60 words correct per minute would be ready to move on to more difficult materials (assuming a low error rate). Fuchs and Deno (1982) recommend an instructional placement range for third through sixth grade materials of 70 to 100 words correct per minute with fewer than seven errors.

Mathematics

There are two primary types of CBM mathematics probes: mixed-skill and single-skill. Mixed-skill probes sample a variety of mathematics operations within a particular curricular or grade level. Mixed-skill probes can be used as an initial survey procedure to sample the full range of mathematics operations the client is currently expected to have mastered or in which he or she is being instructed. Mixed-skill probes are typically developed based on the scope and sequence chart for the client's mathematics curriculum. The scope and sequence chart will specify the order in which mathematics skills are presented. Mixed-skill CBM math probes can also be developed based on readily available references (e.g., a scope and sequence chart for a readily available mathematics text). The utility this approach is increased by the general consistency across mathematics curricula in the sequence of presentation of *primary* mathematics skills. Examination of recent assignments can be used to estimate where in the mathematics curricular sequence the client is currently being instructed. Single-skill probes are prepared to assess client skill with a single mathematics operation and are typically used to provide more detailed follow-up for initial mixed-skill probes.

CBM mathematics probes are used to assess fundamental mathematics tool skills such as addition facts or completing long division problems. Probes are prepared with mathematics problems printed on a page with sufficient space provided for necessary calculations. Probes can be prepared by hand, with a word processor, or with software designed for this purpose (e.g., Math Sequences, Milliken Publishing). Additionally, commercially prepared materials such as *Basic Skill Builders* (Beck, Conrad, & Anderson, 1995) are available.

Once relevant probes have been selected or prepared, they are administered in a quiet room with minimal distractions. The examiner informs the client of the types of mathematics problems presented in the probe and instructs the client not to skip around within the probe. Specifically, the client is instructed to begin with the problem in the top left hand corner to work problems from left to right within rows and work down the page one line at the time. The client is also told that he or she may place an "X" over any problem that he or she does not know how to complete. The examiner monitors the client's progress as he or she works through the probe to ensure compliance.

CBM mathematics probes are scored on the basis of digits correct rather than problems correct. Digits correct has two important advantages over problems correct. Digits correct provides a consistent metric for academic skill across a range of mathematics tasks. Second, digits correct is more sensitive to learning than problems correct. When scoring, a correct digit is assigned for each digit in the final answer as well as for each digit that a client would record if they "showed their work" when completing the problem. So for example, adding two and three would result in a single correct digit (five). Alternatively, multiplying four and seven would result in to correct digits (28, 2 and 8). The problems presented in Figure 4.1 illustrate scoring for digits correct for a long division problem and a multiplication problem. If a client provides the correct answer he or she is given credit for the maximum number of correct digits. So if a client provides the correct answer it is not necessary to check his or her work in arriving at the answer.

Long Division	Multiplication
32 7)224 -21 14 -14 0	1 32 x 17 224 32 544
9 Digits Correct	9 Digits Correct

Figure 4.1. Examples of Scoring Digits Correct for Multiple-Step Mathematics Operations.

The two primary considerations for interpreting CBM mathematics probes are the extent to which the client has acquired basic mathematics tool skills and the extent to which the client has developed fluency. Acquisition of a skill is indicated when the client completes problems correctly, but slowly. Evaluating the data inevitably raises questions about what level of accuracy and what rate of correct responding constitute acquisition of mathematics skills. It is imperative that basic mathematics operations such as addition facts and division facts be mastered with 100% accuracy. These types of basic tool skills provide the building blocks for more elaborate mathematics skills and applications. For example, if clients learn basic fact operations to 90% accuracy and then use those facts to solve 4-step problems, fact errors alone will result in clients completing only 66% of those operations accurately. Any standard below 100% accuracy for basic tool skills places children at a high risk of subsequent academic failure (White & Haring, 1982).

A child has developed fluent responding when he or she can maintain fast accurate responding for the task. Fluency is an important part of academic competence because academic work is typically time limited and fluency is important in preparing clients to retain and apply skills (Daly, Martens, Kilmer, & Massie, 1996; Wolery, Bailey, & Sugai, 1988). The mastery criteria proposed for various tasks vary rather widely across tasks and authors. For example, Shapiro (1996) proposes 20 digits correct per minute as mastery criteria for a range of third grade tasks while Howell Fox, and Morehead (1993) propose 80 digits correct per minute as a standard for addition facts. The variety of tasks included within mathematics contributes to the range of mastery criteria. Obviously, clients will need to achieve a higher fluency in reading numbers than in solving for one unknown within linear equations.

Three general approaches are most practical for selecting fluency standards. First, accept standards established by the client's school district, curriculum publisher, or teacher when they are available. Second, consult a standard assessment reference that provides criterion standards (e.g., Howell et al., 1993 or Shapiro, 1996). Finally, develop a standard based on the performance of competent individuals. This procedure may be least useful for outpatient based clinicians because they may not have ready access to several competent children to provide a benchmark.

Written Expression

The construction of probes for written expression is extraordinarily simple. A CBM writing probe consists of a brief sentence fragment that is described as a story starter. For example, the fragment, "When I went to the zoo..." can be used as a story starter. When a probe is administered the client is told that the examiner would like him or her to write a story. The story starter is read to the client and the client is allowed one minute to think about a story. The client is then allowed to write for three minutes. The client is asked to do his or her best work and is told to guess when he or she is unsure how to spell a word.

The standard scoring metrics for CBM written expression are total words written per three minutes and words correct per three minutes. Total words written is scored by simply counting the total number of recognizable words excluding digits (e.g., 87). For total words written the accuracy of the spelling of the word is not taken into consideration. Words correct per three minutes is scored in the same way as total words written except that only words spelled correctly are counted. These simple metrics have been found to have moderate ($r = .45$) to strong ($r = .92$) correlations with standardized tests of writing skills and with holistic teacher ratings (Marston, 1989). Clients with stronger writing skills typically produced a greater volume of content in three minutes than those with weaker writing skills.

CBM writing samples are primarily useful for obtaining an initial estimate of writing production and for obtaining a writing sample under standardized conditions. This sample can subsequently be examined for additional indicators of writing skill such as use of capitalization, punctuation, sentence complexity, clarity of exposition, and organization. Although formal indices of syntactic and semantic maturity are available they are rarely used. For practical reasons teachers are more likely to evaluate the developmental appropriateness, syntactic maturity, and semantic maturity on the basis of a holistic impression than through a rather complex and time-consuming formal process. Simply examining the writing sample for adequacy of production, basic technical characteristics (e.g., complete sentences), and general development appropriateness can provide useful initial assessment data.

Summary

CBM provides clinicians and educators a collection of brief reliable measures that have been shown to be correlated with more complex time-consuming measures of academic achievement. CBM has been shown to be sensitive to client learning and to contribute to improve the educational outcomes when it has been used as part of a progress monitoring plan (Fuchs, Fuchs, & Stecker, 1989; Hintz et al., 1998). Poor performance on CBM probes can indicate significant deficits in basic academic tool skills. Positive outcomes for CBM measures can indicate the absence of academic concerns or may suggest the absence of concern for only fundamental tool skills. For example, the client may have adequate mathematics calculation skills and still struggle with math applications. Although CBM can be an important element of assessing a client's instructional needs, it is unlikely to be sufficient in isolation. The following section describes a multi-dimensional approach to academic assessment that can place a client's academic functioning in a meaningful context and clarify the client's educational needs.

CBM procedures appear to be practical for incorporation into clinical practice. For many types of skills commercially prepared probes are available that can be readily used on an outpatient basis. Additionally, it is frequently possible to prepare probes based on the client's textbooks. The brevity and simplicity of CBM probes increase their practicality for administration during a relatively brief office visit. Finally, standards for acceptable performance on probes can be developed based on locally available information (e.g., such as the school district's standards for grade promotion) as well as standard assessment references (e.g., Howell et al., 1993; Shapiro, 1996).

MOVING BEYOND TESTING TO ASSESSMENT: SEEING THE FOREST

Testing a client's academic performance in isolation has little clinical or educational utility. A useful assessment requires evaluating the meaning of that performance, which inevitably requires consideration of the school context. For example, assessment data indicating that a client reads 48 words correct per minute (WCPM) in grade level texts has little meaning out of context. If the instructional range in those texts is 40 to 60 WCPM and the average peer at the client's school reads 52 (WCPM), the assessment result is encouraging. In contrast, if the instructional range is 70 to 100 WCPM for that level of text and the average peer is reading 97 WCPM, then 48 WCPM suggests significant reading problems. Traditionally, educational assessment has focused disproportionately and sometimes exclusively on describing the client's skills in reference to either criteria or norms. However, describing a client's academic skills provides only a small portion of the information needed to develop an effective educational program.

Understanding how a client's academic performance fits within the school context is an important element of an academic assessment, but it is not sufficient. Completing an assessment of academic performance that can guide development of an adequate instructional program requires consideration of why the client behaves as he or she does. However, completing an inclusive assessment that considers the full range of variables that may influence a client's performance is a daunting task because of the tremendous range of variables that can influence a child's learning. For example, parental academic skills, parental involvement in homework, classroom arrangement, lesson presentation, curricular materials, sensory abilities (e.g., vision and hearing), motivation, and the client's current academic skills can all influence academic success.

An additional consideration for the broad scope of the client's concerns is the extent to which cultural or linguistic differences may be related to current concerns or influence assessment results. Obviously, if a student has a limited English proficiency, tasks presented in common English-language American classrooms will be more challenging. Additionally and more subtly, if clients' developmental experience has not provided them the many social and behavioral competencies that schools expect, value, and take for granted, they will be at a distinct disadvantage. Although no standard assessment for these factors has been developed, a careful examination of how well clients' competencies match educational expectations can address this issue, at least in part. This process is described below.

Cultural or linguistic differences may also influence assessment results. Although this has been a crucial concern in the broad educational assessment literature (see Shinn, Collins, & Gallagher, 1998), it has not been a primary consideration for direct behavioral assessments that focus on specifying students' needs. These types of assessments are largely descriptive and consistently rely on very low levels of inference. Normative constructs with their attendant vulnerability to bias are rarely relevant. The focus of this type of assessment is on describing a client's needs and the type of services that will meet those needs. Broader issues of how culture and bias can influence behavioral assessment are equally relevant for direct academic assessment as they are to any clinical interview or observation. Space limitations preclude a detailed examination of these issues other than to acknowledge their importance. Readers interested in a further discussion of these issues as they relate to behavioral assessment of academic concerns may find Shinn et al. (1998) and Baker, Plasencia-Peinado, and Lezcano-Lytle (1998) helpful.

Requiring that an academic assessment consider every contextual, individual, familial, or cultural factor that may influence achievement will result in an assessment design that is too impractical to complete. Organizing academic assessment so that it is focused on clarifying the client's current educational needs can help make it more manageable. Explicitly focusing on the client's contemporary educational needs emphasizes the client's current skills, educational context, and examination of changeable environmental conditions. This type of assessment is relatively focused, specific, and is likely to have immediate relevance to treatment planning. The five questions below can be used as a heuristic for guiding an initial academic assessment.

1. What is the client expected to do and to learn?
2. What is the client's current academic performance and behavior?
3. What mismatches between expected and actual performance were observed?
4. What skills are within the client's repertoire?
5. What conditions result in the client meeting educational expectations?

These questions can be regarded as an organizational heuristic that permits a focused, systematic approach to instructional assessment. The following sections describe issues that are critical to answering each question as well as some prototypical assessment methods.

1. What Is the Client Expected to Do and to Learn?

Simply finding out what it is that the client is expected to do can be a challenging element of completing an academic assessment for practitioners who work outside of schools. Parents and the client may be the only immediately available sources of information and they may have a poor understanding of the school's expectations. In point of fact, misunderstandings regarding what is expected of the client may be contributing to the current problems. In order to complete an adequate academic assessment it is necessary to know what the school expects of the client. The persons who are in the best position to provide this information are the client's teachers. Frequently, it is possible to obtain critical assessment data about performance expectations and other issues in a brief focused interview with the client's teacher(s) (Shapiro, 1996).

When gathering information regarding instructional expectations from teachers, clinicians should consider at least three dimensions of academic behavior: accuracy, fluency, and quality. The accuracy of a client's work is frequently the first dimension of behavior that comes to mind when describing instructional expectations. Because not all schools or teachers use the same grading scales or systems it is important to ask if percentage correct is the basis for grade assignment and if so, what those standards are. Second, standards for the fluency of academic work are consistently important because of the ubiquitous nature of time limits and deadlines in schools. As a result it is always important to consider how quickly a client is expected to work as well as how accurately. For some clients the most important mismatch between their skills and educational expectations will be the fluency rather than the accuracy of their work.

Even though they may not be readily apparent, all teachers have some qualitative expectations regarding students' work. These may include clarity of handwriting, complexity of sentence structure, simplicity of a proof, and the level of spoken vocabulary. Qualitative expectations may be difficult to specify clearly, but can be an important element of the assessment picture. It can be highly frustrating for a client to begin completing a weekly journal assignment and still receive poor grades because the content of the entries are too immature, too repetitive, or unstructured. When gathering information about academic expectations it is important to consider whether or not qualitative dimensions of the client's work are a significant concern.

School districts' published educational expectations are an additional source of information regarding expected academic performance. Published standards can be a stable and useful source of important information regarding educational expectations. Published curricular standards are particularly useful for clinicians in outpatient settings for several reasons. First, they provide important benchmarks that clients' educational assessment data can be compared to. For example, a school district's standard that kindergarten students must accurately count 20 objects in less than 30s before being promoted to first grade may be an important element of assessing a young child's academic skills. Similarly, a school district's or state department of education's published standards for physical science knowledge that must be demonstrated in order to graduate from high school may put a client's skills into a meaningful context.

In addition to providing important benchmarks, school districts' curricular expectations are uniquely useful because they are available prior to contact with a specific referral. This type of information may be available from local teachers, principals, and school districts' central offices. Contacting local school districts periodically to gather data on curricular standards, student performance expectations, and promotion requirements can provide clinicians with valuable information that is available when new referrals are received. Additionally, this type of information may be especially useful because it may be relevant to a large number of referred children.

2. What Is the Client's Current Academic Performance and Behavior?

As with any domain of behavioral assessment the first element of treatment planning is describing the client's current functioning. Describing a child's current academic functioning requires gathering data about behavior in the instructional context. These data should examine both the process and products of academic engagement. By process the authors are referring to behaviors such as task engagement and following directions. Task engagement, compliance with directions, and appropriate help seeking are all behaviors that can facilitate children developing academic skills and meeting academic expectations.

It is important to recognize that behaviors such as compliance and task-engagement are only related to learning; they are not synonymous with it. Some children are capable of learning and producing high quality academic products with little task engagement and frequent non-compliance. For example, Harold was a young man who was referred for treatment of non-compliance, disruption, and over-activity at school. During in class observation he was on-task less than 25% of the observation and ignored some teacher directions. Despite these poor "process behaviors" Harold completed assignments with an acceptable level of accuracy. What Harold was doing while he was off-task and his non-compliance were regarded as highly problematic despite the quality of his academic products. In contrast to Harold, some referred children will exhibit high levels of on-task behavior, compliance, and appropriate help seeking and still fail to meet instructional expectations.

The several assessment strategies commonly used for assessing clients' functioning in the academic context are the same assessment strategies used more broadly in academic functioning: interviews, observations, permanent products, and ratings. As with other areas of behavioral assessment the greatest weight is given to those assessment tools that are most direct. Therefore, review of a client's work products is stronger evidence of academic performance than are interview reports. Data collection forms and guides for this stage of assessment are available from several sources (e.g., Witt et al., 2000). Figure 4.2 presents a classroom observation grid that can be used to record data regarding work habits, teaching, and in-class behavior. Detailed description of the observation grid's use in available in Witt et al. (2000). The goal of this stage of assessment is to accurately describe the client's current academic performance considering both behaviors related to the academic process and its outcomes.

3. What Mismatches between Expected and Actual Performance Were Observed?

The next stage of the assessment consists of comparison of the client's academic performance to the expected academic performance. Experienced clinicians and educators will readily recognize that this is actually a complex multidimensional process that includes objective and subjective dimensions of a client's behavior. For example, a particular client may be described by her parents and teacher as "disruptive and not working up to her potential." Review of assessment data may reveal that she is passing all of her classes with at least a C, she exceeds all of the district's performance standards, and she completes her assignments on time. In this case it is likely that the referral concerns are focused on behaviors related to academic achievement such as task engagement and compliance.

Classroom Observation Grid

Student: ________________ Date: ________ Subject Area: __________ Beginning Time: ________

Task to Be Completed: ____________________________________

	Teacher Behaviors				Target Student Behaviors				Teacher and Peer Behaviors					
Time:	Ask Question	Presents	Shows	Prompts	Verb Resp	Writt Resp	Raises Hand	Disrupts	Praise	Repri-mand	Redirect	Correct Error	Deliver Reward	Peer Attn
0:00-1:00														
1:01-2:00														
2:01-3:00														
3:01-4:00														
4:01-5:00														
5:01-6:00														
6:01-7:00														
7:01-8:00														
8:01-9:00														
9:01-10:00														
Totals														

Ending Time: ______________ Length of Observation (in minutes): ________

Total/Length of Observation x 10 = Rate per 10 Minutes

Rates per 10 Minutes for Each Column:

____ per 10 min.	____ per 10 min.	____ per 10 min.	____ per 10 min.	____ per 10 min.	____ per 10 min.	____ per 10 min.	____ per 10 min.	____ per 10 min.	____ per 10 min.	____ per 10 min.	____ per 10 min.	____ per 10 min.	____ per 10 min.

Figure 4.2. A Classroom Observation Grid.

Note: Reprinted from Witt, Daly, & Noell (2000) *Functional assessments: A step-by-step guide to solving academic and behavior problems*. Copy right 2000 Sopris West, Longmont, CO, reprinted by permission.

The primary goal of answering this assessment question is to precisely describe any mismatches between the school's expectations and the client's behavior. This description should describe the problematic behavior and the dimension of that behavior that is problematic. For example, Matt and Sal both performed substantially below their teachers' expectations during independent seatwork in mathematics. Although the referrals were similar globally, the specific nature of the mismatch between expected and actual performance suggested different follow-up assessments. Matt typically completed only a small portion of his assignments, but the work he completed was accurate. This suggested considering whether Matt needed assistance to develop fluency, whether there was some behavior he was engaging in that was interfering with assignment completion, and examination of motivation. Sal completed assignments, but did so with very poor accuracy. The crucial assessment concerns for Sal were the extent to which he possessed the basic tool skills needed to complete the task as well as the extent to which he was actually attending to his work as opposed to simply rushing through his assignments. The precise description of the referral concern will then set the occasion for a focused and specific assessment of the client's academic skills.

4. What Skills Are within the Client's Repertoire?

Once assessment has determined what the client is expected to do, what the client actually does, and how those are incongruent—assessment should shift to consideration of what the client knows how to do. The fact that a client does not produce acceptable academic products in the classroom does not mean that the client does not know how to do so (Noell, Roane, VanDerHeyden, Whitmarsh, & Gatti, 2000). A range of variables can interfere with performance in the classroom. For example, no reinforcing contingencies may exist for the client to complete the work and as a result he or she may choose not to do the work. Relatedly, the client may have modest motivation to do the work, but there may be strong immediately reinforcing consequences for doing something other than school work (e.g., talking with friends).

The authors recommend following the ecologically focused phase of the assessment (i.e., expectations and performance at school) with a child-focused assessment. The child-focused assessment should be designed to obtain an estimate of the client's academic skills. The authors describe this assessment as an estimate because it is a logical and practical impossibility to know absolutely what skills a child possesses (Noell et al., 2000). It is always possible that asking the question in another way in a different context would have elicited skilled behavior. The intent of this phase is to conduct an assessment that is optimized for that client to elicit an optimal academic performance. The goal is to determine what the client "knows" rather than how the client responds to a set of previously defined test conditions.

Accurately assessing a client's academic skills is an assessment rather than testing activity. It requires consideration of the individual and what conditions are likely to elicit the client's optimal performance. For example, a highly anxious client might perform best in an emotionally supportive context that offers a great deal of reassurance and little time pressure. Although optimizing an assessment context for an individual client is clearly an idiographic process that may require some individual experimentation, the professional literature does suggest some consistent considerations. Many clients are likely to perform better when directions explicitly request that the client do his or her best (Rodriguez, Nietzel, & Berins, 1980), limit distracting stimuli (e.g., noise; Zental & Shaw, 1980) and limit reinforcement available for behaviors other than the academic work (Martens & Houk, 1989). Additionally, an optimized assessment context for many clients will include clear directions and reinforcing consequences for completing the task at hand (Noell, Freeland, Witt, & Gansle, in press).

For some clients the combination of a quiet room with few distractions, clear directions, and a strong incentive to do well will result in substantially improved performance. In both research and practice this combination of conditions has been used to demonstrate that a referred child could perform the targeted academic skills despite the fact that they did not do so at school (Noell, Witt, Gilbertson, Ranier, & Freeland, 1997; Noell, Freeland, Witt, & Gansle, in press). When a client does meet expectations in an optimized assessment context, but does not do so in the criterion environment the behavioral deficit can be described as a performance deficit. In this instance the skill is within the client's repertoire, but he or she does not perform the skill in the target environment. This type of outcome data suggests a motivational approach to intervention. These issues will be discussed below.

If the client does not perform well in the individual assessment, a more "fine grained" analysis of his or her skills may be needed. This analysis should examine the skills that make up the target skill and the client's competencies for these subordinate skills. The subordinate skills that make up the target skill previously may have been identified by the client's curricula, teacher, or school. Alternatively, the clinician may choose to complete a task analysis of the problematic activity. A task analysis is the process of breaking down a complex behavior into a series of discrete, measurable, and teachable components (Cooper, Heron, & Heward, 1987). For example, completing multiplication problems requires that clients read the numbers, read the operation sign, identify the correct answer, and write the correct answer. Similarly, completing a word problem will include at least a reading component, identification of the question being asked, identification of relevant data, selection of appropriate operations, completion of those operations, and written reporting of the correct answer. Howell et al. (1993) provides task analyses of a range of academic skills that span a range of levels of academic tasks.

Several strategies can be used for completing a task analysis. First, the performance of competent individuals can be watched and the steps they use to complete the task recorded. This approach can be readily accomplished in educational contexts because of the availability of competent students who are not the focus of the referral, but may prove problematic in an outpatient context. A second approach is to consult an expert. For educational concerns the client's teacher(s) may be a helpful source of information. A third approach is to perform the task yourself and record each of the steps needed to complete the task. Interested readers can consult Cooper et al. (1987) for a more extensive and detailed description of task analysis techniques.

Once the relevant academic skills have been identified the assessment should focus on describing the client's current level of skill for those component skills. For example, an assessment focused on word problems in mathematics might examine reading decoding, identification of the question being asked, identification of relevant data, selection of appropriate operations, completion of those operations, and written reporting of the correct answer. The component skill analysis should clarify instructional and treatment needs for the client. For example, a client whose deficit is in reading comprehension has different needs than a client whose deficit is in mathematics calculations. At the conclusion of this phase of the assessment the clinician should have a clear description of what skills the client does and does not demonstrate in an assessment context that has been optimized for that client.

5. What Conditions Result in the Client's Meeting Relevant Educational Expectations?

The final stage of the assessment focuses on the most important question: What can be done to help the client to meet the educational expectations at his or her school? The identification of an effective treatment plan will require integration of assessment data from the previous activities as well as collection of additional assessment data. The diversity of referred children's educational needs precludes an exhaustive coverage in this volume, this section will focus on a broadly applicable process.

Perhaps the most encouraging answer to the fourth question (What are the client's skills?) is that the client has the necessary skills, but does not use them at school. This suggests a treatment plan designed to increase the client's motivation to complete academic demands and to reduce his or her motivation to engage in other behaviors. Ideally the details of the treatment plan will be developed collaboratively with the client's parents and teacher(s). For example, providing rewards based on academic performance may result in improved performance (e.g., Noell et al., 1998). Additionally, for some clients it may be important to reduce reinforcement for behaviors that compete with schoolwork. For example, it may be important to move the client's seat in the classroom away from preferred peers to reduce off-task socialization. Similarly, it may be necessary to stop sending the client to the school counselor when he or she is disruptive if the counselor's supportive approach may be inadvertently reinforcing disruption.

Intervention for clients who do not possess the prerequisite skills is more complicated. Obviously an important element of the intervention plan will be to provide the client effective remedial instruction designed to improve skills. This may require using lower level materials and teaching skills that have already been covered. The clinical practitioner will rarely, if ever, be the individual providing the remedial instruction. Typically this element of the treatment plan will be implemented by the client's parents, a tutor, or by school personnel. From the authors' perspective the most crucial element of intervention planning for the clinical practitioner is assuring that frequent progress monitoring data are being collected and reviewed to ensure that the instruction is beneficial to the client. Interested readers can consult Howell et al. (1993), Shapiro (1996), Stoner, Shinn, and Walker, (1991), or Witt et al., (2000) for detailed descriptions of academic intervention approaches.

Remedial instruction can be described as addressing the client's long term educational and developmental needs. It should be designed to ensure that the client acquires the academic skills he or she needs to be successful at school. However, despite the crucial importance of the teaching element of the intervention it will frequently be inadequate to address the client's immediate needs. Tutoring may strengthen the client's reading skills or help him learn his addition facts, but that will take time. It is unlikely to solve the referral concern on Monday morning. Most clients will need both a long term and a short-term treatment strategy. The short-term strategy should be designed to permit the client to meet with success immediately with the skills he or she already possesses.

Suppose for example that a client can write adequate prose, but does so too slowly. Intervention should focus on building fluency so that the client can meet the school's expectations in the long term. However, in the short term it may be helpful to negotiate a reduction in the length of the client's writing assignments until he can build up sufficient writing fluency. Similarly, a client who understands mathematics word problems, but has not mastered her fact operations might be allowed to use a calculator until tutoring has allowed her to master those facts. It is also important to bear in mind that using a short-term solution alone is not in the client's long-term best interest. The client who has reduced writing expectations is likely to have less practice writing and fall further behind his peers. The client who uses the calculator may never learn her math facts. The short-term solution should be conceptualized as an immediate way to break the cycle of frustration and failure for the child, educators, and parents. It is a way of buying time so that the long-term solution has the opportunity to benefit the client.

TWO CASE ILLUSTRATIONS

Jeremy

Jeremy was a second grade student who was referred due to disruptive behavior, poor quality academic work, and noncompliance. His teacher's primary goals were that he would complete his assignments, would do so with at least passing grades (i.e., 70% correct), and would work quietly enough that he would not disturb others (e.g., question 1 expectations). Observation and review of permanent products were used to describe Jeremy's current functioning (question 2). Observation in class revealed that he was frequently off task and disrupted other students' work. Additionally, review of his permanent products revealed that he rarely completed more than half of any assignment and that the work he did complete was below 70% accuracy.

Examination of the mismatch between expected and actual performance revealed two concerns. First, the quality of his academic work was unacceptable in both quantity and accuracy. Second, his work habits were viewed by his teacher as unacceptable and disruptive. An assessment of Jeremy's skills (question 4) conducted using CBM indicated that Jeremy lacked some of the prerequisite skills required by his assignments. Specifically, Jeremy's reading rates in both first and second grades were substantially below the typical instructional range of 40 words correct per minute. Additionally, he made more than 4 errors per minute and exhibited few word attach skills (e.g., phonics) when he confronted words he did not know. Jeremy's reading rates were also substantially below the available CBM reading norms that had been collected by his school building.

In addition to significant deficits in reading Jeremy was struggling in mathematics. He completed less than 10 digits correct per minute on grade level mixed math, addition, and subtraction probes. Jeremy also committed computational errors. The assessment results indicated that Jeremy lacked basic reading decoding skills (i.e., phonics skills, sight word fund, and reading fluency) as well as basic grade level computational skills. Based on the assessment data it appeared that the most probable means of helping Jeremy meet his teacher's expectations (question 5) in the short term would be to provide him lower difficulty worksheets during independent seat work. This proved to be effective. In order to meet teacher's expectations in the long term, Jeremy needed additional instruction to build up his deficient academic skills.

Glen

Glen was a young man referred to an outpatient summer treatment program for children exhibiting Attention Deficit Hyperactivity Disorder.[1] Although he was not in school at the time, one of his parents' many concerns was his reading performance. Because no teacher was available, expectations for the assessment were based on published criterion referenced standards for CBM reading assessments (Fuchs & Deno, 1982). Current performance data were limited to school records, but these indicated poor grades in reading and poor performance on standardized reading tests. An initial CBM screening also indicated performance substantially below grade level.

During the individual assessment, Glen's reading in lower grade materials improved when he could earn access to rewards for doing well. For example, when Glenn read from

[1]The case of Glen is drawn from the published study by Noell et al., 1998. A complete graphic presentation of Glen's data is available in that source.

second grade materials across several sessions his median score was 31 words correct per minute. When he was allowed to earn a small reward for beating his score from his previous session his median across five sessions improved to 73 words correct per minute. This indicated a change in performance from the frustrational range to the mastery range for this level of materials. This suggested that for relatively easy tasks his poor motivation may result in an underestimate of his skills.

For materials at the grade level he had just completed rewards did not result in improved reading performance. Glen's median under standard conditions was 67 words correct per minute and with the reward it was 62. Based on these results a reading intervention was tested at this grade level that included two elements that are strongly supported in the research literature. First, the passage was previewed for Glen; it was read to him. Then Glen was allowed to practice the passage with corrective feedback as he read. Finally, Glen read the passage for a timed score. This teaching intervention resulted in steady substantial improvements in Glen's reading fluency over seven sessions. He improved from approximately 70 words correct per minute to 100 words correct per minute.

SUMMARY

For children, academic, social, emotional, and vocational success are all interrelated. Effective treatment of children's mental health concerns will frequently need to consider the child's academic needs. Unfortunately, traditional norm-referenced assessment tools are a sub-optimal approach for assessing children's academic needs. These assessment tools provide data at too global a level to be very useful for planning instruction and give insufficient consideration to the role of the child's environment. Additionally, these types of instruments have not been shown to have treatment utility (Braden & Kratochwill, 1997).

More recent approaches to academic assessment have been more promising in their ability to clarify children's educational needs. These approaches (e.g., CBM) have emphasized the direct assessment of specific targeted behaviors using brief probes that can be repeated frequently. These probes can then be used to evaluate the efficacy of instructional interventions. Additionally, recent innovations that layer planned environmental manipulations such as testing the impact of motivational manipulations or instructional interventions have demonstrated increased treatment utility (Daly et al., 1998; Noell et al., in press).

Integrating the types of assessment practices described in this chapter into outpatient practice presents some new challenges. Some elements of the direct assessment of client's instructional needs using contemporary assessment practices are quite simple and others are rather complex. Obtaining and preparing standardized CBM type measures or using the client's texts to set up CBM measures is not complicated. The individual measures themselves are also quite simple to administer. However, simply shifting from standardized measures to direct behavioral measures of academic performance is only a portion of the challenge. Obtaining data about educational expectations and actual performance in class is crucially important and can be challenging. Some schools and teachers can be quite defensive about collaborating with professionals outside the school context. It is also important to acknowledge that at times it can be amazingly simple to gather data from schools. In some cases, a simple note delivered to the school by the parent can result in a host of useful information.

Perhaps the most challenging element of the approach described herein may not be collecting or interpreting the data. The most challenging element may be establishing working collaborations with clients, parents, and schools that permit the data to be collected. However, this is likely to be time well spent, because the challenge presented by collaborative work in the assessment phase will be modest compared to the challenge presented when treatment is initiated. Treatment may require behavior change on the part of teachers, parents, and the client. Supporting and ensuring behavior change across all the relevant individuals who will be participating in the treatment can be extraordinarily challenging. Establishing a positive collaborative relationship during the assessment may help set the occasion for the really hard work of treatment implementation. In the end it is the implementation of the treatment and the assessment of its efficacy that is the goal of the entire process.

REFERENCES

Baker, S. K., Plasencia-Peinado, J., & Lezcano-Lytle, V. (1998). The use of curriculum-based measurement with language-minority students. In M. R. Shinn (Ed.), *Advanced applications of curriculum-based measurement* (pp. 175–213). New York: Guilford.

Beck, R., Conrad, D., & Anderson, P. (1995). *Basic skill builders handbook.* Longmont, CO: Sopris West.

Bell, P. F., Lentz, F. E. & Graden, J. L. (1992). Effects of curriculum-test overlap on standardized test scores: Identifying systematic confounds in educational decision making. *School Psychology Review, 21,* 644–655.

Braden, J. P., & Kratochwill, T. R. (1997). Treatment utility of assessment: Myths and realities. *School Psychology Review, 26,* 475–485.

Cooper, J. O., Heron, T. E., & Heward, W. L. (1987). *Applied Behavior Analysis.* Upper Saddle River, NJ: Prentice Hall.

Daly, E. J., III, Martens, B. K., Dool, E. J., & Hintze, J. M. (1998). Using brief functional analysis to select interventions for oral reading. *Journal of Behavioral Education, 8,* 203–218.

Daly, E. J., III, Martens, B. K., Kilmer, A., and Massie, D. R. (1996). The effects of instructional match and content overlap on generalized reading performance. *Journal of Applied Behavior Analysis, 29,* 507–518.

Deno, S. L. (1985). Curriculum-based measurement: The emerging alternative. *Exceptional Children, 52,* 219–232.

Deno, S. L., Mirkin, P. K., & Chiang, B. (1982). Identifying valid measures of reading. *Exceptional Children, 49,* 36–45.

Espin, C. A., & Tindal, G. (1998). Curriculum-based measurement for secondary students. In M. R. Shinn (Ed.), *Advanced applications of curriculum-based measurement* (pp. 214–253). New York: Guilford.

Fuchs, L. S., & Deno, S. L. (1982). *Developing goals and objectives for educational programs.* Washington, DC: American Association of Colleges for Teacher Education.

Fuchs, L. S., & Deno, S. L. (1991). Paradigmatic distinctions between instructionally relevant measurement models. *Exceptional Children, 57,* 488–500.

Fuchs, L. S., Fuchs, D., Hamlett, D. L., Wlaz, L., & Germann, G. (1993). Formative evaluation of academic progress: How much growth should we expect? *School Psychology Review, 22,* 27–48.

Fuchs, L. S., Fuchs, D., & Stecker, P. M. (1989). Effects of curriculum-based measurement on teachers' instructional planning. *Journal of Learning Disabilities, 22,* 51–59.

Hintze, J. M., Shapiro, E. S., & Daly, E. J., III (1998). An investigation of the effects of passage difficulty level on outcomes of oral reading fluency progress monitoring. *School Psychology Review, 27,* 433–445.

Howell, K. W., Fox, S. L., & Morehead, M. K. (1993). *Curriculum-based evaluation: Teaching and decision making.* Pacific Grove, CA: Brooks/Cole.

Kaufman, A. S. (1994). *Intelligent testing with the WISC-III.* New York: Wiley.

Kern, L., Childs, K. E., Dunlap, G., Clarke, S., and Falk, G. D. (1994). Using assessment-based curricular intervention to improve the classroom behavior of a student with emotional and behavioral challenges. *Journal of Applied Behavior Analysis, 27,* 7–20.

Marston, D. B. (1989). A curriculum-based measurement approach to assessing academic performance: What it is and why do it. In M. R. Shinn (Ed.), *Curriculum-based measurement: Assessing special children* (pp. 18–78). New York: Guilford.

Martens, B. K., & Houk, J. L. (1989). The application of Hernstein's law of effect to disruptive and on-task behavior of a retarded adolescent girl. *Journal of the Experimental Analysis of Behavior, 51,* 17–27.

Macmann, G. M., & Barnett, D. W. (1997). Reliability interpretations for Kaufman's "intelligent testing" approach to the WISC-III. *School Psychology Quarterly, 12,* 197–234.

Noell, G. H., Freeland, J. T., Witt, J. C., & Gansle, K. A. (in press). Using brief assessments to identify effective interventions for individual students. *Journal of School Psychology.*

Noell, G. H., Gansle, K. A., Witt, J. C., Whitmarsh, E. L., Freeland, J. T., LeFleur, L. H., Gilbertson, D. A. & Northup, J. (1998). Effects of contingent reward and instruction on oral reading performance at differing levels of passage difficulty. *Journal of Applied Behavior Analysis, 31,* 659–664.

Noell, G. H., Roane, H. S., VanDerHeyden, A. M., Whitmarsh, E. L., & Gatti, S. L. (2000). Programming for communication in the classroom following an assessment of skill and performance deficits. *School Psychology Review, 29,* 429–442.

Noell, G. H., Witt, J. C., Gilbertson, D. N., Ranier, D. D., & Freeland, J. T. (1997). Increasing teacher intervention implementation in general education settings through consultation and performance feedback. *School Psychology Quarterly, 12,* 77–88.

Patterson, G. R. (1993). Orderly change in a stable world: The antisocial trait as a chimera. *Journal of Consulting and Clinical Psychology, 61,* 911–919.

Rodriguez, R., Nietzel, M. T., & Berins, J. I. (1980). Sex-role orientation and assertiveness among female college students. *Behavior Therapy, 11,* 353–367.

Sattler, J. M. (1988). *Assessment of children* (3rd ed.). San Diego: Jerome M. Sattler.

Shapiro, E. S. (1996). *Academic skills problems: Direct assessment and intervention* (2nd ed.). New York: Guilford.

Shinn, M. R. (1989). *Curriculum-based measurement: Assessing special children.* New York: Guilford.

Shinn, M. R., Collins, V. L., & Gallagher, S. (1998). Curriculum-based measurement and its use in a problem-solving model with students from minority backgrounds. In M. R. Shinn (Ed.), *Advanced applications of curriculum-based measurement* (pp. 143–174). New York: Guilford.

Standardized reading passages measures for screening and progress monitoring. (1987). Minneapolis: Children's Educational Services, Inc.

Stoner, G., Shinn, M. R., & Walker, H. W. (1991). *Interventions for achievement and behavior problems.* Silver Spring, MD: National Association of School Psychologists.

Wechsler, D. (1991). *Manual for the Wechsler Intelligence Scale for Children—Third Edition (WISC-III).* San Antonio, TX: Psychological Corp.

White, O. R., & Harring, N. G. (1982). *Exceptional teaching* (2nd ed.). Columbus, OH: Merrill.

Witt, J. C., Daly, E., & Noell, G. H. (2000). *Functional assessments: A step-by-step guide to solving academic and behavior problems.* Longmont, CO: Sopris West.

Wolery, M., Bailey, D. B., & Sugai, G. M. (1988). *Principles and procedures of applied behavior analysis with exceptional children.* Boston: Allyn & Bacon.

Zentall, S. S., & Shaw, J. H. (1980). Effects of classroom noise on performance and activity of second-grade hyperactive and control children. *Journal of Educational Psychology, 72,* 830–840.

Part II
Assessment Instruments

Chapter 5

Summary Grid of Review Measures

Shannon Self-Brown

INSTRUMENT	GENERAL PURPOSE	POPULATION	METHOD/ INFORMANT(S)	ADMINISTRATION	NORMS	STRENGTHS/ LIMITATIONS	FEE
Name and Abb.	General purpose-Screen/ Diagnosis; Tx. Planning and Evaluation	For whom intended	Questionnaires, Observation, Interview	Time	yes, no	Strengths/limitations	YES/NO
Achenbach System of Empirically Based Assessment Child Behavior Checklist (CBCL) Teacher Report Form (TRF) Youth Self-Report (YSR)	To assess emotional and behavioral problems in children.	Ages 2–18 years (CBCL) Ages 5–18 years (TRF) Ages 11–18 years (YSR)	CBCL is a behavior rating scale completed by parents. TRF is a behavior rating scale completed by teachers. YSR is a self-report form completed by youths.	10–17 min.	Yes	Strong treatment utility. ——— Fails to distinguish between attentive and hyperactive behaviors, as well as anxiety and depression.	YES
Achenbach System of Empirically Based Assessment Child Behavior Checklist: 11/2–5 Caregiver-Teacher Report Form	To assess the behavioral, emotional, and social functioning of preschoolers across settings.	Ages 11/2–5 years	Behavior rating scale completed by parents.	10–15 min.	Yes	Well-researched. Items are clearly written and easy to understand.	YES
Achievement Motivation Profile (AMP)	To measure student's motivation to achieve, as well as personality characteristics, interpersonal attributes, work style, and other qualities related to school success.	Students aged 14 years and older	Self-Report Questionnaire	20–30 min.	Yes	Useful for assessing student motivation. ——— Scoring is complicated. Minorities were underrepresented in the normative sample.	YES
Achieving Behavioral Competencies: Teacher Rating Scale	Measure social skills deemed important by classroom teachers. May be useful for descriptive purposes.	School Aged Children	Questionnaire/ Completed by teacher only.	10 min.	None Reported	Good face validity. ——— Lacks adequate psychometric data.	YES

ADD-H Comprehensive Teacher's Rating Scale-2nd Edition-Parent and Self Report Form (ACTeRS)	To identify children with attention deficit, with or without hyperactive behavior.	Grades: K-8	Teacher-Report Screening Measure	<10 min.	Yes	Easy to administer. Has adequate psychometric properties. ——— Inadequate for diagnostic purposes.	Unknown
Adjustment Scales for Children and Adolescents (ASCA)	To aid mental health professionals in the assessment of behavioral syndromes and degree of adjustment.	Ages 5–17 years	Behavior Rating Scale	15–20 minutes	Yes	Provides multi-situational information. ——— Low reliability estimates.	YES
Adolescent Psychopathology Scale (APS)	To provide a comprehensive assessment of the severity of psychological disorders and social-emotional problems in adolescents.	Ages 12–19 years	Self-Report Measure	45–60 minutes	Yes	Provides a comprehensive evaluation of adolescents. ——— More information is needed on the diagnostic utility of this measure.	YES
Assessment of Interpersonal Relations (AIR)	To assess children's perceptions of the quality of their relationships with parents, peers, and teachers.	Ages 9–19 years	Rating Scale	20 min.	Yes	Reliable and valid instrument that is easy to administer. ——— Item generation process was questionable.	YES
The Attention Deficit Disorders Evaluation Scale-2nd Ed. (ADDES)	Assess for ADHD Symptoms according to DSM-IV criteria. Used an aid to diagnosing and treatment planning.	Ages 3–19 years	School and Home Questionnaires/ Multi-informant-Parents and Teachers	15–20 min.	Yes	Behaviorally anchored items. ——— No self -report form.	YES
Attention Deficit Hyperactivity Disorder Rating Scale-IV- Home and School Versions	To aid in clinicians in obtaining parent and teacher ratings of behavior that is representative of ADHD symptomatology according to the DSM-IV.	Ages 4–20 years	Rating Scale	10–20 min.	Yes	Easy to administer. Has strong psychometric properties.	YES

(Continued)

INSTRUMENT	GENERAL PURPOSE	POPULATION	METHOD/ INFORMANT(S)	ADMINISTRATION	NORMS	STRENGTHS/ LIMITATIONS	FEE
Name and Abb.	General purpose- Screen/Diagnosis; Tx. Planning and Evaluation	For whom intended	Questionnaires, Observation, Interview	Time	yes, no	Strengths/limitations	YES/NO
Attention-Deficit/Hyperactivity Disorder Test (ADHDT)	To aid clinicians in obtaining parent and teacher ratings of behavior that is representative of ADHD symptomatology as found in the DSM-IV.	Ages 3–23 years	Behavioral Checklist	5–10 minutes	Yes	Strong psychometric properties. ——— Fails to make a unique contribution distinctive from other measures available for the assessment of ADHD.	YES
Behavior Assessment Systems for Children (BASC)	To provide a thorough and comprehensive assessment of emotional and behavioral problems in children and adolescents.	Ages 4–18 years	School, Home, and Self-Report Rating Scales	Approx. 30 min.	Yes	Assesses self-reliance, leadership, and other adaptive behaviors that are not included in similar assessment systems. ——— Fails to provide a mechanism for integrating the multi-informant information.	YES
The Behavior Dimensions Scale-Home and School Versions (BDS)	To document the characteristics of ADHD, ODD, CD, APD, and MDD in children.	Ages 3–19 years Home version Ages 5–16 years School version	Rating Scale	20 min.	Yes	Useful as a screening tool. Easy to administer and score. ——— Lacks usefulness as a diagnostic tool that validly differentiates between DSM disorders.	YES
Behavior Disorders Identification Scale-Home and School Version (BDIS)	Contributes to early identification and service delivery for students with behavior disorders/emotional disturbance according to PL94–142.	Ages 4.5–21 years	School and Home Rating Scale/ Multi-Informant-Parents and Teachers or other School personnel	20 min.	Yes	Useful for identifying behavior disorders. Useful for making placement decisions. ——— No self-report form.	YES

The Behavior Evaluation Scale, 2nd Ed. (BES-2)	To assess for behavioral and emotional problems in accordance with PL94–142 criteria for special education, behavioral disorders, or emotional disturbance.	Ages 5–18 years Grades: K-12	School and Home Questionnaires/Multi-Informant-Parents and Teachers or other School personnel	20 min	Yes	Useful for clinical and research purposes. ——— No self-report form.	YES
Behavior Rating Profile-2nd Edition-Parent, Student, and Teacher Rating Scale (BRP-2)	To evaluate student behavior at home, school, and in interpersonal relationships.	Ages 6–6 through 18–6 years	Battery includes five rating scales and a sociogram.	60 min.	Yes	Provides both multi-informant and multi-situational information. ——— Paucity of research available regarding the instrument's validity.	YES
Burks' Behavior Rating Scale (BBRS)	To identify patterns of pathological behaviors that occur in children exhibiting behavioral problems in school or at home.	Grades: Pre-K-9th	School and Home Rating Scale/Multi-Informant-Parents and Teachers	No time specified	Standardized but the data is skewed.	Useful in assessing the behavioral characteristics of children. ——— Lack of adequate normative data.	YES
The Carey Temperament Scales (CTS)	To assess temperamental characteristics in infants and children.	Ages 1 month to 12 years.	Instrument includes 5 questionnaires according to age.	No time estimates were provided.	Yes	Items are behaviorally worded and the scales are easy to complete. ——— Lack of normative data for differing ethnic and SES populations.	YES
Child and Adolescent Functional Assessment Scale (CAFAS)	To rate impairment in children referred for emotional and behavioral problems.	Ages 5–17 years	Assessment Scale completed by parents or primary caregivers.	10 min. for CAFAS. Raters should complete the Self-Training Manual which takes 3 hours.	Yes	Useful in school settings or other settings where program evaluation is needed. ——— Scale may be lengthy for beginning raters.	YES

(*Continued*)

INSTRUMENT	GENERAL PURPOSE	POPULATION	METHOD/ INFORMANT(S)	ADMINISTRATION	NORMS	STRENGTHS/ LIMITATIONS	FEE
Name and Abb.	General purpose-Screen/Diagnosis; Tx. Planning and Evaluation	For whom intended	Questionnaires, Observation, Interview	Time	yes, no	Strengths/limitations	YES/NO
Children's Action Tendency Scale (CATS)	Provides a self-report measure of children's aggressiveness, assertiveness, and submissiveness.	Ages 6–12 years	Self-report/ Contains vignettes with 3 pairs of response alternatives.	15–20 min.	Yes	Good internal consistency, test-retest reliability, and construct validity. ——— Needs more research on gender factors.	NO
Children's Attention and Adjustment Survey (CAAS)	To measure behaviors related to ADHD in children.	Grades: K-5th	Rating Scale/ Completed by school psychologists or intake administrators.	2–5 min.	Yes	Good for screening and identifying those who need further assessment. ——— Should not be used as a primary diagnostic tool.	YES
Children's Personality Questionnaire	To assess various dimensions of personality in children and adolescents.	Ages 8–12 years	Self-Report Questionnaire	60 min.	None reported.	May aid in diagnosis and treatment. ——— Poor Psychometric support.	YES
Children's Problems Checklist (CPC)	To aid in the evaluation and assessment of children by providing a written documentation of presenting problems.	Ages 5–12 years	Checklist/ Completed by parents or guardians.	10–20 min.	None reported.	Can provide the clinician with a general idea of what the parental concerns are regarding a child. ——— No test manual or psychometric information.	YES
Conducting Functional Behavioral Assessments: A Practical Guide	To assist school personnel with conducting functional behavioral assessments and with developing behavioral intervention plans based on those assessments.	No specific age range for target students was specified in the manual.	Recording forms and guide to contribute to a functional behavioral assessment.	Varies according to target concerns.	None.	Straightforward tool for collecting information pertinent to a functional analysis of behavior. ——— Requires a high level of expertise in functional assessment to correctly use this tool.	YES

Conners' Rating Scale (CRS)	To assess Attention Deficit Hyperactivity Disorder and co-morbid disorders.	Ages 3–17 years	Rating Scales/Multi-informant-Parents and Teachers, Adolescent Self-Report		Yes. Includes norms for African Americans.	Allows for comparison across informants. ——— Former versions lack standardization.	YES
The Devereux Rating Scale-School Form	To determine the extent to which a child/adolescent's behaviors fall within or outside normal range.	Ages 4–18 years	Rating Scale/Completed by parent or teacher	15–45 min.	Standardized, but the data is positively skewed.	Useful for assessing for placement in Special Education. ——— Statistical soundness of subscales.	YES
The Diagnostic Interview for Children and Adolescents-Revised (DICA-R)	To classify childhood psychiatric disorders according to DSM-IV or ICD-10.	Ages 6–17 years	Structured Interview. Based on parent and child report.	1 hour–1.5 hours	Yes but limited data is available.	DICA-R consists of objectively worded items and comes with an easy to read technical manual. ——— Time consuming	YES
Differential Test of Conduct and Emotional Problems (DT/CEP)	To assist teachers and school personnel in screening for and differentiating children with emotional and conduct problems.	Grade: K-12th	Rating Scale/ Completed by teachers of other school personnel.	15–20 min.	Yes	Measure and manual are easy to understand. ——— Limited standardization data, and reliability and validity data.	YES
The Early Childhood Behavior Scale	To identify emotional disturbance and behavior disorders in children.	Ages 3–6 years	Rating Scale/ Completed by school teachers	15 min.	Yes	Can be used to assess effectiveness of school based interventions. ——— Questionable standardization process, Does not include parents as raters.	Unknown

(Continued)

INSTRUMENT	GENERAL PURPOSE	POPULATION	METHOD/ INFORMANT(S)	ADMINISTRATION	NORMS	STRENGTHS/ LIMITATIONS	FEE
Name and Abb.	General purpose-Screen/ Diagnosis; Tx. Planning and Evaluation	For whom intended	Questionnaires, Observation, Interview	Time	yes, no	Strengths/limitations	YES/NO
Early Childhood Inventory-4 (ECI-4)	To screen for behavioral, emotional, and cognitive difficulties in preschool-aged children.	Ages 3–5 years	Rating Scale/ Completed by parents and teachers.	10–15 min.	Yes	Broad screening tool that allows for multi-informant assessment ——— Validity data not representative of all disorders assessed.	Yes
The EcoBehavioal Assessment Systems Software, Ver. 3.0 (EBASS)	To provide a computerized data entry and analysis tool that is designed to aid in the collection, analysis, and management of classroom observation data.	Grades: K-12th	Observational tool	Varies	N/A	Includes detailed training materials. ——— Places temporal distance between events which may lead to inaccuracy.	YES
Emotional and Behavior Problem Scale (EBPS)	To provide a method of early identification of students with behavior disorders or emotional disturbance.	Ages 4.5-21 years	Rating Scale/ Completed by teachers or other school personnel	15 min.	Yes	Easy to administer, Reliability is strong. ——— Limited validity, Poor manual.	YES
Emotional or Behavior Disorder Scale (EBDS)	To assess behavioral and emotional problems of students for the purposes of early identification and provision of educational services.	Ages 4.5–20 years	Rating Scale/Home and School Versions.	20 min.	Yes	Assists in developing individualized education programs and treatment for children meeting PL 94:142 criteria. ——— Standardization and psychometric properties are of concern.	Unknown

Eyberg Child Behavior Inventory (ECBI) Sutter-Eyberg Student Behavior Inventory-Revised (SESBI-R)	To assess degree of conduct problems in children, assist in treatment planning, monitor treatment progress, and measure treatment outcome.	Ages 2–16 years	ECBI-report measure completed by parents. SESBI-report measure completed by teachers.	5–10 min.	Yes	Useful for targeting specific behaviors for treatment. ——— Needs additional research to expand norms to broader racial and SES populations.	NO
Functional Assessment and Intervention Program (FAIP)	To assist school personnel in conducting and interpreting functional assessments for students' problem behaviors.	No specific age range is provided in the manual.	Computer program completed by school personnel.	15–30 min.	No	FAIP provides intervention recommendations. ——— FAIP is limited by the clinical/educational skills of and data available to the respondent.	YES
Home Situations Questionnaire-Original and Revised (HSQ and HSQ-R) School Situations Questionnaire-Original and Revised (SSQ and SSQ-R)	To aid clinicians in the identification of different situations that may present difficulties for children with behavior problems.	HSQ: Ages 4–16 years HSQ-R: Ages 6–12 years SSQ: Ages 4–11 years SSQ-R: 6–12 years	School and Home Questionnaires	5 minutes	Yes	Easy to administer and score. Ample psychometric support makes them useful for a variety of clinical and research purposes. Caution when using norms tables for traditionally underrepresented groups.	YES
Individualized Classroom Education Questionnaire (ICEQ)	To measure perceptions of the classroom environment among secondary school students and teachers.	High School Students and Teachers	Multi-informant Questionnaire	15–30 min.	Yes	Good face validity. ——— Unclear how the measure would foster the classroom environment with regards to learning and performance.	Unknown
Interview Schedule for Children and Adolescents (ISCA)	To assess childhood-onset affective disorders using a semi-structured, symptom-oriented psychiatric interview format.	Ages 8–17 years	Intake interview version and follow-up assessment version. Administered by an experienced clinician.	Intake 2–2.5 hours Follow-up interview varies.	Yes	Can aid in diagnostic decision. ——— Needs more psychometric support and is lengthy.	Unknown

(Continued)

INSTRUMENT	GENERAL PURPOSE	POPULATION	METHOD/ INFORMANT(S)	ADMINISTRATION	NORMS	STRENGTHS/ LIMITATIONS	FEE
Name and Abb.	General purpose-Screen/ Diagnosis; Tx. Planning and Evaluation	For whom intended	Questionnaires, Observation, Interview	Time	yes, no	Strengths/limitations	YES/NO
Louisville Behavior Checklist (LBC)	To aid in conceptualizing behavior and communicating concerns about children.	Ages 4–17 years	Checklist completed by parents.	20–30 min.	Yes.	Small sample standardization and lack of reliability and validity.	YES
Manifestation of Symptomatology Scale (MOSS)	To assess self-reported behavioral and emotional problems in adolescents.	Ages 11–18 years	Self-Report Questionnaire	15–20 min.	Yes	User-friendly screening instrument. ——— Age-based norms are not provided.	Unknown
The Matson Evaluation of Social Skills with Youngsters (MESSY)	To measure social skills, identify potential problem behaviors, and measure treatment gains.	Ages 4–18 years	Rating scale/ Completed by teachers and through self-report.	15–30 min.	Yes	Easy to administer and score. ——— Norms and factor structure require further investigation.	YES
Multidimensional Self Concept Scale (MSCS)	Comprehensive assessment of self concept in youth.	Ages 9–19 years Grades: 5–12	Self-Report Rating Scale	20–30 min.	Yes	Strong theoretically and easy to administer and score.	YES
Personality Inventory for Children (PIC)	To provide comprehensive and clinically relevant descriptions of child behavior, affect, cognitive status and family characteristics.	Ages 3–16 years	Inventory/Completed by parents or guardians.	Not time limit provided.	Yes	Well researched and has strong psychometric properties. ——— Lengthy and limited by the True/False response method.	YES
Piers-Harris Children's Self-Concept Scale	To assess self-concept of children and adolescents based on self-report.	Ages 8–18 years	Self-Report Questionnaire	15–20 min.	Yes	Useful as a screening instrument, can aid in diagnosis and treatment. ——— Limitations due to the specific standardization sample.	YES

The Portland Problem Behavior Checklist-Revised (PPBC-R)	To aid in identifying problem behaviors, making diagnostic decision, and assessment of treatment procedures.	Grades K-12th	Rating Scale/ Multi-informant-teachers, parents, and students.	15–20 min.	Yes	May be used for screening or descriptive purposes ——— Lack of adequate normative data, sample is small and regionalized.	YES
Preschool and Kindergarten Behavior Scales (PKBS)	To identify children at risk for developing behavior or social problems.	Ages 3–6 years	Rating Scale/ Multi-informant-teachers, parents, or adults familiar with the child.	8–12 min.	Yes	Useful for screening young children. ——— Weak reliability; Doesn't contribute to treatment planning.	YES
Revised Behavior Problem Checklist (RBPC)	To screen for common school-based behavior problems.	Ages 5–18 years	Rating Scale/ Completed by parents and teachers.	10 min.	Yes.	Provides a good framework to identify behavior problems. ——— Poor representativeness of norms.	Unknown
School Archival Records Search (SARS)	To systematically code and quantify school records to assist with school-based decision making for students at risk.	Elementary school aged children	Screening Tool to be used in conjunction with the Systematic Screening for Behavior Disorders.	15–30 min.	Limited.	Provides a method for aggregating information found in school records. Initial psychometric properties are adequate. ——— Needs further validation.	YES
School Social Behavior Scales (SSBS)	To provide a screening measure for social skills and antisocial behavior in an academic setting.	Grades: K-12th	Rating Scale/ Completed by educational personnel	10–15 min.	Yes	Useful as a screening tool. ——— May not be appropriate for use with minority children.	YES

(*Continued*)

INSTRUMENT	GENERAL PURPOSE	POPULATION	METHOD/ INFORMANT(S)	ADMINISTRATION	NORMS	STRENGTHS/ LIMITATIONS	FEE
Name and Abb.	General purpose-Screen/ Diagnosis; Tx. Planning and Evaluation	For whom intended	Questionnaires, Observation, Interview	Time	yes, no	Strengths/limitations	YES/NO
School Social Skills Rating Scale (S3)	To assist in determining a student's social skill acquisition and aid in the development and evaluation of intervention plans.	Grades: K-12th	Rating Scale/ Completed by teachers of other school personnel	Approx. 10 min.	No standardization data available	Provides a list of important prosocial behaviors. / Lack of standardization and psychometric support.	YES
Semistructured Clinical Interview for Children and Adolescents (SCICA)	To assess behavioral and emotional problems in children and adolescents.	Ages 6–18 years	Standardized interview in for child or adolescent. Interviewer must be at least master's level.	45–60 min.	Yes. However, standardization is needed for adolescents.	High clinical utility / No norms for adolescents and small N for children.	YES
Social Behavior Assessment Inventory (SBAI)	To assess performance level of social behaviors exhibited in the classroom.	School Aged Children	Curriculum-based measure	30–45 min.	No	Good face validity / Poor psychometric support	YES
Social Competence and Behavior Evaluation-Preschool Edition (SCBE)	To aid clinicians in the assessment of patterns of social competence, affective expression, and adjustment difficulties in preschoolers.	Ages 30–78 months	Questionnaire completed by teacher	15 min.	Yes	Aids in treatment planning for interpersonal skills development. / Geographic limitations of the standardization sample.	YES
Social Skills Rating System (SSRS)	The Social Skills Rating System (SSRS) is designed to assist professionals in screening and classifying children suspected of having social behavior problems and aid in the development of appropriate interventions	Grades: Pre-K-12th	Rating Scale	15–25 min.	Yes	Psychometrically sound, user friendly, and links assessment data to intervention.	YES

Strengths and Difficulties Questionnaire (SDQ)	Screening instrument for evaluating behavioral and emotional concerns.	Ages 4–17 years	Questionnaire	5 min.	Yes	Useful for screening purposes. ——— A more complete discussion of the standardization process, and the measures reliability and validity needed.	NO
Student Adjustment Inventory (SAI)	To assess emotional and social problems in adolescents and young adults.	Upper elementary, middle school, high school, and beginning college students	Questionnaire	No time specified	Yes	Provides valuable information regarding target behaviors for treatment. ——— Standardization is not representative, which limits the measure's value.	YES
Student Self-Concept Scale (SSCS)	To measure self-concept and related psychological constructs.	Grades: 3-12th	Self-Report Measure	20–30 min.	Yes	Strong psychometrically, easy to administer and score.	YES
Systematic Screening for Behavior Disorders	To screen and identify elementary-aged students at risk for school dropout and behavior disorders.	Grades: K-6th	Observational system	Approx. 2 hours	No standardization for stage 1, Standardization for stages 2 & 3	Reduces the subjectivity of this type of assessment. ——— Only moderate levels of reliability and validity.	YES

(Continued)

INSTRUMENT	GENERAL PURPOSE	POPULATION	METHOD/ INFORMANT(S)	ADMINISTRATION	NORMS	STRENGTHS/ LIMITATIONS	FEE
Name and Abb.	General purpose-Screen/ Diagnosis; Tx. Planning and Evaluation	For whom intended	Questionnaires, Observation, Interview	Time	yes, no	Strengths/limitations	YES/NO
Teacher-Child Rating Scale	To assess children's school problem behaviors and competencies.	Grades: Pre-K-8th	Rating Scale completed by teacher	5 min.	Yes	Useful as a quick screening tool. No cut-off scores provided. Lacks validity as a diagnostic tool.	YES
Tennessee Self-Concept Scale: 2nd Edition-Adult Form and Child Form (TSCS:2)	To assist clinicians in measuring multidimensional self-concept.	Ages 7–90 years	Rating Scale	10–20 min.	Yes	Reliable and valid instrument. Scoring is time consuming	YES
Transition Behavior Scale (TBS)	To provide a measure of student readiness for transition into employment or independent living.	Grades: 11-12th	Multi-informant Rating Scale/ Completed by teachers or employers.	15 min.	Yes	Unique in that it measures behavior in the school and employment setting. Scoring guidelines are somewhat confusing.	YES

Chapter 6

Measures of Externalizing and Attentional Problems in Children

ACHENBACH SYSTEM OF EMPIRICALLY-BASED ASSESSMENT: CHILD BEHAVIOR CHECKLIST, TEACHER REPORT FORM, AND YOUTH SELF-REPORT

Reviewed by: Stephen D. A. Hupp and David Reitman

Purpose

To assess a wide range of emotional and behavioral problems in children based on parent report. The measure is a part of a set of instruments that include the Teacher's Report Form (Achenbach, 1991b) and the Youth Self Report (Achenbach, 1991c). A semi-structured interview and direct observation form are also available.

Population

The Child Behavior Checklist (CBCL) is intended for use with parents or caretakers of children and adolescents aged 4 to 18 years. The Teacher's Report Form (TRF) is intended for teachers of youths aged 5 to 18 years. The Youth Self-Report (YSR) is designed for use with children and adolescents aged 11 to 18 years.

Description

The CBCL consists of 113 items that the parent rates as 0 (not true in the past 6 months), 1 (somewhat or sometimes true), or 2 (very true or often true). Eight narrowband factors (i.e., Withdrawn, Somatic Complaints, Anxious/Depressed, Social Problems, Thought Problems, Attention Problems, Delinquent Behavior, and Aggressive Behavior) and two broadband factors (i.e., Internalizing and Externalizing) were derived during the development of the scale and have been supported through confirmatory factor analyses (Greenbaum & Dedrick, 1998). The CBCL also includes a "competency" component in which parents rate the quantity and quality of recreational (e.g., sports), social (e.g., peer relationships) and academic (e.g., grades) performances.

The current version of the CBCL is accompanied by a technical manual that describes the purposes of the checklists, normative data, and present reliability and validity information. Raw scores on each of the subscales can be converted into standard scores and percentile ranks. Achenbach (1991a) suggested that T-scores below 67 are within the normal range, 67 to 70 are in the borderline clinical range, and above 70 are in the clinical range. Recent research suggests that T-scores as low as 65 may indicate clinically significant impairment.

The 113-item TRF contains 93 of the original 113 items from the CBCL and yields problem behavior scores comparable to those of the CBCL. Teachers also rate the child's academic performance on a five-point scale ranging from "far below grade level" to "far above grade level" as well as evaluating their overall adaptive functioning. Appropriate technical information is provided in the manual and interpretation is consistent with the CBCL.

The 112-item YSR contains all items from the CBCL except those deemed inappropriate for adolescents (e.g., "wets the bed"). Youths rate themselves for how true each item is now or has been over the past six months. Scoring and interpretation of the YSR is similar to the CBCL.

Administration

Parents or adolescents with at least fifth grade reading skills can complete the CBCL or YSR in approximately 10 to 17 minutes. An interviewer can also read the instrument to the rater if there are questions about the individual's reading ability. The TRF can be completed in less than 15 minutes by most teachers.

Scoring

The CBCL, TRF, and YSR can be scored somewhat cumbersomely by hand; however, a computer program has been developed for more efficient scoring and has been recommended by some reviewers (see Doll, 1998; Furlong & Wood, 1998).

Psychometric Properties

Norms: The 1991 version of the CBCL was normed on 2,368 non-referred children and adolescents aged 4 to 18 years. The sample was generally representative of the U.S. population regarding gender, ethnicity, socioeconomic status, geographic region, and area of residence. Subsamples of 1,391 and 1,315 youths drawn from the larger sample were used to norm the TRF and YSR, respectively.

Reliability: The internal consistency of most of the CBCL subscales was reported to be greater than .80, and 1-week test-retest reliability was reported to be .89 for the behavior ratings and .87 for social competence component (Achenbach, 1991a). Reports of interparent agreement have ranged from .52 to .99. Internal consistencies are generally very good for problem behavior scores but modest to poor for competence scales (Furlong & Wood, 1998). Test-retest reliability for the TRF over a 15 day interval was .92 and agreement between teacher pairs has been estimated at .60. One week test-retest reliability for the YSR was estimated at .79. The reliability estimates above refer to total scores unless otherwise indicated. Subscale reliability estimates are likely to be lower but generally are acceptable.

Validity: The discriminative validity of the CBCL has been demonstrated by studies showing that it distinguishes between clinic-referred and non-referred children (Achenbach, 1991a). Nevertheless, 30% of youths from a nonreferred sample have scored in the clinical range using this instrument, so the CBLC should be used in addition to other measures child behavior (e.g., interview, the teacher report (TRF), and self-report (YSR)). In fact, it has been consistently recommended that the CBCL be used as part of a multi-method assessment (McConaughy, 1993). Using the computerized scoring option allows for the generation of cross-informant constructs (using 89 items common to the CBCL, TRF, and YSR), yielding more reliable and potentially valid estimates of problem behavior than are possible using single-informant constructs. Subscales of the CBCL correlate with subscales on other instruments, such as the Conner Ratings Scales and the Revised Problem Behavior Checklist, designed to measure similar constructs (Achenbach, 1991a). However, the validity of the Social Competence scales has been called into question and may need further development (Furlong & Wood, 1998). Validity studies of the TRF and YSR have generally been supportive but concerns about the rather low correlations across informants (e.g., parents, teachers, and youths) and the absence of validity indicators to detect lying (especially for youths) or response sets have been the subject of some debate.

Clinical Utility

High. The CBCL, TRF, and YSR are most useful as screening tools for a wide range of problems associated with childhood. The instruments are worded behaviorally, and the subscales provide a continuous analogue to the categorical approach taken by the DSM authors. Children older (18–30 years) or younger (2–3 years) may also be assessed using more recently developed versions of the CBCL. One should strongly consider computer scoring to reduce scoring errors. In addition, while expensive ($450), computer scorings of the CBCL, TRF, and YSR are unlimited and interpretative diagnostic aides such as the cross-informant constructs and age and gender appropriate norm-referenced graphs are made available as well.

Strengths/Limitations

The CBCL, TRF, and YSR are well-known instruments that are easily interpreted by most professionals and educated laypersons. Collectively, they have strong treatment utility and facilitate diagnostic decision-making and treatment planning. Unlike the CPRS-R and the BASC, however, the CBCL does not distinguish between inattentive and hyperactive behaviors and does not make a clear distinction between anxiety and depression. The social competence scales could be improved and the availability of validity indicators would be a welcomed addition to the existing battery of measures. Finally, interpretation of some protocols may need to be done cautiously as CBCL norms may be limited in their applicability outside of Caucasian, and/or primarily middle- and upper-class populations (Sandberg, Meyer-Bahlburg, & Yager, 1991). Despite these limitations, it remains the best known and most extensively researched instrument available.

Author: Thomas M. Achenbach.

Publication Year: 1991.

Source: University of Vermont, 1 S. Prospect St., Burlington, VT 05401.

Fee: Yes.

ADDITIONAL INFORMATION/REFERENCES

Achenbach, T. M. (1991a). *Manual for the Child Behavior Checklist/4–18 and 1991 Profile.* Burlington, VT: University of Vermont Department of Psychiatry.

Achenbach, T. M. (1991b). *Manual for the Teacher's Report Form and 1991 Profile.* Burlington, VT: University of Vermont Department of Psychiatry.

Achenbach, T. M. (1991c). *Manual for the Youth Self-Report and 1991 Profile.* Burlington, VT: University of Vermont Department of Psychiatry.

Doll, B. (1998). [Review of the Child Behavior Checklist.] In J. C. Impara and B. S. Plake (Eds.), *The thirteenth mental measurements yearbook* (pp. 217–220). Lincoln, NE: Buros Institute of Mental Measurements.

Furlong, M. J., & Wood, M. (1998). [Review of the Child Behavior Checklist.] In J. C. Impara and B. S. Plake (Eds.), *The thirteenth mental measurements yearbook* (pp. 220–224). Lincoln, NE: Buros Institute of Mental Measurements.

Greenbaum, P. E., & Dedrick, R. F. (1998). Hierarchical confirmatory factor analysis of the Child Behavior Checklist, 4–18. *Psychological Assessment, 10,* 149–155.

McConaughy, S. H. (1993). Evaluating behavioral and emotional disorders with the CBCL, TRF, and YSR cross-informant scales. *Journal of Emotional and Behavioral Disorders, 1,* 1993.

Sandberg, D. E., Meyer-Bahlburg, H. F., & Yager, T. J. (1991). The Child Behavior Checklist nonclinical standardization samples: Should they be utilized as norms? *Journal of the American Academy of Child and Adolescent Psychiatry, 30,* 124–134.

ACHENBACH SYSTEM OF EMPIRICALLY BASED ASSESSMENT-PRESCHOOL: CHILD BEHAVIOR CHECKLIST 1½–5 AND CAREGIVER–TEACHER REPORT FORM

Reviewed by: Mary Lou Kelley

Purpose

To assess the behavioral, emotional, and social functioning of preschoolers across settings.

Population

Children aged 1–1/2 to 5.

Description

The CBCL 1½–5 is a revised version of the CBCL-2/3. The scale contains 110 problem items that are rated on a three point scale: 1 (Not True), 2 (Somewhat or Sometimes True), or 3 (Very True or Often True). The vast majority of the items are the same as those on the CBCL-2/3 although several items were revised, deleted, or substituted with a new item.

A unique feature of the CBCL-1½–5 scale is that it also contains a Language Development Survey (LDS) component for ages 18–35 months. The authors recommend that this component be completed on all children under the age of three or any child with a suspected language delay.

The first page asks parents questions about the child's birth history, ear infections, and language development. This page also asks parents to list the child's best multi-word phrases. The second page lists 310 words that often are the first words spoken by children. Respondents are asked to circle all words that the child says spontaneously.

The TRF is completed by a caregiver or teacher who observes the child in groups of at least four. The scale also contains 100 items that generally are the same as those on CBCL 1½–5 although are substituted some family items with items that occur in groups.

Administration

The CBCL 1½–5 is completed by a guardian or parent and the TRF is completed by a caregiver or teacher who observes the child in groups of at least four children. Each form can be completed in 10–15 minutes and is available in English and Spanish.

Scoring

As with the other ASEBA scales, CBCL 1½–5 items are grouped into syndromes derived from factor analysis. The seven narrowband factors are Emotionally Reactive, Anxious/Depressed, Somatic Complaints, Withdrawn, Sleep Problems, Attention Problems, and Aggressive Behavior. Items also are grouped into three broadband factors: Internalizing, Externalizing, and Total Problems. The TRF scales are identical to those of the CBCL 1½–5 with the exception that it does not contain the Sleeping Problems factor.

In addition the Syndrome Scales, the CBCL 1½–5 and the TRF problem items are scored according to DSM-IV-oriented scales. These scales are: Affective Problems, Anxiety Problems, Pervasive Developmental Problems, Attention Deficit/ Hyperactivity Problems, and Oppositional Defiant Problems.

Scores for both the Syndrome Scales and the DSM-Oriented Scales can be compared across informants using the computer scoring system available thru the authors. One nice feature of the computer scoring system is scores from up to 8 informants can be plotted on bar graphs in such a way that elevations across informants on each scale can be compared. Correlations between informants is also calculated using the computer program. In addition to computer scoring, both measures can be hand scored and plotted on a profile sheet. Scores for the CBCL 1½–5 does not have separate norms based on gender or age as the authors state the differences were minimal in the standardization sample. Separate norms for boys and girls are obtained on the TRF Attention Problems and Aggressive Behavior scales.

The LDS provides two measures of language development: average length of multi-word phrases and number of words used spontaneously. Scores are plotted on scales based on six different age/gender groupings. Only the CBCL 1½–5 contains the LDS component.

Psychometric Properties

Norms: The CBCL 1½–5 was normed on a heterogeneous sample of non-referred children (n = 700). The TRF was normed on 1,395 non-referred children. The sample was representative of the U.S. population regarding ethnicity, socioeconomic status, and geographic region.

Reliability: Test-retest reliability was .85 for the CBCL 1½–5, .76 for the C-TRF, and $\leq$ .90 for the LDS vocabulary test. Interparent agreement was .61 and intercaregiver agreement was .65. Agreement between parents and teachers was only .40.

Validity: Numerous validity studies were reported in the technical manual. The measures have good discriminant, construct, and criterion-related validity. The scales discriminated referred and non-referred children and scores were correlated with those of similar measures.

Clinical Utility

High. The CBCL 1½–5 and the C-TRF are very useful screening measures for assessing a wide range of problems seen in preschool children. The instrument is worded behaviorally, and the subscales provide a continuous analogue of symptom clusters. The inclusion of the DSM-oriented scales and the LDS component adds to the clinical utility of the instruments.

Strengths/Limitations

The CBCL 1½–5 and the C-TRF are well-designed instruments representing the culmination of research conducted over many years by the authors. The items are easily understood, as are the factors. The technical manual was very easy to read and informative. The addition of the LDS is likely to be a useful feature.

Authors: Thomas M. Achenbach and Leslie A. Rescorla.

Source: ASEBA, 1. South Prospect St. Burlington, VT 05401-3456.

ADDITIONAL INFORMATION/REFERENCES

Achenbach, T. M. (1992). *Manual for the Child Behavior Checklist/2–3 and l992 Profile.* Burlington, VT: University of Vermont Department of Psychiatry.

Achenbach, T. M., & Rescorla, L. A. (2000). *Manual for the ASEBA Preschool Forms & Profiles.* Burlington, VT: University of Vermont Department of Psychiatry.

ACHIEVEMENT MOTIVATION PROFILE

Reviewed by: Kathy Ragsdale and Mary Lou Kelley

Purpose

To measure a student's motivation to achieve, along with related personality characteristics, interpersonal attributes, work style, and other qualities important for school success.

Population

The Achievement Motivation Profile (AMP) is intended for use with students, ages 14 and older, in high school, junior college, and college settings.

Description

The AMP is designed for use in educational and industrial evaluations. It was developed to serve as a multidimensional personality test. The AMP is a self-report questionnaire that consists of 140 brief, self-descriptive statements. All items are worded at a fourth grade reading level. The items are grouped into four general areas: Motivation for Achievement, Inner Resources, Interpersonal Strengths, and Work Habits. These four general areas comprise 15 subscales: Achiever, Motivation, Competitiveness, Goal Orientation, Relaxed Style, Happiness, Patience, Self Confidence, Assertiveness, Personal Diplomacy, Extroversion, Cooperativeness, Planning & Organizing, Initiative, and Team Player. Three validity scales are also derived: Inconsistent Responding, Self-Enhancing, and Self-Critical. The AMP items are rated on a 5 point likert-scale which ranges from 1 = Always True to 5 = Always false. The person completing the questionnaire is instructed to fill in the background information and the date, and to read the directions carefully.

Administration

The AMP may be administered in either paper-and-pencil or computer format. Administration can be completed in 20–30 minutes in group or individual settings.

Scoring

The AMP may be either hand or computer scored. Separate forms are available for the scoring method chosen. Hand scoring is accomplished by transferring values circled, to columns representing the scales. Raw score values are converted to T-scores and percentiles for each scale.

Computerized scoring options include mail-in scoring, fax-in scoring or microcomputer-based scoring. An interpretive report is generated with each of the computer scoring options. Each of the computer based scoring options has a specific answer sheet that must be used for each one of the options.

Psychometric Properties

Norms: The scale was normed on 1,738 high school, junior college, and university students, ages 14 and older in both the United States and Canada. The students sampled were 45% male and 55% female. Ten-percent of the students were from ethnic minorities.

Reliability: Internal consistency for the scales ranged from .58 to .84 (median = .75). Test-retest reliabilities for the AMP scale scores ranged from .61 to .89 (median = .83).

Validity: Various forms of validity data, as reported by the authors, were supportive of the measure. However, the correlations may have been inflated because 58 of the items are used in 2 or more subscales. Content validity was not evidenced.

Clinical Utility

Limited. The scale is difficult to score and the standardization data is limited.

Strengths/Limitations

The AMP may be useful in assessing students' motivation to achieve. However, the AMP's hand scoring is complicated and requires many steps. Minority populations are also underrepresented in the norm sample. In addition, item generation for the AMP was theoretically driven. Final items selected for the scale was based on interterm correlations, factor analysis, correlations with external measures, and professional judgement.

Authors: Jotham G. Friedland, Ph.D., Sander I. Marcus, Ph.D., and Harvey P. Mandel, Ph.D.

Publication Year: 1996.

Source: Western Psychological Services, 12031 Wilshire Boulevard, Los Angeles, CA 90025-1251 (310) 478-2061 or (800) 648-8857 FAX: (310) 478-7838.

Fee: Yes.

ADDITIONAL INFORMATION/REFERENCES

Owen, S. V. (2001). Review of the Achievement Motivation Profile. In: *Mental Measurements Yearbook: Volume 14,* pp. 8–10.

Stewart, J. R. (2001). Review of the Achievement Motivation Profile. In: *Mental Measurements Yearbook: Volume 14,* pp. 10–12.

ACHIEVING BEHAVIORAL COMPETENCIES: TEACHER RATING SCALE

Reviewed by: Mary Lou Kelley

Purpose

To provide a measure of social skills deemed important by classroom teachers. The measure is one component of a three-part social skills program that includes the assessment instrument, social skills curriculum, and program evaluation.

Population

School-aged children.

Description

The Achieving Behavioral Competencies consists of three components: the Teacher Rating Scale and the Social Skills Curriculum that corresponds to the scale, and a computer program for assessment data summarization. The Teacher Rating Scale is an 80-item checklist of social behaviors that are rated by teachers on a 5-point Likert scale which ranged from 1 (Never) to 5 (Always). Teachers are asked to complete the rating scale on a single student based on an indeterminant time period. Items are fairly specific, behavioral, and positively written. Items from the scale are grouped into four categories: Relating to Others, Personal Responsibility, Coping with Stress, and Personal/Affective Development. It was not clear how the fourth factor was determined as it was added later to account for problems with anxiety and depression that are often manifested by at-risk youth.

The curriculum that accompanies the instrument and contains skills training modules covering each of the factor domains is fairly straightforward. The curriculum is attractively presented and provides teaching instructions that are logical and clearly described. Within each domain, five skills are included. For example, in the Relating to Others domain, the following skills are included: building friendships, maintaining friendships, compromising/negotiating, giving/accepting praise or criticism. Each skill contains instructional guides for promoting: student self-awareness, teacher instruction, teacher demonstration, student interaction, self-management and generalization.

Administration

Approximately 10 minutes by a classroom teacher.

Scoring

The only method of scoring the instrument is through the use of the computer program provided. The computer scoring offers cut-off scores for whom social skills training might be recommended due to weaknesses in a given skill area. Statistical justification for the cut-off scores was not provided.

Psychometric Properties

Norms: None reported.

Reliability: Alpha reliabilities were adequate but the sample was not described. Other reliability indices were not provided.

Validity: Only initial factor analysis data collected on undescribed sample.

Clinical Utility

Limited. This is mainly due to the lack of adequate psychometric and normative data. However, questionnaires or the questionnaire might be used for descriptive purposes and the curriculum might be very useful in a clinical setting. Strongly recommend against using the instrument in any diagnostic manner.

Strengths/Limitations

The measure has good face validity but lacks psychometric support. The curriculum seems reasonable and is presented in a logical, sequential manner. It is unclear, however, whether a teacher untrained in conducting social skills groups could effectively administer the curriculum.

Authors: Lawrence T. McCarron, Ph.D., Kathleen McConnell Fad, Ph.D., and Melody B. McCarron, M. S.

Publication Year: 1992.

Source: McCarron-Dial Systems, P. O. Box 45628, Dallas, TX 75245.

Fee: Yes.

ADDITIONAL INFORMATION/REFERENCES

Kuhlenschmidt, S. (1998). Review of Achieving Behavioral Competencies. In *Mental Measurement Yearbook, Volume 13,* pp. 23–25.

Leark, R. A. (1998). Review of Achieving Behavioral Competencies. In *Mental Measurement Yearbook, Volume 13,* pp. 25–27.

ADD-H COMPREHENSIVE TEACHER'S RATING SCALE—2nd EDITION: PARENT REPORT FORM, SELF REPORT FORM

Reviewed by: Sara E. Sytsma & Mary Lou Kelley

Purpose

To identify children with attention deficits with or without hyperactive behavior.

Population

Children in grades kindergarten through eighth grade.

Description

The ADD-H Comprehensive Teacher's Rating Scale (ACTeRS) is a 24-item teacher-report screening measure of attention problems and hyperactive behavior. Suggested uses include screening by teachers and physicians to identify children who may benefit from intervention and to monitor medication effects. The ACTeRS measures behavior in four different domains: Attention, Hyperactivity, Social Skills, and Oppositional Behavior. Items in each scale are scored using Likert-type ratings ranging from 1 (Almost Never) to 5 (Almost Always). Lower scores on the Attention and Social Skills factors suggest more problematic behavior whereas higher scores on the Hyperactivity and Oppositional scales suggest more problematic behavior.

A parent-report form of the ACTeRS was developed in 1996 (MetriTech, 2001a). It consists of the same four factors as the teacher-report form and includes a fifth scale, reporting on early childhood behavior. The parent form is available in both English and Spanish versions.

A manual is available from the publisher that provides information about the teacher and parent forms of the ACTeRS. Computerized scoring and report generation can also be purchased in quantities of 50 and 100 administrations (MetriTech, 2001b).

A self-report form of the ACTeRS was also developed in 1998 and is marketed as a diagnostic measure of ADD in adolescents and adults (MetriTech, 2001c). It consists of 35 items comprising three scales: Attention, Hyperactivity/Impulsivity, and Social Adjustment, which are also scored on a 5-point Likert-type scale. It can be completed in 10–15 minutes. Normed on over 1000 individuals, the ACTeRS Self Report is reported to have adequate reliability. A technical manual is also available for this form.

Administration

The ACTeRS can be completed in less than 10 minutes.

Scoring

Items within each domain are summed and can be easily converted to percentile ranks and plotted on profiles on the back of the rating form. Raw scores are compared to other children of the same gender from the standardization sample. The protocol can be scored and plotted according to gender norms in less than 5 minutes.

Psychometric Properties

Norms: The ACTeRS was normed on approximately 4,000 elementary and middle school students, mainly from Illinois. Further information on standardization is available in the test manual.

Reliability: The teacher report form of the ACTeRS was found to have excellent internal consistency, good test-retest reliability, and adequate interrater reliability (MetriTech, 2001b). The parent report form also yielded adequate reliability, averaging .86 across subscales (MetriTech, 2001a).

Validity: Factorial validity of the ACTeRS was supported (Ullman, Sleator, & Sprague, 1984a). Furthermore, the ACTeRS was sensitive to medication effects (Ullman & Sleator, 1985; Ullman & Sleator, 1986), supporting its use as a measure of treatment outcome. A variety of other validity tests have been conducted and found to be adequate. Additional information on the validity of the ACTeRS can be found in the test manual.

Clinical Utility

Adequate. The ACTeRS has utility as a briefly administered, easily scored screening device for use by teachers and physicians. Its utility is enhanced by the recent development of a parent-report form, but limited by its lack of relationship to current diagnostic criteria.

Strengths/Limitations

The ACTeRS has been found to have adequate psychometric properties and is easy to administer and score. It was, however, developed as a screening measure and its lack of correspondence to current diagnostic criteria renders it inadequate for diagnostic purposes.

Authors: Rina K. Ullmann, M.Ed., Esther K. Sleator, M. D., & Robert L. Sprague, Ph.D.

Publication Year: 1991.

Source: MetriTech, Inc., 4106 Fieldstone Road, Champaign, Illinois 61821. (217) 398-4868, Fax (217) 398-5798. Internet: www.metritech.com.

ADDITIONAL INFORMATION/REFERENCES

MetriTech, Inc. (2001a). *ACTeRS Parent Form.* Online: www.metritech.com/Metritech/Products/acters_parent.htm. Champaign, IL: MetriTech, Inc.

MetriTech, Inc. (2001b). *ACTeRS Teacher Form.* Online: www.metritech.com/Metritech/Products/acters_teacher.htm. Champaign, IL: MetriTech, Inc.

MetriTech, Inc. (2001c). *ACTeRS Self-Report.* Online: www.metritech.com/Metritech/Products/acters_self_report.htm. Champaign, IL: MetriTech, Inc.

Ullman, R. K. (1985). ACTeRS useful in screening Learning Disabled from Attention Deficit Disordered (ADD-H) children. *Psychopharmacology Bulletin, 21,* 339–344.

Ullman, R. K. & Sleator, E. K. (1985). Attention Deficit Disorder Children with or without Hyperactivity: Which behaviors are helped by stimulants?. *Clinical Pediatrics, 24,* 547–551.

Ullman, R. K. & Sleator, E. K. (1986). Responders, nonresponders, and placebo responders among children with Attention Deficit Disorder. *Clinical Pediatrics, 25,* 594–599.

Ullman, R. K., Sleator, E. K., & Sprague, R. L. (1984a). A new rating scale for diagnosis and monitoring of ADD children. *Psychopharmacology Bulletin, 20,* 160–164.

Ullman, R. K., Sleator, E. K., & Sprague, R. L. (1984b). ADD children: Who is referred from the schools? *Psychopharmacology Bulletin, 20,* 308–312.

ADJUSTMENT SCALES FOR CHILDREN AND ADOLESCENTS

Reviewed by: Aaron Clendenin & Mary Lou Kelley

Purpose

To aid mental health professionals in the assessment of behavioral syndromes and degree of adjustment

Population

School children from 5–17 years old.

Description

The Adjustment Scales for Children and Adolescents (ASCA) is a standardized behavior rating scale containing 97 problem and 26 prosocial behavior indicators. The ASCA purports to be multi-situational, in that rated behaviors are presented within the context of interactions with authority, peers, smaller or weaker youths, recreation, learning, or confrontation. It assesses behavior relevant to six Core Syndrome subscales: Attention-Deficit Hyperactivity Disorder, Solitary Aggressive (Provocative), Solitary Aggressive (Impulsive), Oppositional Defiant, Diffident, and Avoidant; two Supplementary Syndrome subscales: Delinquent and Lethargic

(Hypoactive); and two Overall Adjustment subscales: Overactivity and Underactivity. The ASCA is available in male and female versions.

Administration

Approximately 15 to 20 minutes to a teacher.

Scoring

The scoring keys are printed on the reverse side of the cover and last pages of the protocol form. Item endorsements are automatically transferred to corresponding symbols (star, square, diamond, etc.) for each syndrome scale. Raw scores for a syndrome scale are obtained by counting the number of endorsed symbols for the appropriate syndrome. Raw scores are compared to T scores in either a cutoff score format that yields functional levels or as a syndromic profile.

Psychometric Properties

Norms: The standardization sample consisted of 1,400 children and adolescents aged 5 through 17 years. Stratified random sampling with matrix blocking was used to construct the ASCA sample. Substantial effort was expended to insure accurate representation of the major demographic characteristics of the national population.

Reliability: Correlation coefficients for internal consistency ranged from .67 to .86; interrater reliability scores ranged from .65 to .85; and test-retest correlations, conducted at an interval of 30 school days, ranged from .66 to .91.

Validity: Exploratory and confirmatory factor analysis generally supported the syndrome structure. Convergent validity was established through correlations with the revised Conners Teacher Rating Scale (Trites et al., 1982) and the Child Behavior Checklist (Achenbach & Edelbrock, 1983). Divergent validity was supported through the analysis of the relationship between the ASCA and the Differential Ability Scales (Elliot, 1990) and Learning Behaviors Scale-Revised (McDermott, Green, Francis, & Stott, 1993).

Clinical Utility

Adequate. The low reliability estimates preclude the use of this measure in diagnostic decisions.

Strengths and Limitations

The authors supply an ample amount of validity evidence for the measure. Select subscales, however, are not to be used with certain populations (Lethargic: females > 12 years old; Delinquent: females < 12 years old).

Authors: Paul A. McDermott, Marston C. Neville, & Denis H. Stott.

Publication Year: 1993.

Source: Edumetric and Clinical Science, Ed & Psych Associates, PMB 900, 2071 South Atherton St., State College, PA 16801, Fax: (814) 235-9115.

Fee: Yes.

ADDITIONAL INFORMATION/REFERENCES

Achenbach, T. M. & Edelbrock, C. (1983). *Manual for the Child Behavior Checklist and Revised Child Behavior Profile.* Burlington, VT: University of Vermont.

McDermott, P. A., Green, L. F., Francis, J. M. & Stott, D. H. (1993). *Learning Behaviors Scale-Revised.* Philadelphia: Edumetric and Clinical Science.

Trites, R. L., Blouin, A. G. A., & Laprade, K. (1982). Analysis of the Conners Teacher Rating Scale based on a large normative sample. *Journal of Consulting and Clinical Psychology, 50,* 615–623.

ADOLESCENT PSYCHOPATHOLOGY SCALE

Reviewed by: Kellie Hilker & Mary Lou Kelley

Purpose

The Adolescent Psychopathology Scale (APS) provides a comprehensive assessment of the severity of psychological disorders, personality disorders, and social-emotional problems and competencies in adolescents.

Population

Adolescents between the ages of 12 and 19.

Description

The APS is a 346-item, self-report measure consisting of 4 major domains: Clinical; Personality Disorder; Psychosocial Problem Content; and Response Style Indicators. The majority of the scales fall under the Clinical Domain and correspond to DSM-IV diagnoses. The Clinical Domain includes the following scales: Attention-Deficit/ Hyperactivity Disorder; Conduct Disorder; Oppositional Defiant Disorder; Adjustment Disorder; Substance Abuse; Anorexia Nervosa; Bulimia Nervosa; Sleep Disorder; Somatization Disorder; Panic Disorder; Obsessive-Compulsive Disorder; Generalized Anxiety Disorder; Social Phobia; Separation Anxiety Disorder; Posttraumatic Stress Disorder; Major Depression; Dysthymic Disorder; Mania; Depersonalization Disorder; and Schizophrenia. The Personality Disorder Domain was created to evaluate somewhat stable and enduring maladaptive personality traits. Five scales (Avoidant Personality Disorder, Obsessive-Compulsive Disorder, Borderline Personality Disorder, Schizotypal Personality Disorder, and Paranoid Personality Disorder) are included in the APS. The Psychosocial Problem Content Domain assesses psychological characteristics that may create significant distress for adolescents. There are a total of 11 scales including Self-Concept, Psychosocial Substance Use Difficulties, Introversion, Alienation-Boredom, Anger, Aggression, Interpersonal Problems, Emotional Lability, Disorientation, Suicide, and Social Adaptation. The Lie Response, Consistency Response, Infrequency Response, and Critical Item Endorsement scales comprise the Response Style Indicator Domain. Internalizing, Externalizing, and Personality factor scores also can be obtained from the APS.

The adolescent completing the APS is instructed to indicate how often they experience a variety of symptoms. A multiple response format is utilized, therefore, some items have a true/false format, while others require a choice from 3, 4, or 5 potential frequencies (e.g., "never", "almost never", "sometimes", and "nearly all the time"). Additionally, the items are broken down by time frame of symptoms, for example, items are endorsed based on the occurrence of the symptoms in the previous 2 weeks, 1 month, 3 months, 6 months, or 1 year.

Administration

Administration of the APS takes 45–60 minutes and can be administered either individually or in a group setting.

Scoring

The APS Scoring Program and the Key Disk are used to score the APS. The Key Disk is provided with each test packet that is ordered. The Clinical Score Report generated by the scoring program includes various sources of information including a summary of scale elevations, a score summary table, and a critical items summary form. Raw scores on the APS are converted into T-scores for interpretation. The mild clinical symptom range is from 65 to 69, the moderate clinical symptom range is from 70 to 79, and severe clinical symptom range includes T-scores of 80 and greater.

Psychometric Properties

Norms: Standardization was based on 1,827 adolescents and the author attempted to match the standardization sample with 1990 Census estimates. The sample was approximately equal with regards to gender. The majority of the sample was Caucasian (72%) followed by African-American (18.3). Asian and Hispanic adolescents also were represented in the standardization sample. Normative data is provided according to the total standardization sample, gender, age, and age by gender.

Reliability: Internal consistency was calculated for all the scales for the total standardization sample and the clinical sample. In general, internal consistency estimates for the Clinical Disorders, Personality Disorders, and Psychosocial Problem Content domains were moderate to high ranging from .69 to .95 for the total standardization sample. Estimates for the clinical sample ranged from .70 to .95. Moderate item-with-total scale correlations were calculated providing additional support for homogeneity of item content for each scale. Test-retest reliability was evaluated in a 2-week interval and the majority of coefficients were greater than .76.

Validity: Initial content validity was obtained through review of items by an expert panel. The factor analysis of the APS provided support for the construct validity of the APS and was consistent with the hypothesized division of internalizing and externalizing symptoms. Discriminant validity was evaluated by comparison of the APS to IQ scores and social desirability. No significant correlations were found between IQ and scales of the APS, and low, but significant correlations were found between social desirability and the APS scales. Overall, support for discriminant validity was found. Moderately strong correlations were found between scales of the APS and the scales of the MMPI providing support for concurrent validity. Concurrent validity also was calculated with a variety of more specific measures including the Beck Depression Inventory, the Suicide Ideation Questionnaire, the Reynolds Adolescent Depression Scale, and other self-report psychosocial measures. In general, support for concurrent validity also was found with these correlations. Clinical validity, or contrasted groups validity, was obtained by demonstrating significantly different APS scores for the school and the clinical sample.

Clinical Utility

Adequate. This measure can contribute to the process of clinical diagnosis and may be used to screen for psychopathology. The author also suggests that the APS can be used for treatment planning, however, no information about how treatment planning would follow from a clinical profile is indicated in the manual.

Strengths/Limitations

The APS is a comprehensive measure that evaluates psychopathology and psychosocial problems in adolescents. One limitation of the standardization process is the representativeness of the clinical group. Many of the disorders assessed with the APS are not well represented in the clinical sample and others over represented, for example, Substance Abuse Disorder and Conduct Disorder are both present in approximately 20% of the clinical sample. The manual presents a thorough review of issues related to the use of self-report measures, technical information, and administration guidelines. Overall, the data presented by the author provide support for the psychometric integrity of this instrument, however, there is a lack of information regarding the validity of the individual clinical, personality disorder, and psychosocial problem scales. Additionally, more information about the utility in differentiating between individuals with and without different clinical diagnoses is needed. Finally, there was no attempt at obtaining multi-informant data, which may be beneficial with regards to adolescent externalizing problems.

Authors: William M. Reynolds, Ph.D.

Publication Year: 1998.

Source: Psychological Assessment Resources, Inc. P.O. Box 998 Odessa, FL 33556-9908, (813) 968-3003.

Fee: Yes.

ASSESSMENT OF INTERPERSONAL RELATIONS

Reviewed by: Mary Lou Kelley

Purpose

To assess children's perceptions of the quality of their relationships with parents, peers, and teachers.

Population

Children between the ages of 9 and 19.

Description

The AIR was co-developed and co-normed with the Multidimensional Self-Concept Scale (MSCS) with both based on the premise that psychosocial adjustment is multidimensional and context-dependent. More specifically, children's interpersonal behavior are shaped by the environment and that their behavior and quality of their relationships vary depending on the context. The AIR assesses interpersonal relations in three contexts: Social (Male and Female Peers subscales), Family (Mother and Father subscales), and Academic (Teachers subscale). Each subscale assesses children's and adolescents' perceptions of the quality of their relationships with that person or group of people. Interestingly, the author presents developmental characteristics of relationships. For example, graphic displays of age and gender differences in interpersonal relationships indicated that both boys' and girls' perceptions of their relationship with their mothers and fathers decline and later stabilize across the ages from 9–19.

Items are rated on a four-point scale (Strongly Agree to Strongly Disagree) and presented in both positively and negatively connoted contexts. Each subscale contains the same 35 items. Items are concise, written at a third grade reading level, and constructed to reflect 15 literature-based factors shown to affect relationship quality (i.e., companionship, emotional support, guidance, trust, conflict). The response booklet is very easy to complete and the manual is very easy to read.

Administration

The AIR can be administered individually or in a group format, taking approximately 20 minutes to complete.

Scoring

Items for each subscale are assigned a number from 1–4 with every fifth item for each subscale being worded negatively and therefore being reversed scored. Scores are summed for each subscale and totaled for the Total Relationship Index (TRI) score. Raw scores are converted into standard scores based on respondent age and gender. Standard scores are classified according to relationship quality (Very Positive Relationship to Very Negative Relationship). Ipsative interpretations are also obtained by comparing the average subscale score to actual standard scores and classifying as relationship strength or weakness for each of the subscales.

Ipsative profiles allow the examiner to assess relationship strengths and weaknesses rather than solely interpret scores from a norm-referenced perspective.

Psychometric Properties

Norms: The scale was normed on 2,501 children from range of geographic, demographic, and ethnic backgrounds. Both regular and special education students were included.

Reliability: Internal consistency and test-retest reliability was above .90 for each of the subscales.

Validity: Validity data were supportive of the measure but were limited. The age and gender differences discussed earlier supported the measures sensitivity to developmental changes. Validity data also were supported by a study employing contrasted groups and factor analysis of the scale.

Clinical Utility

High. The AIR gives a broad look at strengths and weaknesses of interpersonal functioning.

Strengths/Limitations

The AIR appears to be a reliable and valid instrument that is easy to complete and score. My biggest concern is with the item generation process, which was theoretically driven for the most part.

Author: Bruce A. Bracken.

Publication Year: 1993.

Source: PRO-ED, 8700 Shoal Creek Boulevard, Austin, TX 78757 (800) 897-3202.

Fee: Yes.

THE ATTENTION DEFICIT DISORDERS EVALUATION SCALE, 2nd ED.: HOME AND SCHOOL VERSIONS, EARLY CHILDHOOD HOME AND SCHOOL VERSIONS, AND SECONDARY-AGE STUDENT, SCHOOL VERSION

Reviewed by: Mary Lou Kelley

Purpose

To assess Attention Deficit Hyperactivity Disorder (ADHD) symptoms based on parent and teacher report in a manner that corresponds to DSM-IV diagnostic criteria.

Population

The ADDES School and Home Versions are intended for use with children and adolescents aged 3.0–19.0. The Early Childhood ADDES School and Home Versions are for use with children aged 2.0–6.11. The ADDES Secondary-Age Student, School Version is for use with 11–18. School Versions are completed by teachers and Home Versions are completed by parents or guardians.

Description

The Attention Deficit Disorders Evaluation Scale (ADDES) Home and School, Versions, Early Childhood (ADDES) Home and School Versions are separate, but similarly formatted questionnaires. All versions consist of objectively worded items that load on either the Inattentive or the Hyperactive-Impulsive subscales. Unlike most other measures used to assess ADHD, items are rated based on frequency in which the child was observed exhibiting the behavior. Items are rated as either, 0 = Does not engage in the behavior; 1 = One to Several Times Per Month; 2 = One to Several Times Per Week; 3 = One to Several Times Per Day; or, 4 = One to Several Times Per Hour. The ADDES Home Version contains 46 items and the School version contains 60 items. The Early Childhood ADDES Home Version contains 50 items and the School Version contains 56 items. Many of the items in the Early Childhood Versions are similar or the same as the items on the more comprehensive versions. However, the Early Childhood ADDES contains items and item examples that reflect the behavior of a young child. For example, the Early Childhood Versions do not contain items about assignments. The versions also makes references to preschool and kindergarten activities such as preparing for lunch or playing games.

The ADDES Secondary Age Student, School Version is identical to the ADDES School Version with one exception. It contains only three item qualifiers instead of four. The qualifier, "One-to-Several Times Per Day" is omitted as middle and high school teachers generally have a student for only one hour a day.

The ADDES instructions are very explicit and easy to understand. The items on the ADDES describe specific, observable behavior and often provide examples of the behavior so that misunderstanding of item content is minimized. The ADDES items directly correspond to DSM-IV groupings of ADHD-Primarily Inattentive Type and Impulsive-Hyperactive Type. All versions of the ADDES are accompanied with an easy to read technical manual that describes the purposes of the test, normative data, and data on the measures reliability and validity.

The second edition of the ADDES Home and School Versions appears to have addressed problems associated with an earlier version. The earlier version was criticized (Silverthorn, 1994) because it contained items that did not correspond with ADHD diagnostic criteria and because a third factor was artificially created by dividing Hyperactive and Impulsive Behavior items.

Administration

The ADDES can be completed by parents or guardians and teachers who are quite familiar with the child's behavior. The respondent should be one who observes the child on a regular, consistent basis (McCarney, 1995). The instrument can be completed within 15–20 minutes.

Scoring

For all versions, scores are summed separately for the two subscales. Raw scores are converted to subscale standard scores and percentile ranks. Standard scores are such that lower scores represent more symptomatology. This is dissimilar from most other measures and was a bit confusing. Standard scores are derived for different age and gender groupings for all scales.

Psychometric Properties

Norms: The ADDES Home Version was normed on 2,415 children and youth from 23 states and included ADHD and non-ADHD individuals. The ADDES School Version was normed on 5,795 students from 137 school systems and 30 states. The Early Childhood Home Version was normed on 1,896 and the school version on 2,887 students. The Secondary School Aged Student Version was normed on 1,280 students. The publisher indicated that new norms will be available in the spring of 2002. The sample demographics for all ADDES versions corresponded to national census data and were collected in many different states. Norms are available at different age and gender groupings for all scales.

Reliability: Internal consistency for all versions for both subscales was above .85 and usually was above .90. Test-retest reliability also was very high and generally was above .90 for each of the age and gender groups. Inter-rater reliability was .80 or above for all age levels for the Home and School versions but ranged from .64–.72 for the Early Childhood versions.

Validity: Considerable attention was made by the author to ensure the content validity of both scales. The construct validity of the two subscales for all ADDES versions was very high with factor analysis strongly supporting the two factor scale. Criterion related validity for the ADDES Home and School Versions was established by correlating scores with corresponding measures having good psychometric properties (e.g., Achenbach Child Behavior Checklist and the Achenbach Teacher Report Form, Achenbach & Edelbrock, 1991). Good to moderate correlations were obtained. Criterion related validity also was adequate for the Early Childhood ADDES Versions when scores were compared to scores from the Conner's Rating Scales and the Attention Deficit/Hyperactivity Test. Finally diagnostic validity was evaluated by comparing a group of ADHD children to a corresponding group from the normative sample. Significant differences between the two groups were obtained.

Clinical Utility

High. All versions of the ADDES represent scales that are worded behaviorally and are evaluated based on the frequency in which the behavior is observed. This feature directly corresponds to DSM-IV diagnostic criteria for ADHD. The instruments can be completed in only a few minutes, are psychometrically sound and well normed, and thus can be used for a variety of clinical and research purposes.

Strengths/Limitations

The ADDES Home and School versions have very good clinical utility and may aid in diagnosis and treatment planning. Intervention books that correspond to the items of the scales are available separately. Items are behaviorally worded and objectively anchored which makes the ADDES different form many other scales. The items also directly reflect diagnosis.

A self-report version is not available. Limitations of a previous version have been addressed in the current versions of the ADDES. It would be helpful to have information on which version to administer to teachers and parents when age overlap of versions exists.

Author: Stephen B. McCarney, Ed.D.

Publication Year: 1995.

Source: Hawthorne Educational Services, Inc., 800 Gray Oak Dr., Columbia, MO 65201, Call: (573-874-1710).

Fee: Yes.

ADDITIONAL INFORMATION/REFERENCES

Achenbach, T. M. & Edelbrock, C. (1991). *Manual for the child behavior checklist/4–18 and 1991 Profile*. Burlington VT: University of Vermont.

Silverthorn, P., (1995). Assessment of ADHD Using the ADDES. *Child Assessment News, 4,* 1, 5 and 12.

ATTENTION DEFICIT/HYPERACTIVITY DISORDER RATING SCALE—IV: HOME AND SCHOOL VERSIONS

Reviewed by: Aaron Clendenin & Mary Lou Kelley

Purpose

To aid clinicians in obtaining parent and teacher ratings of behavior that is representative of Attention Deficit/Hyperactivity Disorder (ADHD) symptomatology as found in the Diagnostic and Statistical Manual of Mental Disorders-IV (DSM-IV; American Psychiatric Association, 1994).

Population

School children aged 4–20 years old.

Description

The Attention Deficit Hyperactivity Disorder Rating Scale-IV (ADHD Rating Scale-IV) is comprised of 18 items that were adapted explicitly from DSM-IV criteria. There are two versions—Home and School. Both versions are composed of two empirically derived subscales, Inattention and Hyperactivity-Impulsivity, which are believed to be the key dimensions of ADHD.

Administration

Approximately 10 to 20 minutes by a parent or teacher.

Scoring

A raw score is derived from each subscale by tallying the odd-numbered items for Inattention and the even-numbered items for Hyperactivity-Impulsivity. These scores are added together to yield a Total raw score. Raw scores can are converted to percentile ranks according to age and gender. It is possible to do this either by individual subscales or as a Total score.

Psychometric Properties

Norms: Normative data for the Home Version were collected from a subsample of the initial factor analytic sample. This group consisted of 2,000 (1,043 girls, 930 boys, and 27 unspecified) individuals ranging in age from 4 to 20 years ($M = 9.63$; $SD = 3.53$) representing kindergarten through 12th grade ($M = 4.21$; $SD = 3.46$). Participants approximated U.S. Census data for region and ethnicity. There is, however, a slight underrepresentation of the Southern part of the United States and overrepresentation of African-Americans.

The normative data for the School Version was collected in a similar fashion and also consisted of 2,000 (1,040 boys, 948 girls, and 12 unspecified) individuals ranging in age from 4 to 19 years ($M = 10.6$; $SD = 3.6$) representing kindergarten through 12th grade ($M = 5.1$; $SD = 3.5$). Again, the normative sample closely resembles the U.S. Census data, but with a slight underrepresentation of the Western part of the United States and overrepresentation of African-Americans.

Reliability: Coefficient alphas for internal consistency ranged from .88 to .96 for the School Version and .86 to .92 for the Home Version. Pearson product-moment correlations for test-retest reliability ranged from .88 to .90 for the School Version and .78 to .86 for the Home Version.

Validity: Criterion validity was established through Pearson correlation coefficients between the School Version and CTRS and the Home Version and CPRS, which ranged from .22 to .88 and .10 and .81, respectively. The strongest correlations were between factor scores for each version and CTRS and CPRS Hyperactivity Index scores. Discriminant validity was established by comparison of mean ratings between ADHD-Combined, ADHD-Inattentive, and clinical control groups. Statistically significant differences were found between the three groups for parent Inattention and Hyperactivity–Impulsivity ratings and teacher Inattention and Hyperactivity–Impulsivity ratings ($F(2,87) = 23.57$, $p < .0001$). Furthermore, predictive validity studies were conducted in clinical and school settings that supported the ADHD Rating Scale as a measure that could differentiate the two ADHD subtypes from each other and controls based on subscale scores.

Clinical Utility

High. Given the strong psychometric properties, the ADHD RS-IV is an adequate aid in making diagnoses.

Strengths/Limitations

The ADHD Rating Scale is easy to administer and understand due to its derivation from the DSM-IV. Furthermore, its technical adequacy makes it useful as a clinical and research instrument.

Authors: George J. DuPaul; Thomas J. Power; Arthur D. Anastopolous; & Robert Reid.

Publication Year: 1998.

Source: The Guilford Press, 72 Spring St., New York, NY 10012, www.guilford.com

Fee: Yes.

ADDITIONAL INFORMATION/REFERENCE

American Psychiatric Association. (1994). *Diagnostic and statistical manual of mental disorders (4th ed.)*. Washington, DC: Author.

ATTENTION-DEFICIT/HYPERACTIVITY DISORDER TEST

Reviewed by: Aaron Clendenin & Mary Lou Kelley

Purpose

To aid clinicians in obtaining parent and teacher ratings of behavior that is representative of Attention Deficit/Hyperactivity Disorder (ADHD) symptomatology as found in the Diagnostic and Statistical Manual of Mental Disorders-IV (DSM-IV; American Psychiatric Association, 1994).

Population

Children, adolescents, and adults from 3–23 years old.

Description

The Attention-Deficit/Hyperactivity Disorder Test (ADHDT) is a 36-item standardized behavioral checklist that was derived from the DSM-IV definition of ADHD. The ADHDT consists of three subscales, Inattention, Hyperactivity, and Impulsivity, which are believed to be the key components of ADHD. For each item, the subject's behavior is rated as either "not a problem", "mild problem", or "severe problem", which are coded as 0 to 2, respectively. This instrument is designed to be given at home or school.

Administration

Approximately 5 to10 minutes by a parent or teacher.

Scoring

A raw score is derived from each subscale by adding the item scores in each domain. These scores can then be converted to percentile ranks and standard scores by means of tables provided in the manual. Additionally, the subtest standard scores can be totaled for an ADHD Quotient and composite percentile rank.

Psychometric Properties

Norms: Normative data were collected on a sample of 1,279 children and young adults previously diagnosed with ADHD. Teachers (n = 638), parents (n = 391), professionals ((psychiatrists/diagnosticians), (n = 104), spouses (n = 13), and others (n = 133) from 47 states and Canada completed the ADHDT regarding participants that were a representative approximation of 1990 U.S. Census Data.

Reliability: All Cronbach's alphas for internal consistency were above .90. Test-retest reliability scores ranged from .85 to .94.

Validity: Content validity was established through item discrimination coefficients, which had median values of .71 for the Hyperactivity subscale, .72 for the Impulsivity subscale, and .69 for the Inattention subscale. Criterion-related validity was established through the correlations of the ADHDT with seven other tests that are commonly used in the assessment of ADHD and other emotional and behavior problems. Moderate to strong correlations were found between the ADHDT and several other scales including the Conners' Teacher Rating Scales-28, Conners' Teacher Rating Scales-39 (Conners, 1990), Attention Deficit Disorders Evaluation Scale-School Version (McCarney, 1989), and the ADD-H Comprehensive Teacher's Rating Scale-Second Edition (Ullmann, Sleator, & Sprague; 1991). The ADHDT was also able to discriminate with 92% accuracy those who had ADHD from those who did not. Furthermore, it could differentiate among groups of persons who are ADHD, mentally retarded, emotionally disturbed, and learning disabled.

Clinical Utility

Limited. While the ADHDT has good psychometrics, it does not seem to offer much to the assessment process beyond other well-known measures of this construct.

Strengths/Limitations

The ADHDT is unique in that it is one of the few measures that are entirely normed on individuals with ADHD.

Author: James E. Gilliam.

Publication Year: 1995.

Source: Pro-Ed, 8700 Shoal Creek Blvd., Austin, TX 78757-6897, (800) 897-3202, Fax: (800) 397-7633.

Fee: Yes.

ADDITIONAL INFORMATION/REFERENCES

American Psychiatric Association. (1994). *Diagnostic and statistical manual of mental disorders (4th ed.).* Washington, DC: Author.

Conners, C. K. (1989). *Conners' Rating Scales Manual.* North Tonawanda, NY: Multi-Health Systems.

McCarney, S. B. (1989). *Attention Deficit Disorders Evaluation Scale-School Version.* Columbia, MO: Hawthorne.

Ullmann, R. K., Sleator, E. K., & Sprague, R. L. (1991). *ADD-H Comprehensive Teacher's Rating Scale (2nd ed.).* Champaign, IL: MetriTech.

THE BEHAVIOR ASSESSMENT SYSTEM FOR CHILDREN: PARENT RATING SCALE, SELF-REPORT OF PERSONALITY, STRUCTURED DEVELOPMENTAL HISTORY, STUDENT OBSERVATION SYSTEM, AND TEACHER RATING SCALE

Reviewed by: Nichole Jurbergs & David Reitman

Purpose

To provide a more thorough and comprehensive assessment of emotional and behavioral problems in children and adolescents. The BASC may be utilized in home, school, or clinical settings, and has aspired to meet high psychometric standards.

Population

The BASC Teacher Rating Scale (TRS), Parent Rating Scale (PRS), Structured Developmental History (SDH), and Student Observation System (SOS) are intended for use with children and adolescents aged 4–18. The BASC Self-Report of Personality (SRP) is intended for children aged 8–18.

Description

The Behavioral Assessment Schedule for Children consists of three separate rating scales– the Teacher Rating Scale, Parent Rating Scale, and Self-Report of Personality– which make up the core of the BASC. The TRS and PRS have alternate versions appropriate for pre-school (2.5 to 5 years), child (6 to 11 years), and adolescent (12 to 18 years) populations, and share similarly formatted items rated in 4-point, Likert-type format (1 = "never" to 4 = "almost always"). The SRP has two versions, child and adolescent, which require True-False responses. The SOS and SDH provide a standardized format for conducting observations and interviews. The five components may be used alone or in various combinations to suit the needs of the user. All ratings scales contain an "F" scale which assesses extremely negative responding (e.g., faking bad). The SRP has additional validity indicators to assess nonsensical and unusually positive responding.

Administration

The TRS is completed by a teacher or other school administrator that is familiar with the student and the student's behavior, and the PRS is completed by his or her parent or guardian.

The SRP is filled out by the child or adolescent and may take up to 30 minutes to complete. The SDH may be administered as a questionnaire or a structured interview and is lengthy. The SOS assesses child or adolescent behavior in the classroom. Those administering the BASC system are required to have had formal academic training and supervised experience with similar testing instruments.

Scoring

The hand-scoring procedures, though more complex than in other similar rating scales, are well-developed and straightforward. There is also computer-scoring software available. The raw scores from the TRS, PRS, and SRP may be converted to T-scores and percentile scores. Higherscores represent greater symptomatology or higher levels of problem behavior.

Psychometric Properties

Norms: The TRS and PRS were normed on over 1,400 and the SRP on over 4,800 children and adolescents from both clinical and non-clinical populations. Norms are provided for males and females. The standardization was intended to correspond to 1988 US Census data in terms of race, gender, and level of parental education.

Reliability: Internal consistency for all three of the rating scales is impressive, averaging between .70 and .90 across scales and composites. Two to eight-week test-retest reliability estimates were acceptable across all forms. Unfortunately, no reliability (or validity information, for that matter) data is provided for the SOS. Nevertheless, the manual suggests that reliability may be enhanced by retesting the child on multiple days in different classrooms.

Validity: Factor analytic data generally support the scale construction of the TRS, PRS, and SRP with only minor variations across scales. As a possible exception, Hoza (1994) noted that scores on the Depression scale of the PRS and TRS might be inflated by problems with peers that may be more characteristic of aggression than depression. Alternately, the pattern of the relations between the rating scales and other measures of similar content (e.g., the Child Behavior Checklist) are strong. Also, somewhat surprisingly, the TRS was not correlated with the Conners Teacher Rating Scale or the Behavior Rating Profile suggesting that the content of the TRS is inequivalent to that of other popular teacher rating scales.

Clinical Utility

Adequate. The BASC rating scales are psychometrically sound and well-normed, and may be useful for a variety of research and clinical purposes. However, with no clear means of combining the data from the separate components of the BASC, the large data yield may not result in substantial increases in clinical utility over other (separate) measures of problem behavior (Reitman, Hummel, Franz, & Gross, 1998).

Strengths/Limitations

The BASC assesses several constructs that do not appear in other similar assessment systems, such as self-reliance, leadership, and other forms of adaptive behavior. The BASC's weaknesses include poorly worded items on the SRP-C (ages 8–11) that may be difficult for the children to understand and hand-scoring sheets that are complicated could result in computational errors. Additionally, while computer scoring is available, the data entry fields are relatively inflexible and not well suited to research purposes (Hoza, 1994). The procedure for recording behavior in the SOS is unusual and the authors offer no rationale for its methodology. Finally, although the BASC purports to function as a "system" it fails to provide a mechanism for integrating the obtained information.

Authors: Cecil R. Reynolds and Randy W. Kamphaus.

Publication Year: 1998.

Source: American Guidance Services, Inc., 4201 Woodland Road, Circle Pines, MN 55014-1796., Call: (1-800-328-2560).

Fee: Yes.

ADDITIONAL INFORMATION/REFERENCES

Adams, C. D. & Drabman, R. S. (1994). BASC: A critical review. *Child Assessment News, 4,* 1–5.

Sandoval, J., & Echinadia, A. (1994). Behavior Assessment System for Children. *Journal of School Psychology, 32,* 419–425.

Hoza, B. (1994). Review of the Behavioral Assessment System for Children. *Child Assessment News, 4,* 5–10.

Kamphaus, R., & Reynolds, C. (1998). *Behavior Assessment System for Children Manual.* Circle Pines, Minnesota: American Guidance Service.

Reitman, D., Hummel, R., Franz, D., & Gross, A. M. (1998). A review of methods and instruments for assessing externalizing disorders: Theoretical and practical considerations in rendering a diagnosis. *Clinical Psychology Review, 18,* 555–584.

THE BEHAVIOR DIMENSIONS SCALE: HOME AND SCHOOL VERSIONS

Reviewed by: Nichole Jurbergs & Mary Lou Kelley

Purpose

To document the characteristics of Attention-Deficit/ Hyperactivity Disorder, Oppositional Defiant Disorder, Conduct Disorder, Avoidant Personality Disorder, and Major Depressive Episodes in children.

Population

The Behavior Dimensions Scale (BDS) Home Version is intended for use with children age 3–19. The School Version is intended for children age 5–16.

Description

The BDS consists of two separate rating scales, the Home and School Version Rating Forms. The Home Version consists of 108 behaviors, and the School Version consists of 99 behaviors. The forms are similarly formatted with items rated in a 5-point, Likert-type format using "quantifiers" (0 = does not engage in the behavior, 4 = one to several times per hour). The BDS Technical Manuals for both Home and School Versions are fairly comprehensive and contain normative data and psychometric information. The instructions for the rating scales are simple and straightforward. Items are stated plainly and often include concrete examples to illustrate the behaviors, minimizing the possibility of misunderstanding. The BDS includes an Intervention Manual to be used in conjunction with the rating scales. It offers goals and objectives for children in the classroom based on common behavior problems exhibited in school.

Administration

The School Version is completed by a teacher with primary observation opportunities, and the Home Version is completed by a parent or other primary care giver. Each form takes approximately 20 minutes to complete.

Scoring

The BDS is hand-scored using a Scoring Form that is quick and simple. Seven raw subscale scores (Inattentive, Hyperactive-Impulsive, Oppositional Defiant, Conduct, Avoidant Personality, Anxiety, and Depression) are calculated which may be converted to standard scores, which may be summed and converted to a percentile score. This percentile score is intended to provide an overall reference of the child's behavior to the standardization sample, but it has very little clinical utility without the subscale scores.

Psychometric Properties

Norms: The scales were normed on 7,383 children distributed equally across age between 5 to 19 years. The standardization sample reflected national statistics of race, residents, gender, geographic area, and occupation of parents. The children represented both clinical and non-clinical populations, with the clinical children having a diagnosis of one of the six disorders measured by the BDS. However, there is inadequate description of how many children were diagnosed with each of the specific disorders.

Reliability: Interrater reliability for both versions was reported greater than .90, although no data is provided measuring the interrater reliability between the two versions. A 30-day test-retest reliability for all six subscales were higher than .76. Internal consistency was reported at .98 for the total score.

Validity: Criterion validity was established between the BDS and the Child Behavior Checklist which ranged from approximately .34 to .91 on the various subscales of each. The strongest correlations were between factor scores of the Inattentive, Oppositional, Conduct, and Anxiety subscales. There is no evidence of diagnostic validity to discriminate between the individual disorders.

Clinical Utility

Limited. The total percentile score derived from the BDS may be useful in screening children for behavior disorders in general. However, there is no evidence that the subscale scores are able to differentiate between the six disorders the scale purports to measure. By no means should this scale be used to diagnose disorders, it may only be sufficient as a screening tool. The intervention manual may also have limited utility due to the ambiguous nature of many of the interventions.

Strengths/Limitations

The BDS is quick and easy to administer and score. The total score appears to be effective in differentiating clinical from non-clinical children. One weakness of the scale is its inability to differentiate between the six DSM-IV diagnoses.

Author: Stephen B. McCarney, Ed.D.

Publication Year: 1995.

Source: Hawthorne Educational Services, Inc., 800 Gray Oaks Drive, Columbia, MO 65201, Call: (1-800-542-1673), Fax: (1-800-442-9509).

Fee: Yes, $148 for the complete kit including the Home and School Version technical manuals, the intervention manuals, 50 rating forms, and computerized scoring disk.

ADDITIONAL INFORMATION/REFERENCES

McCarney, S. B. (1995). *The Behavior Dimensions Scale Home Version Technical Manual.* Columbia, MO: Hawthorne Educational Services.

McCarney, S. B. (1995). *The Behavior Dimensions Scale School Version Technical Manual.* Columbia, MO: Hawthorne Educational Services.

McCarney, S. B., and McCain, B. R. (1995). *The Behavior Dimensions Intervention Manual.* Columbia, MO: Hawthorne Educational Services.

BEHAVIOR DISORDERS IDENTIFICATION SCALE—HOME AND SCHOOL VERSION

Reviewed by: Shannon Self-Brown & Mary Lou Kelley

Purpose

To contribute to the early identification and service delivery for students with behavior disorders/emotional disturbances based on the federal definition that appears in PL 94–142.

Population

The BDIS Home and School versions are intended for use with children and adolescents aged 4.5–21.

Description

The BDIS Home and School versions are two separate but similarly formatted questionnaires. The BDIS Home Version contains 73 items and the School Version contains 83 items. The BDIS Home and School versions consist of items that are characteristic of behavior disorders that can be observed in the home and school environment. The items are grouped according to the following subscales: Learning/Self-Control, Interpersonal/Social, Inappropriate Behavior Under Normal Circumstances, Unhappiness/Depression, Physical Symptoms/Fears. These subscales represent the five areas of impairments in which a child is required to meet the criteria in order to receive special education due to PL 94–142 (Seriously Emotionally/Behavioral Disturbed). The PL 94–142 criteria also require the documentation of the frequency, intensity, and context of behavior. To address this mandate, the BDIS is designed to provide a frequency rating of student behavior in an efficient and accurate way determined by parents, teachers, etc, who are in the best position to provide such information. The BDIS items are rated on a 7- point scale which ranges from 1= Not in My Presence to 7-More Than Once an Hour.

The BDIS instructions for both the Home and School versions are very explicit and easy to understand. Both versions are accompanied by an easy to read technical manual that describes purposes of the test, test administration, and psychometric information.

Administration

The BDIS Home version is completed by parents or guardians. The BDIS School version is completed by teachers or other school personnel who are very familiar with the student's behavior. Both the School and Home version can be completed in approximately 20 minutes.

Scoring

For both the BDIS Home and School version, scores are summed separately for the five subscales to compute raw scores. Raw scores are converted to subscale standard scores and percentiles using tables located in the technical manual.

Psychometric Properties

Norms: The School version was normed on 3,188 students by 867 teachers from 23 states. The Home version was normed on 1,769 with 1,845 parents or guardians rating the students. The author used a heterogeneous sample.

Reliability: Internal consistency for the Home and School versions for all subscales was adequate. Test-retest and inter-rater reliability was good.

Validity: Various forms of validity data were obtained that supported the utility of the measure. To assure the integrity of content validity, the author initially created an item based on a careful literature review, and the input from diagnosticians, educational personnel, and parents/guardians of over 200 students with serious behavior problems. The construct validity for subscales was supported for the most part via factor analysis, diagnostic validity, subscale interrelationships, and item validity. Criterion related validity for the BDIS Home and School versions was established by correlating scores with the Behavior Rating Profile, another measure of emotional disturbance and behavior disorders in youth (Brown & Hamill, 1983).

Clinical Utility

High. The most appropriate use of the BDIS is to document the existence of behaviors that meet the criteria for identifying a student as behaviorally disordered. The BDIS Home and School versions represent scales that are worded behaviorally and are evaluated based on frequency in which the behavior is observed. This feature directly corresponds to legal definitions of behavioral/emotional disorder and thus, is useful to placement decisions. The instruments can be completed in only a few minutes, are well-normed and may prove useful for both clinical and research purposes. The BDIS also goes a step further than many tests by providing a manual for developing a student's Individual Educational Plan which assists teachers in complying with legal requirements of PL 94–142.

Strengths/Limitations

Strengths of the BDIS are that the kit provides the examiner with all the materials necessary to comply with PL 94–142 requirements, it relies on behavioral observations from both the school and home environment, and it is well-normed. The BDIS is unique in its focus on evaluating behaviors associated with behaviorally disordered children within the school setting. One limitation of the BDIS is that the components analyses were conducted without breaking down the sample by characteristics such as sex, SES, and ethnicity, which are related to the prevalence of emotional disturbance/behavior disorders (Fairbank, 1995). Another limitation is that some of the items on the BDIS are 35 to 40 words long. This may affect the accuracy of teacher and parent judgments of behavior.

Authors: Fred Wright and Kathy Wunderlich.

Publication Year: 1998.

Source: Hawthorne Educational Services, Inc., 800 Gray Oak Dr., Columbia, MO 65201., Call: (573-874-1710).

Fee: Yes.

ADDITIONAL INFORMATION/REFERENCES

Fairbank, D. W. (1995). Review of Behavior Disorders Identification. In: *Mental Measurement Yearbook Volume 12*, pp. 115–117.

Stientjes, H. J. (1995). Review of Behavior Disorders Identification. In: *Mental Measurement Yearbook: Volume 12*, p. 117.

THE BEHAVIOR EVALUATION SCALE, 2nd ED.: HOME AND SCHOOL VERSIONS

Reviewed by: Mary Lou Kelley

Purpose

To assess behavioral and emotional problems in school age children in accordance with PL 94–142 criteria for the special education category, behavior disorders/emotional disturbance. The authors states six primary purposes of the Behavior Evaluation Scale (BES-2): screen for behavior problems, assess behavior of referred children, assist in the diagnosis of behavior disorders/emotional disturbance, contribute to the development of individual education programs for students in need of special education, document progress resulting from behavioral interventions, and collect data for research purposes.

Population

The BES-2 Home version is intended for use with children and adolescents aged 5.0 - 18; the School Version is used with children in grades Kindergarten thru 12th.

Description

The BES-2 Home and School versions are two separate but similarly formatted questionnaires. The BES-2 Home and School versions consist of objectively worded items that are grouped according to following subscales: Learning Problems, Interpersonal Difficulties, Inappropriate Behaviors, Unhappiness/Depression, Physical Symptoms/Fears. These subscales represent the five areas of impairments of which one is required to meet the criteria for the special education criteria for Seriously Emotionally/Behavioral Disturbed (PL 94–142). Thus significant scores on the various subscales provide substantiation for an *educational diagnosis* and not a DSM-V diagnosis.

Unlike many other measures, items are rated based on frequency of occurrence in which the child was observed exhibiting the behavior. Items are rated on a 7 point scale which ranges from 1 = Does Not Occur in My Presence to 7 = More Than Once an Hour. The BES-2 Home version contains 73 items and the School version contains 76 items. A unique feature of the BES-2 is the weighting of items with differing levels of severity, which was based on considerable input from teachers and parents.

The BES-2 instructions for both the Home and School versions are very explicit and easy to understand. Both versions are accompanied with an easy to read technical manual that describes purposes of the test, test administration, normative data, and data on the measures reliability and validity.

Administration

The BES-2 Home version is completed by parents or guardians and the BES-2 School version is completed by teachers or other school personnel very familiar with the student's behavior. The instrument can be completed in approximately 20 minutes.

Scoring

The score for each item is derived from multiplying the frequency rating by the severity weight. For both versions, scores are summed separately for the five subscales. Raw scores are converted to subscale standard scores and percentile ranks. Standard scores are such that lower scores represent more symptomatology, which is dissimilar from most other measures and was a bit confusing. For the BES-2 School version, raw scores are converted into standard scores using four grade groupings that span Kindergarten to 12th grade. For the BES-2 Home version raw scores are converted into standard scores using four male and four female age groupings.

Psychometric Properties

Norms: The School version was normed on 2,700 students from 31 states and the Home version was normed on 1,769 students from 59 school systems. The author used a heterogeneous sample. Additionally, item weightings were determined by having 276 teachers rate each item on a 9-point scale.

Reliability: Internal consistency for the Home and School versions for all subscales was adequate. Test-retest and inter-rater reliability was good.

Validity: Various forms of validity data were obtained that supported the utility of the measure. The construct validity for subscales was supported for the most part via factor analysis. Criterion related validity for the BES-2 Home and School versions was established by correlating scores with the Behavior Rating Profile (Brown & Hamill, 1983). Diagnostic validity was evaluated by comparing a group of children identified as behaviorally disordered and who attended special education to those that were in regular education on the School version only. Significant differences between the two groups were obtained on all five subscales.

Clinical Utility

High. The BES-2 Home and School versions represent scales that are worded behaviorally and are evaluated based on frequency in which the behavior is observed. This feature directly corresponds to legal definitions of behavioral/emotional disorder and thus, is useful to placement decisions. The instruments can be completed in only a few minutes, are well-normed and may prove useful for both clinical and research purposes.

Strengths/Limitations

The BES-2 is unique in its focus on evaluating behaviors associated with behaviorally disordered children within the school setting. An intervention book that corresponds to the items of the scale is available separately. A self-report version is not available.

Author: Stephen B. McCarney, Ed.D.

Publication Year: 1994.

Source: Hawthorne Educational Services, Inc., 800 Gray Oak Dr., Columbia, MO 65201., Call: (573-874-1710).

Fee: Yes.

ADDITIONAL INFORMATION/REFERENCES

Brown, L. L. & Hamill, D. D. (1978). Behavior Rating Profile. Austin, TX: Pro-Ed.
Goldman, B. A. (1995) Review of Behavior Evaluation Scale-2. In: *Mental Measurements Yearbook:Volume 12*, pp. 117–120.

BEHAVIOR RATING PROFILE-2nd EDITION: PARENT RATING SCALE, STUDENT RATING SCALE, AND TEACHER RATING SCALE

Reviewed by: Shannon Self-Brown & Mary Lou Kelley

Purpose

To evaluate student behaviors at home, in school, and in interpersonal relationships.

Population

Children and adolescents ranging in age from 6–6 through 18–6 years of age.

Description

The Behavior Rating Profile-Second Edition (BRP-2) is a battery of six instruments, five rating scales and a sociogram, designed to evaluate student behavior at home, in school, and in interpersonal relationships. Three of the rating scales, Student Rating Scales for Home, School, and Peer, are combined into a 60-item, self-report instrument. Items describe behaviors or situations that occur primarily in the home, school, or social settings. An example of a home item is "I often break rules set by my parents". Children are asked to describe their own behavior by responding "True" or "False" to each item.

The other rating scales included in the BRP-2 include the Teacher Rating Scale and Parent Rating Scale. These scales are very similar to one another in format. Both scales contain 30 items which consist of a sentence stem describing behaviors that may be exhibited by the child in the pertinent environment. For example, an item on the Teacher Rating Scale is "Doesn't follow class rules". Respondents classify each item as "Very much like the child", "Somewhat like the child", "Not much like the child", or "Not at all like the child". The Teacher Rating Scale is typically completed by one or more of the student's instructors. However, other school personnel that have regular contact with the students may also complete this form. The Parent Rating Scale is completed by the child's primary care givers.

The Sociogram is a peer nomination technique used for gaining an understanding of peers' perceptions of the target student. Pairs of stimulus questions are posed to a class of students and each student nominates three classmates in response to the questions. The stimulus questions query the students on topics such as "Which of the students in your class would you most like to work with on a school project?" and Which of the students in your class would you least like to work with on a school project?".

Scoring

Explicit instructions for hand scoring are provided in the BRP-2 manual. Total raw scores for each scale are copied onto the BRP-2 Profile and Record Form. Raw scores from the BRP-2 instruments can be converted to percentile ranks and to derived standard scores with a mean of 10. Standard scores ranging from 8–12 are within the average range, with scores above 12 being above average and less than 8 below average.

Administration

The BRP-2 instruments can be administered independent of each other or as a battery of instruments. Total administration time is approximately one hour, including allocations of 15–30 minutes for the Student Rating Scales, 10–15 minutes for the Teacher Rating Scale, 15–20 minutes for the Parent Rating Scale, and 15 minutes for the Sociogram.

Psychometric Properties

Norms: The BRP-2 Student Rating Scales and Sociogram were normed on a sample of 2,682 students ages 6–6 through 18–6 years across 26 states. The Parent Rating Scale was normed on a sample of 1,948 parents and the Teacher Rating Scale was normed on 1,452 classroom teachers. The normative samples were representative of the U.S. population.

Reliability: The reliability of the BRP-2 is well within acceptable ranges. Internal consistency for all the BRP-2 scales met or exceeded .80. Test-retest reliability of the BRP-2 scales was high overall, but was problematic for 1st and 2nd graders.

Validity: In the technical manual, authors of the scale indicate that the data available at this time only serves as preliminary evidence for the measure's validity. The authors provided a lengthy discussion of the empirical item selection criteria for the BRP-2 scales. Research has evidenced statistically significant item discrimination coefficients with medians ranging from .43 to .83. Several studies have been conducted examining the effectiveness of the BRP-2 instruments to accurately discriminate between gifted, average, learning-disabled, and emotionally disturbed students and results have indicated the utility of the battery in distinguishing among these groups of children. Studies assessing the intercorrelation of the BRP-2 instruments have found that the scales appear to measure similar underlying structures.

Clinical Utility

High. The BRP-2 yields information from several contexts and sources, bolstering its usefulness in program development.

Strengths/Limitations

The BRP-2 provides a systematic assessment instrument that provides multi-informant data regarding a specific child's current behavior in both the home and school environment. The instrument can be completed in a time efficient manner and serves as a good screening tool. The main limitation of the BRP-2 is the paucity of research available regarding the instrument's validity.

Authors: Linda Brown and Donald Hammill.

Publication Year: 1990 (most recent version).

Source: PRO-ED, 8700 Shoal Creek Blvd. Austin, TX 78757-6897.

Fee: Yes.

BURKS' BEHAVIOR RATING SCALES

Reviewed by: Shannon Self-Brown & Mary Lou Kelley

Purpose

To identify patterns of pathological behavior shown by children exhibiting behavioral problems in the school or home.

Population

The BBRS is intended for use with children ranging from preschool to 9th grade.

Description

Burks' Behavior Rating Scales (BBRS) consists of two versions. One version is designed for children ages 3–6, in grades preschool through kindergarten. This version contains 105 items. The second version is designed for children in grades 1 through 9 and contains 110 items. Both versions consist of negatively worded items that describe behaviors often displayed by children who have behavioral difficulties. Items are rated from 1 (You have not noticed this behavior at all) to 5 (You have noticed the behavior to a very large degree). The BBRS, Preschool and Kindergarten version, groups items into 18 subscales that measure a particular commonality of conduct. The groupings have been named according to the type of behavior shown and include: Excessive Self-Blame, Excessive Anxiety, Excessive Withdrawal, Excessive Dependency, Poor Ego Strength, Poor Physical Strength, Poor Coordination, Poor Intellectuality, Poor Academics, Poor Attention, Poor Impulse Control, Poor Reality Contact, Poor Sense of Identity, Excessive Suffering, Poor Anger Control, Excessive Sense of Persecution, Excessive Aggressiveness, Excessive Resistance, Poor Social Conformity. The BBRS for grades 1 through 9 is grouped into 19 subscales, adding a grouping for Poor Academics.

Administration

The BBRS consists of a four-page item booklet that is filled out by the rater in order to evaluate the behavior of a particular child. Raters should be someone who is well aquatinted with the child and can include both parents and teachers. Expected time for completion of the BBRS is not reported.

Scoring

For both versions of the BBRS, the manual contains specific instructions for scoring and interpreting the scores. Items are arranged so that boxes descend in a vertical column for each category. The columns are summed for each subscale and transferred to a profile sheet that is divided into not significant, significant, and very significant ranges. The manual also contains intervention approaches for those children who score in the significant or very significant range.

Psychometric Properties

Norms: Both versions of the BBRS are based on studies with small sample sizes and limited populations.

Reliability: Item reliability was established by having teachers rate 95 disturbed children over a ten day period. The average item /item retest correlation coefficient was .705.

Validity: Content validity was established by selecting items from clinical observations of children and evidence in the literature. Extensive modification of the items occurred over a period of four years by twenty-two school psychologists and over 200 teachers. Contrasted-groups validity was shown by a significant difference between children referred for guidance services and those children in a cross sample from regular education classrooms. Factorial validity was indicated by the findings that category ratings on the BBRS differ across age groups. Construct validity was supported by a correlation of scores on the BBRS with measures of internal adjustment, similar ratings on the BBRS by parents and teachers, and factor analysis.

Clinical Utility

Limited. The BBRS can be used to assess the behavioral characteristics of children. However, the BBRS is not recommended as a screening instrument. Additionally, one should be aware that interpretations of the scale provided in the manual focus on internal pathology rather than observable behavior. Such interpretations are especially concerning since the author describes the scale in the beginning of the manual as one that does not assess how the child's inner world is experienced.

Strengths/Limitations

The BBRS can be completed by a variety of informants and is easy to administer and score. However, the usefulness of the BBRS is limited do to the standardization process, which was comprised of a small population that was skewed and unrepresentative of the national census data.

Author: Harold F. Burks.

Publication Year: 1968–1977.

Source: Western Psychological Services, 12031 Wilshire Blvd., Los Angeles, CA 90025-1251.

Fee: Yes.

ADDITIONAL INFORMATION/REFERENCES

Bischoff, L. G. (1992). Review of Burks' Behavior Rating Inventory. In: *Mental Measurement Yearbook: Volume 11*, pp. 121–123.
Zlomke, L. C. (1992). Review of Burks' Behavior Rating Inventory. In: *Mental Measurement Yearbook: Volume 11*, pp. 123–124.

THE CAREY TEMPERAMENT SCALES

Reviewed By: Patrick M. O'Callaghan & Mary Lou Kelley

Purpose

To assess temperamental characteristics in infants and children. Temperamental assessment is used clinically for clarifying the nature of behavioral and parenting issues, and as a tool to assist caregivers learn about the infant's or child's individuality.

Population

The Carey Temperamental Scales (CTS) were intended for use with children from 1 month to 12 years.

Description

The instrument is comprised of five questionnaires assessing nine temperamental traits (Activity, Rythmicity, Approach, Adaptability, Intensity, Mood, Persistence, Distractibility, and Threshold). The questionnaires are divided at the following age levels: 1 to 4 months, 4 to 11 months, 1 and 2 years, 3 to 7 years, and 8 to 12 years. The scales are designed for caregivers to complete, and contain 76 to 110 items rated on a continuum from 1 (almost never) to 6 (almost always).

Administration

The rater (parent, caregiver, or teacher) should have sufficient experience with the child over a four to six week period prior to completing the scale. Items require an early high school reading level, and may be read to individuals if necessary. No administration time estimates were provided.

Scoring

Ratings are entered by hand on a "Scoring Sheet" for each temperament characteristic. Specific directions are provided to tabulate category scores. These scores are transferred to the "Profile Sheet", and are compared to relevant means and standard deviations. Electronic scoring also is available and allows the examiner to directly enter item scores and then generates a "Caregiver Report" and a "Professional Report".

Psychometric Properties

Norms: The Carey Temperament Scales were standardized on 200–500 infants or children representing the intended age range of the measure. Samples were comprised primarily of Euro-Americans living in the Eastern United States. The authors acknowledge that the norms may not apply to " specialized settings" or "special subgroups".

Reliability: Test-retest reliability scores ranged from .64 to .94. Lower reliabilities were associated with scores from the younger children. The increased variability suggests that the CTS may be more valuable with children between 3 and 12. No inter-rater reliability data were provided by the authors.

Validity: The CTS is based on a large body of research examining temperament theory and as such the scales have high construct validity. The authors provide sufficient evidence that quantitative methods were used to ensure item and content validity. Also, the readers are referred to additional literature investigating the use of temperamental data in practice and this data's relationship to external events.

Clinical Utility

Adequate. The Carey Temperament Scales are designed to help learn about a child's individuality in order to prevent "stressful" child-caregiver interactions from occurring. However, the authors caution that data derived from the scales should be used with other sources of information and assessment.

Strengths/Limitations

The scales are easy to administer and may be completed by a number of adult informants. Computer scoring is available and is recommended, as hand scoring may be confusing with a high possibility of human error. Items are worded behaviorally and are clearly written with a number of helpful examples to aid rating. The authors admit several limitations of the scales including the lack of normative data for differing ethnic and socioeconomic status populations. Furthermore, items, graphs, and written temperament descriptions require at least an early high school reading level.

Authors: William B. Carey, Sean C. McDevitt, Barbara Medoff-Cooper, William Fullard, and Robin L. Hegvik.

Publication Year: 1996–1998.

Source: Behavioral-Developmental Initiatives, 14636 North 55th Street, Scottsdale, AZ 85254.

Fee: Yes.

ADDITIONAL INFORMATION/REFERENCES

Langlois, A. (2001). Review of the Carey Temperament Scales. In: *Mental Measurement Yearbook: Volume 114,* pp. 234–236.

Newman, J. (2001). Review of the Carey Temperament Scales. In: *Mental Measurement Yearbook: Volume 14,* pp. 236–238.

CHILD AND ADOLESCENT FUNCTIONAL ASSESSMENT SCALE

Reviewed by: David Reitman and Molly Murphy

Purpose

The Child and Adolescent Functional Assessment Scale (CAFAS) is designed to rate impairment in children referred for emotional and behavioral problems. It is intended for use in assessing outcome over time and directing case management activities.

Population

The CAFAS is intended for use with children aged 5 to 17 years.

Description

The CAFAS assesses a youth's degree of functional impairment due to emotional or behavioral problems. The 316 items are rated Likert-style, from no disruption to severe disruption, with higher scores indicating greater impairment. The scale assesses, performance at school/work, home, and in the community. Behavior toward others, moods/emotions, self-harmful behavior, substance use, and thinking are also assessed. In addition, the resources of the caregiver are evaluated, including; whether or not material needs of the youth are being met and the level of family/social support. The raters may include primary, non-custodial, or surrogate caregivers. At the end of each subscale is a list of strengths or goals. If the child exhibits the stated behavior, it is regarded as a strength, otherwise, it is a considered a goal (e.g., obeys rules routinely).

Administration

According to the manual, The CAFAS requires approximately 10 minutes to complete. Raters should have completed the Self-Training Manual, which is very explicit. Raters train using vignettes supplied in the training manual and should be able to complete training in 3 hours. Computer administration and a scannable version of the CAFAS are also available.

Scoring

The rating involves endorsing items that will lead to a behavior treatment plan. The scores are determined by marking the items that were endorsed by the client on the Profile sheet. For the 5-scale summary of youth functioning, scores can range from 0–10 (no dysfunction), up to 90 or higher, where a restrictive or supervised living situation is recommended. The computer program or the scannable CAFAS Profile is helpful for collecting data on clients over time and assessment of program outcomes through group analysis. The presence of risk behaviors (e.g., fire setting, runaway, or severe substance use) also is featured prominently in the CAFAS scoring summary.

Psychometric Properties

Norms: The CAFAS was developed using over 1,000 children drawn from a community mental health center and a large longitudinal study in the Ohio Valley.

Reliability: Internal consistency estimates using Cronbach's alpha ranged from .63 to .68, indicating marginal scale homogeneity. Good test-retest reliability was found on the CAFAS 1994 version. Inter-rater reliability is good for the individual scales.

Validity: High content validity was shown for scale items (e.g., expelled from school). When compared to the Child Behavior Checklist and the Child Assessment Schedule, significant to moderate correlations were found. Evidence of predictive validity (i.e., type of interventions needed, time spent in care, and cost) was also provided.

Clinical Utility

High. Ranking the level of functional impairment in the child is highly content valid and may be thought of as especially germane to the development of behavior treatment plans. Goals are explicitly noted and strengths are emphasized which may lead to more effective interventions. The availability of a training manual is a plus, and the instrument would probably work well in a multidisciplinary setting due to its high content validity.

Strengths/Limitations

The CAFAS may be especially useful in school settings or in a setting where general program evaluation is needed. Multidisciplinary treatment teams may also find the scales useful. Given the large number of items which must be reviewed and the number of strengths and goals (optional) which might be rated, it seems unlikely that the rating could be completed in 10 minutes; a 30-minute time frame seems more realistic, especially for raters unfamiliar with the instrument.

Author: Kay Hodges, Ph.D.

Publication Year: 1997.

Source: 2140 Old Earhart Road, Ann Arbor, MI 48105 (313) 769-9725 Fax: (313) 769-1434.

Fee: Yes.

ADDITIONAL INFORMATION/REFERENCES

Hodges, K., & Wong, M. M. (1996). Psychometric characteristics of a multidimensional measure to assess impairment: The Child and Adolescent Functional Assessment Scale. *Journal of Child and Family Studies, 5,* 445–467.

Hodges, K., & Wong, M. M. (1997). Use of the Child and Adolescent Functional Assessment Scale to predict service utilization and cost. *Journal of Mental Health Administration, 24,* 278–290.

CHILDREN'S ACTION TENDENCY SCALE

Reviewed by: Molly Murphy and David Reitman

Purpose

To provide a self-report assessment measure of children's aggressiveness, assertiveness, and submissiveness following a behavioral-analytic model.

Population

The Children's Action Tendency Scale (CATS) is intended for use with children between 6 and 12 years old.

Description

The CATS presents the child with 13 vignettes involving frustration, provocation, loss, or conflict. For each situation, the child is provided with 3 pairs of forced-choice response alternatives. The categories include 15 items for aggressiveness, 9 items for assertiveness, or 8 items for submissiveness. Response alternatives are designed to limit socially desirable responding and children must choose the response that is regarded as most probable. A completed protocol results in 39 responses. A child is said to be aggressive, assertive, or submissive according to the type of response (e.g., aggressive, assertive, or submissive) chosen most frequently. The questions are generally easy to understand and worded positively. The child must select an alternative for each pair, even if they find it difficult to choose.

Administration

The length of time necessary to administer the scale is not specified in the description, though 10 to 15 minutes would appear to suffice. The instructions are fairly straightforward. Older children complete the scale independently; the instrument is read aloud to children below a fourth or fifth grade.

Scoring

Children can earn a maximum of 2 points on any CATS subscale for each of the 13 vignettes. Total scores for each dimension can therefore range from 0 to 26. Higher scores indicate "more" of the characteristic.

Psychometric Properties

Norms: The scale was developed and normed on 108 children attending both public and parochial schools in the Buffalo, New York area. The CATS has yet to be standardized in a clinical setting.

Reliability: The internal consistency was .70 for Assertiveness, .92 for Aggressiveness, and .81 for the Submissiveness scale (Scanlon and Ollendick, 1986). Four-month test-retest reliability was .48 for aggressiveness, .60 for assertiveness, and .57 for submissiveness (Deluty, 1979). The scale was shown to have moderate split-half reliability; .63 to .77 (Scanlon and Ollendick, 1986).

Validity: The Children's Action Tendency Scale appears to measure and discriminate between aggressiveness and assertiveness. However, the extent to which the CATS effectively discriminates between submissiveness and assertiveness has not been clearly established. The CATS is correlated with behavioral rating scales and appears to be sensitive to treatment effects (Broad, Burke, Byford, & Sims, 1986).

Clinical Utility

Limited. Further research is still necessary to determine the utility of the CATS in clinical settings and it has not been used as a diagnostic tool. The CATS is a unique instrument in terms of format and content and may provide information about social skills which are not easily obtained with other instruments.

Strengths/Limitations

While the CATS possesses good internal consistency and reasonably good test-retest reliability. It may not reliably distinguish between aggressiveness, assertiveness, and submissiveness, especially in clinical populations where it remains largely untested. Submissive children who might otherwise benefit from assertiveness training might not be detected with this instrument (Scanlon and Ollendick, 1986).

Author: Robert H. Deluty.

Publication Year: 1984.

Source: Robert H. Deluty, Ph. D., Department of Psychology, University of Maryland-Baltimore County, 1000 Hilltop Circle, Baltimore, MD 21250.

Fee: No.

ADDITIONAL INFORMATION/REFERENCES

Broad, J., Burke, J., Byford, S. R., & Sims, P. (1986). Clinical application of the Children's Action Tendency Scale. *Psychological Reports, 59,* 71–74.

Deluty, R. H. (1984). Behavioral validation of the Children's Action Tendency Scale. *Journal of Behavioral Assessment, 6,* 115–130.

Scanlon E. M. & Ollendick (1986). Children's assertive behavior: The reliability and validity of three self-report measures. *Child and Family Behavior Therapy, 7,* 9–21.

CHILDREN'S ATTENTION AND ADJUSTMENT SURVEY: HOME AND SCHOOL VERSIONS

Reviewed by: Patrick M. O'Callaghan and David Reitman

Purpose

The survey is designed to measure behaviors related to Attention Deficit Hyperactivity Disorder (ADHD) in children. The rating scale was constructed as part of a longitudinal study exploring the contributions of internal and peripheral influences to the development of the disorder.

Population

The Children's Attention and Adjustment Survey (CAAS) is intended for school-age children from kindergarten through the fifth grade.

Description

The CAAS is designed to measure inattention, impulsivity, hyperactivity, and conduct problems. The survey is comprised of two forms: the School Form (CAAS-S) and the Home Form (CAAS-H). Each form, which differs only in its respective wording, measures the above factors on the basis of ratings by teachers and parents. The instrument consists of 31-items and incorporates a four-point, Likert-type rating system (*not at all, a little, quite a bit, and very much*) for each item.

Administration

In educational settings, a school psychologist or an administrator in close collaboration with a school psychologist should administer the instrument. In mental health or medical settings, the intake administrator or the individual responsible for diagnostic and/or intervention services should administer the survey. The instrument requires approximately 2 to 5 minutes to complete.

Scoring

The CAAS-S and CAAS-H are scored by hand. Marked responses are transferred onto a response grid and summed for each scale. Detailed instructions for scoring and plotting data are printed on the score sheet and profile.

Psychometric Properties

Norms: The CAAS-S standardization sample consisted of over 4000 children from public, private and parochial elementary school children in Alameda and Contra Costa counties in California from kindergarten through fifth grade. All of these children were participants in the longitudinal study concerning the prevalence of hyperactivity. In addition, the investigators sampled five children from the classrooms in which the hyperactive children were enrolled. The data for the standardization of the CAAS-H were provided by the parents of the children who were not considered to be hyperactive and served as controls in the larger study.

Reliability: The alphas for the home form range from a low of .75 for hyperactivity to a high of .81 for inattention. The school alphas range from .78 for impulsivity to .92 for conduct problems. Alpha levels are also provided for composite scales. Test-retest reliabilities over 3 years yielded correlations ranging from .40 to .82 for the home version (N = 135) and from .32 to .44 for the school form (N = 139).

Validity: The content of the items of the CAAS appears to be valid and is consistent with the literature regarding ADHD. Convergent and divergent validity data was collected by comparing outcomes of the CAAS to other measures of attention including the Pupil Behavior Rating Scale, the Child Behavior Checklist, the WISC-R and the PIAT. Other ratings are also compared, such as, teacher peer, and parent ratings of aggression and hyperactivity.

Clinical Utility

High. The CAAS is brief and easy to administer in a variety of settings. In educational settings, the CAAS can be used to identify students at risk of problems and can also be used as a pre-referral tool. In clinical settings, the CAAS can facilitate the construction of a diagnosis and treatment plan, and track behavior over time. The home and school forms combined can provide valuable information by comparing the child's behavior in different settings.

Strengths/Limitations

The scales of the CAAS are too short for the instrument to be a primary diagnostic tool. However, the instrument's brief administration time lends itself to screening and identification of those who may need further assessment.

Authors: Nadine Lambert, Carolyn Hartsough, and Jonathan Sandoval.

Publication Year: 1990.

Source: American Guidance Service, Inc., 4201 Woodland Road, Circle Pines, MN 55014-1796 1-800-328-2560.

Fee: Yes.

ADDITIONAL INFORMATION/REFERENCES

Arnold, L. E., Barneby, N. S., & Smeltzer, D. J. (1981). First grade norms and cross-correlation for the Conners, Davids, and Quay-Peterson behavior rating scales. *Journal of Learning Disabilities, 14,* 269–275.

Ernhart, C. B., (1995). Review of the Children's Attention and Adjustment Survey. In *Mental Measurement Yearbook, 12,* 184–185.

Koffler, S. L., (1995). Review of the Children's Attention and Adjustment Survey. In *Mental Measurement Yearbook, 12,* 185–187.

CHILDREN'S PERSONALITY QUESTIONNAIRE, EARLY SCHOOL PERSONALITY QUESTIONNAIRE, AND HIGH SCHOOL PERSONALITY QUESTIONNAIRE

Reviewed by: Joy H. Wymer & Mary Lou Kelley

Purpose

To assess various dimensions of personality in children and adolescents.

Population

The Children's Personality Questionnaire (CPQ) is designed for use with children ages 8 through 12 years. There are two additional versions, the Early School Personality Questionnaire (ESPQ) and the High School Personality Questionnaire (HSPQ), which are used with children ages 6 through 8 and 12 through 18, respectively.

Description

The CPQ is a 140-item, self-report questionnaire consisting primarily of two statements from which the child must choose the one that best describes him or her. The format is forced-choice, "yes" or "no" answer with the exception of questions loading on the intelligence factor. The CPQ yields fourteen primary source traits (e.g., Sizothymia/Affectothymia, Low Intelligence/High Intelligence, Emotional Instability/Higher Ego Strength, Phlegmatic Temperament/Excitability, Submissiveness/Dominance, Desurgency/Surgency, Low Superego Strength/Superego Strength, Threctia/Parmia, Harria/Premsia, Zeppia/Coasthenia, Naivete/Shrewdness, Untroubled Adequacy/Guilt Proneness, Low Self-Sentiment/High Strength of Self, and Low Ergic Tension/High Ergic Tension; manual explains each source trait in detail) which may be specifically combined into four second-order factors: Extraversion/Introversion, High Anxiety/Low Anxiety, Tough Poise/Tenderminded Emotionality, and Independence. Each factor is presented on a bi-polar continuum, with the advantageous pole differing depending on the factor. The CPQ, in order to alleviate distortions, was constructed so that the questions appear as neutral as possible with regard to social desirability. Additionally, the items were balanced in order to avoid set responses and items with high face validity were eliminated. Raw scores are converted to n-stens, s-stens, and percentile ranks. The CPQ is accompanied by a handbook that describes its purpose, interpretation and use, and reliability and validity.

The ESPQ and HSPQ are similar in format to the CPQ. The ESPQ consists of 80 items and the HSPQ consists of 142 items. The three personality tests measure the same personality concepts and can, therefore, be used to assess development over time and measure therapeutic gain.

Administration

The CPQ, ESPQ, and HSPQ may be administered either individually or in a small group. If necessary, it is permissible to read individual items to a child or to define words. Time to complete the CPQ and the HSPQ is approximately 50 minutes. The ESPQ, which is read aloud to the child or children, may take 1–1½ hours to administer. All three measures are broken into two parts for ease of administration.

Scoring

The CPQ, HSPQ, and ESPQ can be hand-scored with the use of scoring stencils; the CPQ and HSPQ may also be sent to the publisher for computer scoring.

Psychometric Properties

Norms: The manuals for the CPQ and ESPQ do not define the standardization samples, although they appear to have been normed around 1968. The HSPQ was normed in 1968 on a "representative" sample of more than 9,000 adolescents, 12 to 18 years old.

Reliability: With a retest interval of one week, test-retest reliability of the individual factors of the CPQ ranged from .37 to .87. Studies of internal consistency yielded coefficients of .26 to .86. The CPQ has four forms with equivalence coefficients of .33 to .75.

Validity: The authors of the CPQ found its construct validity to range from .20 to 90 for the various personality factors.

Clinical Utility

Limited. The CPQ, as well as the EPSQ and HSQ, are fairly lengthy to administer, but hand-scoring the answer sheets is relatively simple. The measures are cost efficient as the test booklets are reusable and only answer sheets need to be reordered. Given the lack of standardization data, score interpretation is very limited.

Strengths/Limitations

The CPQ may aid in diagnosis and treatment. The measure's limitations include length to administer and lack of reported standardization sample as well as poor psychometric support.

Authors: Rutherford B. Porter, Ed.D. and Raymond B. Cattell, Ph.D., D.Sc.

Publication Year: Unclear.

Source: Institute for Personality and Ability Testing, Inc., P.O. Box 1188, Champaign, IL 61824-1188; Call: (1-800-225-4728); E-mail: custservice@ipat.com

Fee: Yes.

ADDITIONAL INFORMATION/REFERENCE

Porter, R. B. & Cattell, R. B. (1968). *Handbook for the Children's Personality Questionnaire (CPQ).* Institute for Personality and Ability Testing, Inc: Champaign, IL.

CHILDREN'S PROBLEMS CHECKLIST

Reviewed by: Shannon Self-Brown & Mary Lou Kelley

Purpose

To aid in assessment of children by identifying relevant problems, establishing rapport, and providing written documentation of presenting problems consistent with community standards of care.

Population

Children 5–12 years old.

Description

The Children's Problems Checklist (CPC) is a 202-item checklist consisting of problem behaviors commonly experienced by children. The items survey 11 problem areas: Emotions; Self-Concept; Peers and Play; School; Language and Thinking; Concentration and Organization; Activity Level and Motor Activity; Behavior; Values; Habits; and Health. The CPC is completed by the child's parent or guardian. The person completing the checklist is instructed to place a checkmark beside each statement that describes a problem the child is currently exhibiting and circling the problem that is considered to be the most important.

Administration

The CPC can be completed in 10 to 20 minutes by a parent.

Scoring

Scoring the CPC is completed by summing the amount of problem behaviors endorsed in each of the 11 areas.

Psychometric Properties

Norms: No data were reported in the manual.

Reliability: No data were reported in the manual.

Validity: No data were reported in the manual.

Clinical Utility

Limited. The CPC provides the clinician with no information about a child client that could not be attained by an intake interview or other instruments that have supportive psychometric properties.

Strengths/Limitations

The CPC is a paper and pencil interview that can provide the clinician with a general idea of parental concerns about their child. The CPC is lacking many of the basic properties necessary for an instrument to contribute to the mental health field, such as a test manual, standardization data, and psychometric information.

Author: John A. Schinka, Ph.D.

Publication Year: 1985.

Source: Psychological Assessment Resources, Inc.; 1-800-331-TEST.

Fee: Yes.

ADDITIONAL INFORMATION/REFERENCE

Piersel, W. C. (1989). Review of the Children's Problems Checklist. In *The Tenth Mental Measurement Yearbook*, pp. 165–166.

CONDUCTING FUNCTIONAL BEHAVIORAL ASSESSMENTS: A PRACTICAL GUIDE INTERVIEW/SELF-REPORT FORM, OBSERVATION AND ANALYSIS FORM, TEMPORAL ANALYSIS AND RANKING FORM, AND SUMMARY ANALYSIS FORM

Reviewed by: Kristin A. Gansle & George H. Noell

Purpose

To assist school personnel with conducting functional behavioral assessments and with developing behavioral intervention plans based on those assessments.

Population

The forms are designed for use with students and school personnel. No specific age range for target students is specified in the manual.

Description

Conducting Functional Behavioral Assessments: A Practical Guide provides a single form with four major divisions for recording data that may contribute to a functional behavioral assessment (FBA). The four single-page sections of the record are the Interview/Self-report Form, Observation and Analysis Form, Temporal Analysis and Ranking Form, and Summary Analysis Form. The materials are designed for use with students who are experiencing behavioral difficulties for the purpose of assessing problem behavior, generating solutions, and evaluation of intervention effects. The materials and data collection procedures are derived from the functional assessment literature and are designed to be acceptable to educators. The authors discuss the narrow and specific requirements of the reauthorization of the Individuals with Disabilities Education Act and well as discussing the potential utility of functional assessment with a range of school-based concerns.

The manual provides a short discussion of the possible functions of behavior that have been supported by research and which are important to the development of an effective behavior intervention plan. The forms and manual present three interrelated steps to conduct an FBA. These include Problem Identification, Problem Analysis, and Summarization.

Problem Identification uses the Interview / Self Report Form designed to be completed by either the student or by an adult who has had significant contact with the student. It includes one open-ended question regarding the description of the behavior, as well as several checklists that allow the informant to provide information about events related to the behavior, antecedents, and consequences to the behavior.

Problem Analysis uses the Observation and Analysis Form and the Temporal Analysis and Ranking Form. The Observation and Analysis Form and procedures are built around an antecedents-behavior-consequences chart. The observation form contains charts on which to record observation information from three different observations. It is recommended, however, that observations be conducted until the target behavior is observed on at least three occasions. The form also contains a summary section in which the information collected during the observations is written in short, narrative form. The Temporal Analysis and Ranking form contains a format for recording information regarding the times and situations in which the behavior is most likely and least likely to occur. Additional recording forms are likely to be needed if an more detailed observational analysis such as interval recording is used or the target behavior occurs several times per observation.

A functional hypothesis is developed and recorded using the Summary Analysis Form to aggregate the information collected on the previous forms and to suggest potential functions of the target behavior. It is this information which should guide the choice of intervention components.

Administration

The functional behavioral assessment is not administered per se, but is a process whose duration will vary considerably dependent upon the nature, number, severity, and frequency of targeted concerns. *Conducting Functional Behavioral Assessments: A Practical Guide* is designed to support this process and as a result is not a single instrument.

Scoring

There is no scoring, per se, for this instrument. All information is used in raw form to generate hypotheses about the functions of the behaviors of interest. Once the information is collected, it is used in its raw form.

Psychometric Properties

Norms: None.

Reliability: No information regarding the reliability of the instrument is provided.

Validity: No validity evidence for this particular manual or recording form is provided. However, the conceptual basis for the assessment process has been developed in numerous published studies. Additionally, functional assessment is a complex process that can draw data from a range of sources. As a result, traditional psychometric validation procedures may be more immediately relevant to specific functional assessment tools than to a guide for the process.

Clinical Utility

High. *Conducting Functional Behavioral Assessments: A Practical Guide* provides a basic framework for collecting information relevant to a functional behavioral assessment.

Strengths/Limitations

Conducting Functional Behavioral Assessments: A Practical Guide is a straightforward tool for collecting information that is pertinent to a functional analysis of behavior. However, the procedures outlined in *Conducting Functional Behavioral Assessments: A Practical Guide* will require a relatively high level of expertise in functional assessment by the clinician using this tool. No firm guidelines are provided regarding integrating varied and sometimes contradictory data to arrive at a functional hypothesis. Additionally, information describing links from the functional assessment to an empirically validated intervention approach is cursory. Rather than providing a tightly scripted procedure, the guide provides a general approach and recording form for a complex process that will require users to make numerous decisions regarding how to proceed at each stage in the process.

Authors: J. Ron Nelson, Maura L. Roberts, Deborah J. Smith.

Publication Year: 1983.

Source: Sopris West, 4093 Specialty Place, Longmont, CO 80504, (303) 651-2829, www.sopriswest.com

Fee: Yes.

CONNERS' RATING SCALES—REVISED: PARENT RATING SCALE—LONG AND SHORT FORMS, TEACHER RATING SCALES—LONG AND SHORT FORMS, AND ADOLESCENT SELF-REPORT SCALE—LONG AND SHORT FORMS

Reviewed by: Mary Lou Kelley

Purpose

To assess Attention Deficit Hyperactivity Disorder (ADHD) and co-morbid disorders. To provide revisions of previously developed scales using a using a large ethnically diverse normative sample, assessing DSM-IV criteria both categorically and dimensionally, and developing a self-report scale for completion by adolescents.

Population

The Conners' Rating Scales-Revised are intended for use with children ages 3–17 years.

Description

The Conners' Rating Scales (CRS) represent an attempt to revise existing scales in order to improve the psychometrics and utility, while retaining the positive features of the previous scales that have been used extensively in research. The historical background on the former and current scales as well as the rationale and intended uses of the questionnaires are thoroughly discussed in the technical manual.

The CRS consist of short and long versions for each of the parent, teacher, and adolescent respondent. The scales are:

Conners' Parent Rating Scale-Revised Long and Short Forms (CPRS-R:L/S)

Conners' Teacher Rating Scales- Long and Short Forms (CTRS-R:L/S)

Conners-Wells' Adolescent Self-Report Scale: Long and Short Forms (CASS:L/S.

Five brief ancillary scales are also included and are useful for screening or treatment monitoring: Conners' Global Index-Parent (CGI-P) or Teacher (CGI-T), Conners' ADHD/DSM IV Scales-Parent (CADS-P) or Teacher (CADS-T), or Adolescent (CADS-A). The ancillary scales consist of scales embedded within the corresponding, long CRS versions.

All CRS are similarly formatted, administered and scored. Items are rated on a four-point scale (0 = Not True at All/Never, Seldom; 1 = Just a Little Bit True/Occasionally; 2 = Pretty Much True/Often Quite a Bit; 3 = Very Much True/Very Often, Very Frequent). References to frequency have been added to the response format to simplify responding (Conners, 1997). All CRS are formatted so that very specific instructions are provided on the scale. Procedures for administering, scoring, and interpreting results are thoroughly described in the technical manual.

The CPRS-R:L is an 80-item instrument with the following subscales: Oppositional (10 items), Cognitive Problems/Inattention(12 items), Hyperactivity (9 items), Anxious/Shy (8 items), Perfectionism (7 items), Social Problems (5 items), Psychosomatic (6 items), Conners' Global Index (10 items), ADHD Index (12 items), DSM-IV Symptoms subscales (9 DSM-IV Inattentive and 9 DSM-IV Impulsive/Hyperactive).

The CTRS-R:L is somewhat shorter (59 items) than the SPRS-R:L but contains the same scales with the exception of the Psychosomatic scale. Items on the teacher and parent scales overlap but are not identical. Most of the factors were derived empirically. The Global Index represents the Hyperactivity Index from the previous scale and contains items that consistently have distinguished clinical and non-clinical samples. The Global Index is considered a brief measure of general psychopathology that consists of two factors: Emotional Lability and Restless-Impulsive. The ADHD Index was developed and validated through a series of studies described in the manual. The ADHD Index consists of items that distinguish ADHD from non-ADHD children. The DSM-IV Symptom subscales were included in the revised scale in order to assess diagnostic symptoms categorically and dimensionally.

The CPRS-R:S and the CPTS-R consist of four subscales: Oppositional, Cognitive Problems/Inattention, Hyperactivity, and ADHD Index. The parent version contains 27 items and the teacher version 28 items.

The CASS-L is suitable for adolescents ages 12–17 and consists of 87 items loading on 10 subscales: Family Problems, Emotional Problems, Conduct Problems, Cognitive Problems/Inattention, Anger Control Problems, Hyperactivity, ADHD Index, and the two DSM-IV subscales paralleling the other measures. The CASS-R contains 27 items and four subscales: Conduct Problems, Cognitive Problems/Inattention, Hyperactive-Impulsive, and ADHD Index. The auxiliary versions of the CRS were developed simultaneously with the revised measures.

The technical manual is very thorough, clearly written and describes clearly rationales for the revised scales, uses and misuses of rating scales in general and the CRS in particular, administration and interpretation of the data. The manual also contains a number of case examples that explicate a multi-method assessment approach that incorporates data from the CRS in order to make diagnostic and treatment decisions. Information on measure development and reliability and validity studies is extensively and clearly presented.

Administration

The long versions of the CRS can be completed in approximately 15–20 minutes. The short versions and auxiliary scales can be completed in 5–10 minutes. The teacher and parent measures are at about 9th grade level and the adolescent self-report scales are at about a 6th grade reading level. When reading level is of concern, Conners recommends eliminating certain items relevant to DSM-IV criteria.

Scoring

Scoring can be accomplished by "QuikScore" forms, fax or mail-in scoring, or computer software scoring. The "QuikScore" format involves multilayered, perforated, carbonless sheets. The respondent writes on the top form, the results transfer to the next layer. Scores are tabulated easily on the second sheet and then plotted according to age and gender norms on the final sheet. This is an easy and efficient scoring method that minimizes errors. The long versions of the CRS take considerable more time to score since these require transferring scores and adding a longer list of numbers. More errors are likely to be made with this format.

Psychometric Properties

Norms: The CRS scales were collected using a very large normative sample of approximately 2000 or more parents, teachers, and adolescents. Data were obtained on children from over 45 states and 10 provinces. Only regular education children were used and they came from diverse socioeconomic, demographic, and ethnic backgrounds. Emphasis was placed on obtaining data on African American children. Norms are available on 10 separate age and gender groupings for the teacher and parent versions. Two age groupings are available on the self-report scales.

Reliability: Internal consistency was high for all subscales. Test-retest was good for almost all of the subscales.

Validity: Considerable validity exists supporting the various CRS. Factor analysis was employed to define items on the majority of the subscales. Convergent and divergent validity data were conducted by comparing the parent and teacher versions of the scales, parent and teacher with adolescents' ratings, and correlating CRS scores with scores from the Children's Depression Inventory. Data in support of the CRS were consistently obtained. However, the authors did not compare the CRS to other measures designed for the same purpose.

Clinical Utility

High. The CRS-R scales are easy to administer and score and allow for comparisons across informants. The inclusion of DSM-IV criteria will aid in diagnosis. Norms for African Americans are available which enhances the utility of the instrument.

Strengths/Limitations

The former versions of the CRS have been extensively criticized for the lack of standardization data, available information on psychometric properties of the scales, and the absence of empirical methods for developing the scales.

Author: C. Keith Conners, Ph.D.

Publication Year: 1989.

Source: Mental Health Systems, 908 Niagara Falls Blvd., Tonawanda, NY 14120-2960.
(800) 456-3003.

Fee: Yes.

ADDITIONAL INFORMATION/REFERENCES

Martens, B. K. (1992). Review of Conners' Rating Scales. In *Mental Measurement Yearbook,* Volume 11, pp. 231–234.
Oehler-Stinnett, J. (1992). Review of Conners' Rating Scales. In *Mental Measurement Yearbook,* Volume 11, pp. 234–241.

DEVEREUX BEHAVIOR RATING SCALE—SCHOOL FORM

Reviewed By: Shannon Self-Brown & Mary Lou Kelley

Purpose

To provide professionals with a structured system of determining the extent to which children's behavior falls within or outside the normal range. It may also be used to monitor and evaluate treatment progress over time.

Population

The Devereux Behavior Rating Scale-School Form is intended for use with children ages 5–18 years.

Description

The instrument contains two rating scales, one for ages 5–12 and another for ages 13–18. Each form contains 40 behaviorally referenced items that are rated along a 5-point continuum (0 = never to 4 = very frequently) according to the frequency of occurrence over the last 4 weeks. The Devereux-School Form is organized into four subscales that correspond to four areas of the federal definition for Serious Emotional Disturbance: Interpersonal Problems, Inappropriate Behaviors/Feelings, Depression, and Physical Symptoms. The scale items are written at a sixth grade level. The scales are completed by persons who have sufficient opportunity to observe the child or adolescent across a variety of setting for at least a four-week period. The Devereux-School Form is a revision of the Devereux Child Behavior Rating Scale and the Devereux Adolescent Behavior Rating Scale.

Administration

Can be completed by a parent, caretaker, or teacher who has had ample opportunity to observe the child's/adolescent's behavior over a four week period. The estimated completion time is between 15 to 45 minutes.

Scoring

A carbon copy is attached to the answer document that is completed by the rater of the Devereux-School Form. Next to each item on the carbon copy, a box is located in one of four columns identifying which subscale the item is part of. Each subscale score is determined by adding up the boxes in each column. The Total score is computed by totaling all items. Guidelines on the answer document provide references to tables in the manual that are used to convert total and subscale standard scores, percentile ranks, and confidence intervals. The authors recommend using a T-score of 60 as the cutoff score for determining that an individual's score is significantly elevated as compared to the standardized sample.

Psychometric Properties

Norms: The Devereux-School Form was standardized on 3,153 children and adolescents, 5–18 years of age. The sample was stratified for age, gender, geographic region, race, ethnicity, socioeconomic status, community size, and educational placement. The data were obtained from a variety of facilities across the United States, including public school districts, private special education settings, and clinical treatment programs. Children and adolescents who attended regular education classes and those who were identified as having learning disabilities, speech and language impairments, and other disorders were included. Children and adolescents receiving part time or full time special education services for serious emotional disturbance and those who were mentally retarded were not included in the normal standardization sample.

Reliability: The reliability of the Devereux-School Form was assessed using multiple methods. Internal reliability coefficients were adequate for the Total Scale and each subscale. Test-retest reliability, Intra-rater Reliability, and Inter-rater Reliability was good.

Validity: Content validity, construct validity, and criterion validity were investigated. To ensure the integrity of content validity, authors selected the items for the measure from a large pool and had adequate representation of the behaviors for each of the four areas specified in the federal definition for serious emotional disturbance. Construct-Related Validity was determined by calculating all item-total correlations. These were significant ($p < .01$) and highly correlated to the total score. Criterion-related validity was assessed by conducting six studies to determine the extent to which the scale ratings discriminate between normal and clinically diagnosed groups. The results of these studies indicate that the Total Scale score on the Devereux-School Form is an accurate identifier of children and adolescents with severe emotional disturbance.

Clinical Utility

High. This instrument may be useful in assessing for placement into special education resources. It may also be useful for screening purposes and for documenting improvement of diagnostic symptoms over time.

Strengths/Limitations

The Devereux School form can be completed by a variety of adult informants and is easy to administer and score. In addition, the test manual is well written and easy to follow. The items are worded behaviorally and are evaluated on the frequency with which the behavior has been observed.

One relative weakness of this measure was the statistical soundness of the subscales. The inter-rater reliability was rather low for the subscales. Since there are only 10 items in each subscale, caution should be exercised in the interpretation of subscale scores.

Authors: Jack A. Naglieri, Paul A. LeBuffe, and Steven I. Pfeiffer.

Publication Year: 1990–1993.

Source: The Psychological Corporation, 555 Academic Court, San Antonio, TX 78204-2498.

Fee: Yes.

ADDITIONAL INFORMATION/REFERENCES

Bloom, L. (1998) Review of the Devereux Behavior Rating Scale-School Form. In: *Mental Measurement Yearbook: Volume 13,* pp. 357–359.
Farmer, R. F. (1998) Review of the Devereux Behavior Rating Scale-School Form. In: *Mental Measurement Yearbook: Volume 13,* pp. 359–360.

THE DIAGNOSTIC INTERVIEW FOR CHILDREN AND ADOLESCENTS—REVISED CHILD, ADOLESCENT, AND PARENT VERSIONS

Reviewed by: Rebecca Currier and David Reitman

Purpose

To classify childhood psychiatric disorders in children and adolescents based on parent and child/adolescent report in a manner that corresponds to DSM-III-R, DSM-IV, and/or ICD-10 diagnostic criteria.

Population

The DICA-R is intended to evaluate children and adolescents aged 6–17. Its three versions consist of the DICA-R-C, which is for use with children ages 6–12 years, the DICA-R-A for use with adolescents aged 13–17, and the DICA-R-P is used in interviewing parents. A computerized version of the 1997 DICA is also available in all three versions.

Description

The DICA-R is a structured interview but allows some of the flexibility of the semi-structured interview. Questioning begins by eliciting general identifying and demographic information and then proceeds to items that are grouped according to DSM-III-R or DSM-IV diagnostic categories (e.g., Behavior Disorders, Mood Disorders, Anxiety Disorders, Eating Disorders). It comes with an easy to read technical manual that describes administration, example interviews, individual item specifications, and scoring procedures.

The DICA-R consists of three versions that are separate but nearly identical. While they ask the same questions in the same order, wording and examples used differ so that they can be age appropriate. The DICA-R consists of objectively worded items that are numerically coded to facilitate later data entry. Items are rated from 1 = "No" to 5 = "Yes". Some questions have special codes that supersede the standard codes (e.g., race of child). Alternative codes are clearly displayed next to the question.

Administration

The DICA-R should take between an hour and an hour and a half to complete and should be administered at a relatively rapid pace. The computerized version requires less time to administer and can also be self-administered.

Scoring

The DICA-R is diagnostic for DSM-III-R, DSM-IV, and/or ICD-10 diagnoses and is, therefore, scored according to specific criteria which must be met to make a diagnosis of each disorder. The criteria is broken up into three categories that include symptom number, the clustering, or co-occurrence, of symptoms, and the duration of symptomatology that can be utilized to determine diagnoses.

Psychometric Properties

Norms: Limited information is available regarding the standardization of the current versions of the DICA-R.

Reliability: Reliability data for the 1997 version demonstrated kappa values that are consistent with those of semistructured interviews, ranging from .32 to .65 in children and .59 to .92 in adolescents. The computerized version of the DICA showed the kappa values to be lower than when the instrument was administered by a trained interviewer. The 1991 version of the DICA-R has been shown to have acceptable internal consistency. This version has also demonstrated acceptable interrater reliability.

Validity: The authors point out that the lack of a gold standard against which to compare interview instruments creates a problem in the development of a valid research interview. The criterion validity of the DICA-R was established by correlating diagnoses obtained with those derived from clinical interview and was found to be low to moderate. It demonstrated high correlations with the Child Behavior Checklist. The DICA-R has been found to discriminate between pediatric and psychiatric samples.

Clinical Utility

Adequate. The DICA-R is a structured interview that can be clearly evaluated based on specific scoring criterion and tied to DSM-III-R, DSM-IV, and/or ICD-10 diagnostic categories. It has been suggested that use of a structured interview may be superior to the clinical interview for research purposes. However, there is no clear evidence to suggest that utilizing a structured interview is superior to a trained clinicians interview. In addition, the instrument can be time-consuming to administer, particularly when interviewing multiple informants.

Strengths/Limitations

The DICA-R consists of objectively worded items that are numerically coded to facilitate later data entry. It comes with an easy to read technical manual that describes administration, example interviews, individual item specifications, and scoring procedures. The training recommended for appropriate administration is lengthy, lasting between 2–4 weeks. In addition, information obtained from various informants often does not correlate highly necessitating clinical judgment.

Author: Barbara Herjanic, M.D.

Publication Year: 1982; revisions in 1984, 1988, 1992, and 1997.

Source: Wendy Reich, Ph.D., Washington University, Division of Child Psychiatry, Spoehrer Tower, 4940 Audubon Ave. St. Louis, MO 63110, (314) 454-2307.

Fee: Yes.

ADDITIONAL INFORMATION/REFERENCE

Reich, W. (2000). Diagnostic Interview for Children and Adolescents (DICA). *Journal of the American Academy of Child and Adolescent Psychiatry, 39, 1*: 59–66.

DIFFERENTIAL TEST OF CONDUCT AND EMOTIONAL PROBLEMS

Reviewed by: Mary Lou Kelley

Purpose

To assist teachers and school personnel in screening for and differentiating children with emotional and conduct problems.

Population

Children grades Kindergarten to 12.

Description

The DT/CEP is comprised for two scales: Conduct problem Scale (29 items) and the Emotional Disturbance Scale. Both scales are rated using a true/false format and items are weighted from 0–2 points. Items were rationally derived based on field-based descriptors of conduct problems and emotional disturbance, DSM-III criteria, and items from behavior rating scales. Items were refined over a 2-year period according to the authors but details about item refinement were not provided.

The instrument was developed in order to differentiate children who are grouped together in special education classrooms and programs for the behaviorally and emotionally disturbed. It is the author's contention that children with conduct problems choose not to conform to rules and therefore do not have a handicapping condition as is required by law for special education services. In contrast, he views children with emotional disturbance as having symptoms that impede school performance such as the case of performance anxiety. Hence, the need to differentiate these groups of children in order to provide more appropriate services.

Administration

The DT/CEP can be completed in 15–20 minutes by teachers or school personnel familiar with the student.

Scoring

Items for each scale are scored from 0–2 with some items weighted as appears on the template. Scores are tallied for each subscale. Five items are not included in the score due to the results of item analyses.

Psychometric Properties

Norms: The scale was normed on 2367 children with varying socioeconomic and racial backgrounds. However, all were from Las Vegas and surrounding area. Some cells were very low with respect to certain ages and ethnic groupings.

Reliability: Internal consistency for the Conduct Disorder scale was adequate. Test-retest reliability was above .85 but was not conducted on a heterogeneous sample which could have led to artificially high correlations (Brozovich, 1995).

Validity: The scale differentiated between children who have conduct problems and emotionally disturbed children. Validity data were supportive of the measure but were limited. The age and gender differences discussed earlier supported the measures sensitivity to developmental changes. Validity data also were supported by a study employing contrasted groups and factor analysis of the scale.

Clinical Utility

Limited. This scale is not employable as a diagnostic tool.

Strengths/Limitations

The measure and manual are very straightforward and easy to understand. Due to the limited standardization data, and reliability and validity data, other measures may be more useful and appropriate.

Author: Gary Vitali.

Source: Slossen Educational Publications, Inc. P.O. Box 280, East Aurora NY 14052.

Fee: Yes.

ADDITIONAL INFORMATION/REFERENCES

Brozovich, R. (1995). Review of the Differential Test of Conduct and Emotional Problems. In J. C. Conoley & J. C. Impara, *The Twelfth Mental Measurement Yearbook,* pp. 309–310.

Westman, A. S. (1995). Review of the Differential Test of Conduct and Emotional Problems. In J. C. Conoley & J. C. Impara, *The Twelfth Mental Measurement Yearbook,* pp. 310–311.

THE EARLY CHILDHOOD BEHAVIOR SCALE

Reviewed by: Kellie A. Hilker & Mary Lou Kelley

Purpose

The Early Childhood Behavior Scale was developed to identify emotional disturbance and behavior disorders in children aged 3 to 6. The measure can be used to identify behaviors for intervention and assess effectiveness of school-based interventions. Additionally, the scale was designed for use in conjunction with the Early Childhood Behavior Intervention Manual to create goals for a child's IEP and identify appropriate interventions.

Population

Children 3 to 6 years old.

Description

Teachers rate each of 53 items on a 7-point Likert-type scale ranging from 0 (Not in My Presence) to 6 (More Than Once an Hour). A total score is obtained as well as three subscores including Academic Progress, Social Relationships, and Personal Adjustment.

Administration

The Early Childhood Behavior Scale is completed by teachers. Administration time is approximately 15 minutes.

Scoring

Raw scores are summed for the three subscale scores and a total score. Standard scores and percentile ranks are also obtained and plotted on a summary table on the front of the measure. The standard scores have a mean of 10 with a standard deviation of 3. Standard scores below one standard deviation are considered clinically significant.

Psychometric Properties

Norms: In the standardization process, 1314 children were rated by 289 teachers. Children were recruited from both behavior disordered and regular classrooms. Recruitment from these classrooms and percent of the sample from each classroom is not clearly outlined.

Reliability: High inter-rater, test-retest reliability, and high internal consistency were found.

Validity: Criterion-related validity is moderate. The author reports high diagnostic validity when identifying those students enrolled in a behavior disordered classroom. Factor analysis does not lend support of 3 separate subscales.

Clinical Utility

Limited. More evidence is needed to support the use of this measure.

Strengths/Limitations

The scale relies on the definition of behavior and emotional problems for school-aged children outlined by Public Law 94–142. Given the fact that more recent classification systems exist, for example, DSM IV, revisions may be warranted. The standardization process is not clearly explained with regards to percent of the sample with and without behavior disorders. Additionally, parents are not identified as potential raters; therefore, eliminating an appropriate source of information. One strength of this measure is that assessment with the ECBS is designed to guide the intervention through the use of the Early Childhood Behavior Intervention Manual.

Authors: Stephen B. McCarney, Ed.D.

Publication Year: 1991–1992.

Source: Hawthorne Educational Services, Inc., 800 Gray Oak Drive, Columbia, MO 65201, (573) 874-1710.

Fee: Yes.

ADDITIONAL INFORMATION/REFERENCES

Paget, K. D. (199). Review of The Early Childhood Behavior Scale. In J. C. Impara & B. S. Plake (Eds.), *The Thirteenth Mental Measurements Yearbook* (pp. 382–383). Lincoln, NE: Buros Institute of Measurements, University of Nebraska.

Sandoval, J. (199). Review of The Early Childhood Behavior Scale. In J. C. Impara & B.S. Plake (Eds.), *The Thirteenth Mental Measurements Yearbook* (pp. 383–384). Lincoln, NE: Buros Institute of Measurements, University of Nebraska.

EARLY CHILDHOOD INVENTORY—4

Reviewed by: Kellie Hilker & Mary Lou Kelley

Purpose

The Early Childhood Inventory—4 (ECI—4) is a screening instrument for behavioral, emotional, and cognitive difficulties in preschool-aged children.

Population

Children between the ages of 3 and 5.

Description

The ECI—4 is a pen and paper measure with versions for both parents and teachers. The items included in the ECI—4 correspond to DSM-IV Diagnoses. Each item is rated on frequency of the symptoms ("never", "sometimes", "often", and "very often"). The developmental information is rated on a 5-point scale ranging from "delayed" to "superior". The items on the ECI—4 assess the following areas: AD/HD Inattentive Type; AD/HD Hyperactive-Impulsive Type; AD/HD Combined Type; Oppositional Defiant Disorder; Conduct Disorder; Peer Conflict Scale; Separation Anxiety Disorder; Generalized Anxiety Disorder; Specific Phobia; Obsessive–Compulsive Disorder; Tic Disorders; Selective Mutism; Major Depressive Disorder; Dysthymic Disorder; Social Phobia; Sleep Problems; Elimination Problems; Posttraumatic Stress Disorder; Feeding Problems; Reactive Attachment Disorder; Pervasive Developmental Disorders; and Developmental Ratings.

Administration

Administration of the ECI—4 takes 10–15 minutes and can be completed by the parents or administered in an interview format.

Scoring

The ECI—4 is scored using the Symptom Count score, which is the total number of symptoms rated as clinically significant ("often" or "very often") within a diagnostic category. This score is compared to the Symptom Criterion score. The Criterion score is the minimum number of items necessary for a diagnosis. A child will receive a Screening Cutoff of "yes" if the minimum number of symptoms necessary to make a diagnosis of that disorder is endorsed. Throughout the manual the authors stress that a comprehensive evaluation should occur if a Screening Cutoff Score is obtained for any of the diagnostic categories. The Symptom Severity score method involves summing the scores in each diagnostic category. Each response is given a number, for example, an endorsement of "often" is given a score of 2. These responses are then summed for each of the diagnostic categories. The Symptom Severity scores are converted to T-scores with scores above 70 indicating high severity of symptoms.

Psychometric Properties

Standardization for the Parent Checklist was based on 431 children. The sample was approximately equal with regards to gender. The majority of the sample was Caucasian (76%) followed by African-American (15%), Hispanic (8%), and other (1%). Socioeconomic status also was calculated for the normative sample. Lower and middle socioeconomic groups were equal (38%) with 24% of the sample falling in the upper socioeconomic group. Standardization for the Teacher Checklist was based on 398 children with slightly more males (n = 228) than females (n = 170). The distribution of races within this sample was similar to the normative group for the Parent Checklist.

Reliability: Test-retest reliability of the Parent Checklist was evaluated over a 3 month period. Coefficients were obtained for each diagnostic category and ranged from .35 for the Peer Conflict Scale to .77 for Posttraumatic Stress Disorder. The majority of coefficients were higher than .6. Minimal test-rest reliability data is presented for the Teacher Checklist. Coefficients ranged from .62 to .90 for the AD/HD and ODD categories, however, this data was obtained in the in conjunction with a stimulant medication evaluation.

Validity: Predictive validity was obtained by comparing scores on the ECI—4 with child psychiatric diagnoses. Sensitivity and specificity information is provided for each of the diagnostic categories. The predictive validity data appear to be adequate for the disorders that are more commonly seen and prevalent in their sample (e.g. AD/HD and Oppositional Defiant Disorder), however, conclusions can not be made with regards to the disorders that are not represented in the clinical sample (e.g., Generalized Anxiety Disorder). Validity for the Parent Checklist also was obtained by evaluating the ability of the measure to distinguish between clinical and nonclinical samples. Overall, the clinic sample resulted in higher scores on the ECI—4 when compared to a nonclinical sample. Concurrent validity was calculated by comparing Symptom Severity scores on the ECI—4 to the Scale Scores from the Teacher Report Form and the Child Behavior Checklist. In general, support for concurrent validity was found with these comparisons.

Clinical Utility

Fair. The ECI—4 appears to be an adequate screening tool for identifying children with disorders that are commonly seen in young children, however, more information is needed before commenting on the adequacy of the measure in screening for less commonly seen disorders.

Strengths/Limitations

The ECI—4 is a broad screening measure based on DSM-IV diagnoses. The ECI—4 has both a Parent and Teacher Checklist allowing for a multi-informant assessment. The psychometric data provide some initial support for the reliability and validity of the measure as a screening instrument. One important limitation is that the clinical sample used for the validity data was not representative of all the disorders being assessed by the ECI—4. The authors discuss the low prevalence rates of various disorders in young children, however, little can be said about the ability of the measure to identify children with these disorders. Many important details are lacking in the Screening Manual, for example, details regarding the Symptom Severity score are not found in this manual, but more information is provided in the Norms Manual. Better organization of this information may make the measure and manual more user friendly.

Authors: Kenneth D. Gadow, Ph.D. & Joyce Sprafkin, Ph.D.

Publication Year: 1997.

Source: Checkmate Plus, Ltd.

Fee: Yes.

THE ECOBEHAVIORAL ASSESSMENT SYSTEMS SOFTWARE, VER. 3.0: CODE FOR INSTRUCTIONAL STRUCTURE AND STUDENT ACADEMIC RESPONSE, MAINSTREAM CODE FOR INSTRUCTIONAL STRUCTURE AND STUDENT ACADEMIC RESPONSE, AND ECOBEHAVIORAL SYSTEM FOR COMPLEX ASSESSMENTS OF PRESCHOOL ENVIRONMENTS

Reviewed by: Gary Duhon & George H. Noell

Purpose

Provide a computerized data entry and analysis tool that is specifically designed to aid in the collection, analysis, and management of classroom observation data.

Population

The EBASS is intended for use with at-risk and handicapped students in a diverse range of classroom contexts.

Description

The EcoBehavioral Assessment Systems Software Ver. 3.0 (EBASS) is designed to assist in the recording of direct observation data taken in the classroom. The EBASS consists of three similar observation protocols. CISSAR (Code for Instructional Structure and Student Academic Response), MS-CISSAR(Mainstream Version of the CISSAR), and ESCAPE (Ecobehavioral System for Complex Assessments of Preschool Environments) are all part of the EBASS package and are designed to address specific circumstances. Each instrument includes a taxonomy of environmental and behavioral events that can be coded. Taxonomies contain operational definitions of student behaviors, teacher behaviors, and classroom ecology. The CISSAR, provides codes for 55 events and is most appropriate for observing general education settings (K–12). The MS-CISSAR, employs an event taxonomy of 101 codes and is most appropriate for observing children with special needs across a range of settings. The ESCAPE uses 92 event codes and is most appropriate for preschool and kindergarten aged children.

A laptop computer's keyboard is used to record student behavior, teacher behavior, and ecological events using momentary time sampling. Due to the large number of codeable events the student behavior, teacher behavior, and class ecology are coded separately on three consecutive intervals. Interval length is dependent upon the instrument used with the CISSAR, MS-CISSAR, and ESCAPE employing 10, 20, and 15-second intervals respectively. The EBASS includes training materials designed to teach observers to use the observation software reliably.

Administration

The EBASS can be completed by a trained individual who is familiar with the taxonomy, has completed basic training using the materials provided, and has met criterion on the reliability standards for a given instrument. Observations of varying lengths can be completed based on clinical and practical considerations.

Scoring

All scoring for the EBASS is completed through computerized data analysis tools. The user can select which analyses are of interest. The analyses range from simple to complex and consist of: percent occurrence for each variable observed by category, graphic display of each variable, a minute by minute engagement analysis, profile analysis of similarity/discrepancy between persons or settings, and an ecobehavioral analysis relying on conditional probabilities. The data obtained can also be exported from the software program for use in other statistical analysis programs.

Psychometric Properties

Reliability: The EBASS provides tools to help ensure that new observers use the software and operational definitions reliably. The EBASS provides training software, video taped observations, and standardization data. In addition, the software can calculate agreement statistics for training data and the authors provide recommendations regarding agreement criteria that indicate the completion of training. The software also allows testing of interobserver agreement directly with the Data Reliability function. This function calculates the percent agreement and the *kappa* statistic between two observers.

Validity: The EBASS is an observation tool and as a result the primary technical consideration is the extent to which observers can accurately measure behavior using this tool. All three instruments provided in the EBASS have undergone prior validations and have been employed in published research. The published research supports the ability of observers to use the EBASS instruments reliably and as well as the instruments' utility.

Clinical Utility

High. The EBASS applies computerized efficiency to old paper and pencil observation technology. The computerized data analysis allows results to be immediately available, saves time, and eliminates the risk of calculation errors. The EBASS provides thorough training procedures and allows the user to customize the observation by reducing the number of codes within a taxonomy. Finally, data exporting procedures allow the user to complete alternative forms of analyses when appropriate, adding flexibility to the assessment.

Strengths/Limitations

The EBASS' strengths are its structure, the large number of codes available, the detailed training materials, and its flexibility of use. However, it is limited by two factors. In order to record the numerous codes employed in the EBASS student behavior, teacher behavior, and classroom ecology are coded on successive intervals. This places some temporal distance between events (up to 60 seconds in the CISSAR) and introduces a degree of inaccuracy (Greenwood, Carta & Dawson, 2000). Another limitation is the need for large amounts of data to complete some statistical analyses. At least 60 sequences of data must be recorded to complete the ecobehavioral analysis. This can require relatively long observation samples that will be difficult to obtain to obtain in some cases.

Authors: Charles R. Greenwood, Judith J. Carta, Debra Kamps, and Joseph Delquari.

Publication Year: 1992.

Source: Juniper Gardens Children's Project, 650 Minnesota Ave., 2ndFloor, Kansas City, KS 66101 (193) 321-3143.

Fee: Yes.

ADDITIONAL INFORMATION/REFERENCES

Greenwood, C. R., Carta, J. J., & Dawson, H. (2000). Ecobehavioral assessment systems software (EBASS) A system for observation in education settings. In T. Thompson, D. Felce, & F. J. Symons (Eds), *Behavioral Observation* (pp. 229–251). Baltimore: Paul H. Brookes Publishing Co.

Greenwood, C. R., Carta, J. J., Kamps, D., Terry, B., & Delquadri, J. (1994). Development and validation of standard classroom observation systems for school practitioners: Ecobehavioral assessment systems software (EBASS). *Exceptional Children, 61,* 197–210.

EMOTIONAL AND BEHAVIOR PROBLEM SCALE

Reviewed by: Monique LeBlanc & Mary Lou Kelley

Purpose

To provide a method of early identification of students with behavior disorders or emotional disturbance.

Population

This measure is designed for children ages 4.5 to 21 years.

Description

The Emotional and Behavior Problem Scale, a 58-item rating scale, is completed by teachers or other educational personnel on a single student. It has a 7-point Likert scale with items ranging from 1 (not in my presence) to 7 (more than once an hour). The instrument contains two sets of subscales. One set, labeled the theoretical interpretation, is based upon the federal definition of "seriously emotionally disturbed" contained in PL 94–142. It consists of five subscales: Learning, Interpersonal Relationships, Inappropriate Behavior, Unhappiness/Depression, and Physical Symptoms/Fears. The second set of subscales, labeled the empirical interpretation, is based upon factor analyses and includes five subscales: Social Aggression/Conduct Disorder. Social-Emotional Withdrawal/Depression, Learning/Comprehension Disorder, Avoidance/Unresponsiveness, and Aggressive/Self-Destructive.

An IEP and intervention manual accompanies the EBPS and contains recommendations for each of the behaviors of the scale. It also contains sample behavioral forms, contracts, and reinforcer menus. This may be helpful in delineating treatment recommendations for students. However, the recommendations would need to be tailored to individual students.

Administration

The EBPS can be completed by teachers of students ages 4.5 to 21 years, or any school personnel who knows the child well. The measure was not designed to be completed by parents as the primary focus is upon school behaviors. The scale takes approximately 15 minutes to complete. All items must be completed in order to score the EBPS.

Scoring

Raw scores, standard scores, and percentile ranks can be obtained for each interpretation and its subscales. Scores below one standard deviation from the mean are considered to imply serious difficulty. Separate norms are provided for males and females in three age groups, 4.5 to 11 years, 12–14 years, and 15–20 years. The manual does not report how many students in each cell. Furthermore, the interpretation section of the EBPS manual is unclear and difficult to read.

Psychometric Properties

Norms: The EBPS was normed on 2,988 students from 23 states. 867 teachers completed the measure. Gender and age frequencies were reported and approached national averages; however, minority groups appear to be underrepresented within this sample. No demographics were reported on the teachers who completed the measure.

Reliability: Internal consistency ranged from .77 to .95 for the theoretical interpretation and .85 to .97 for the empirical interpretation. Test-retest reliability was reported to be conducted after 30 days with 201 students. Correlations ranged from .87 to .93 for both interpretations. Inter-rater reliability was .83 or above for all age levels. No forms of reliability were reported for any of the six normative groups.

Validity: Procedures to achieve content validity are described in the manual. Factor analyses were utilized to create the five subscales of the empirical interpretation. These analyses did not appear to justify the use of the five theoretical interpretation subscales. Criterion-related validity was investigated by correlating the EBPS with another rating scale, the Behavior Evaluation Scale (BES). Correlations between the BES and the theoretical interpretation of the EBPS were moderate. Another attempt to validate the measure involved comparing the standard scores of 284 behaviorally disordered male students with an equal number from the normative sample. Differences were found between groups for both interpretations; however, means were not reported.

Clinical Utility

Limited. The clinical utility of the EBPS appears limited at this time. The scale cannot be used for its intended purpose, classification decisions, until further investigation of validity are conducted.

Strengths/Limitations

Strengths of the EBPS include the ease of administration. Preliminary reliability information appears strong. Limitations include limited investigations of validity, lack of support for the theoretical interpretation, difficult to read manual, and lack of information regarding the normative sample and the subscales. Furthermore, no sensitivity or specificity information was included in the manual. These issues demonstrate the necessity for further investigation prior to the use of the EBPS as a classification tool.

Author: Fredrick Wright.

Publication Year: 1989.

Source: Hawthorne Educational Services, Inc., 800 Gray Oak Dr., Columbia, MO 65201., Call: (573) 874-1710. Fax: 1-800-442-9509.

ADDITIONAL INFORMATION/REFERENCES

Grill, J. J. (1989). Review of Emotional and Behavior Problem Scale. In *Mental Measurement Yearbook, Vol. 12* pp. 342–343.

Reinehr, R. C. (1989). Review of Emotional and Behavior Problem Scale. In *Mental Measurement Yearbook, Vol. 12* pp. 343–344.

EMOTIONAL OR BEHAVIOR DISORDER SCALE—HOME AND SCHOOL VERSIONS

Reviewed by: Nicole Francingues Lanclos and Mary Lou Kelley

Purpose

To assess behavioral and emotional problems of students for the purposes of early identification and provision of educational services. The scale is in accordance with the federal definition of special education classification of emotionally disturbed/behaviorally disordered children represented by PL 94–142.

Population

The EBDS Home Version has been developed for use with school age children $4^1/_2$ to 21 years, and the School Version is standardized for children age $4^1/_2$ to 20 years.

Description

The EBDS consist of Home and School versions that are formatted and scored similarly. The EBDS Home Rating Form consists of 59 items, and the School Rating Form consists of 64 items. The items on the questionnaires describe specific, observable behaviors with examples provided for clarification. Items are rated by frequency of occurrence on a 7-point Likert scale ranging from 1 = Not in my Presence to 7 = More than Once and Hour. The EBDS Home and School Versions yield three subscale scores: Academic, Social Relationships, and Personal Adjustment. Five and six standardization groups are available divided by gender and age levels for the Home and School Versions, respectively.

Administration

The EBDS Home and School Versions can be completed by parents or guardians and teachers who are familiar with the child's behavior. Completion time is less than 20 minutes.

Scoring

Raw scores from the three subscales, Academic, Social Relationships, and Personal Adjustment, are converted into subscale standard scores and percentile rankings. The standard scores are such that lower scores represent higher levels of psychopathology which is opposite from most other assessment measures and may be a point of confusion.

Psychometric Properties

Norms: The EBDS-Home Version was normed on 1,769 children and 1,845 parents/guardians from 18 states. The School Version was normed on 3,188 students and 867 teachers from 23 states. According to the author, the sample demographics approximate those of the national distribution; however, African American children are underrepresented in the sample and other ethnicities were not included. Additionally, demographic characteristics of the sample and sample selection process were not fully described.

Reliability: Internal consistency, inter-rater reliability, and test-retest reliability were high for both scales. Inter-rater reliability averaged .85 and .89 across the subscales for the home and school versions, respectively.

Validity: The validity of the EBDS appears to be adequate with several concerns with both versions of the scale. The factor structures are questionable given the high level of correlation between subscales. For example, the Personal Adjustment and Social Relationships subscales have a correlation coefficient of .907 for the School version and .806 for the Home version. To measure the diagnostic validity of the scales, the author reports a study comparing behaviorally disordered students with randomly selected students from the normative sample and compares subscale mean standard scores between the groups. A more powerful statistical analysis such as discriminant function analyses would provide stronger support for the diagnostic validity of the instrument. Finally, to assess the criterion-related validity of the instruments, the manual reports subscale correlations ranging from .55 to .72 between the EBDS and the Behavior Evaluation Scale (McCarney, Leigh, & Cornbleet, 1983) for the School Rating Form and the Behavior Rating Profile (Brown & Hammill, 1978) for the Home Rating Form.

Clinical Utility

Adequate. In spite of the concerns regarding the validity, the theoretical design of the instrument is commensurate with the federal definition of emotionally disturbed/behaviorally disordered and may prove useful for identification and placement purposes. Items are behaviorally worded and scores reflect the frequency of occurrence.

Strengths/Limitations

The EDBS is unique in its concordance with PL 94:142 criteria rather than DSM-IV criteria for educational diagnostic purposes. An accompanying intervention manual facilitates the development of individualized education programs and treatment. However, the development, standardization, and psychometric properties of the instrument remain a significant concern.

Author: Stephen B. McCarney, Ed.D.

Publication Year: 1991–1992.

Source: Hawthorne Educational Services, Inc., 800 Gray Oak Drive, Columbia, MO 65201, (573) 874-1710.

Fee: Yes.

ADDITIONAL INFORMATION/REFERENCES

Brown, L., & Hammill, D. (1978). *Behavior Rating Profile*. Austin, TX: Pro-Ed.

McCarney, S. B., Leigh, J. E., & Cornbleet, J. E. (1983). *Behavior Evaluation Scale*. Columbia, MO: Educational Services.

EYBERG CHILD BEHAVIOR INVENTORY/SUTTER-EYBERG STUDENT BEHAVIOR INVENTORY—REVISED

Reviewed by: Sara E. Sytsma & Mary Lou Kelley

Purpose

To assess parents' and teachers' perceptions of conduct problems in children.

Population

Children aged 2 to 16.

Description

The Eyberg Child Behavior Inventory (ECBI) is a 36-item parent report measure of commonly occurring, problematic child behavior. The ECBI consists of two scales, the Intensity scale and the Problem scale. The Intensity scale measures the frequency of the child's behavior with item ratings ranging from 1 (Never) to 7 (Always). On the Problem scale, parents report if they find each of the behaviors to be problematic by circling either "Yes" or "No."

The Sutter-Eyberg Student Behavior Inventory—Revised (SESBI-R) is a comparable 38-item teacher report measure of conduct problems in the classroom with two scales identical in format to the ECBI scales. Items on both instruments are simply written, requiring a low reading level.

The ECBI and the SESBI-R measure problem behaviors in which both normal and conduct-problem children engage. The ECBI and SESBI-R are unique from other indices of child behavior problems, as they can be used to identify specific behaviors occurring at a high rate and perceived as problematic that can be targeted for treatment. The instruments also can be used outside of the clinical realm as potentially useful outcome measures of general parent education programs. One caveat of these instruments is that all items are negatively worded, which may lead to response bias and/or a focus on problem behavior rather than appropriate behavior.

The ECBI and SESBI-R are *not* designed to be used diagnostically. Rather, the instruments are to be used to identify children that may benefit from intervention. For diagnostic purposes, the authors recommend using the instruments in combination with more comprehensive measures of child psychopathology.

The manual clearly presents information on the administration, scoring, development, and research supporting the psychometric properties of these scales. The authors have found the SESBI-R to be psychometrically stronger than the original SESBI, with enhanced item variability and a stronger factor structure.

Administration

The ECBI and SESBI-R each can be completed in about 10 minutes.

Scoring

Raw scores are summed separately for the Intensity and Problem scales. Raw scores greater than 131 on the Intensity scale and 15 on the Problem scale are considered to be clinically significant ($T = 60$ for both scales). On the SESBI-R, raw scores greater than 151 on the Intensity scale and 19 on the Problem scale are considered to be clinically significant. Constant cutoffs and consistent items across the age range allow for longitudinal measurement of conduct problem behavior.

Psychometric Properties

Norms: The ECBI was restandardized on an ethnically and socioeconomically diverse sample of 798 children between the ages of 2 and 16 years attending pediatric clinics in the southeastern U.S. Restandardization addressed criticisms of prior normative samples' over-representation of minority and lower SES families.

The original SESBI items were revised with ratings from a sample of 726 5th through 12th-grade students and then standardized on a sample of 415 elementary students in a single geographic location to create the SESBI-R. The sample consisted of students in regular and exceptional student classes, including children identified as having emotional or behavioral problems, learning disabilities, and mental retardation. Approximately half of the children rated were African American and half the children were Caucasian, with 16% living below the poverty level.

Reliability: The ECBI and SESBI-R have demonstrated very high internal consistency and high test-retest reliability. Interrater reliability for the ECBI and SESBI-R has varied (.60 to .97) with parents of preschool children have rating children less reliability than parents of adolescents on the ECBI.

Validity: Sufficient data support the validity of the ECBI and the SESBI-R. Convergent and discriminant validity has been demonstrated through correlations with observational measures and well-validated existing rating scales. Both measures have been shown to be sensitive to behavior change, by significant reductions in intensity and problem ratings following treatment of conduct problem children.

Clinical Utility

High. The ECBI and the SESBI-R are unique from other measures of conduct-problem behavior because they identify specific behaviors occurring at a high rate and viewed as problematic that can be targeted for treatment.

Strengths/Limitations

The ECBI is a well-developed scale with recently updated norms, strong psychometric properties, and high clinical utility for screening, treatment planning, and evaluation of treatment outcome. Although prior criticisms of the standardization sample have been addressed with the 1999 restandardization, further development of the ECBI should include a more geographically diverse normative sample.

The SESBI-R is a promising new scale with good initial psychometric properties and clinical utility for screening and treatment planning. However, additional research is needed to expand the norms to include older students, more geographic locations, greater ethnic diversity, and a broader range of socioeconomic groups.

Author: Sheila Eyberg, Ph.D. & Joseph Sutter, Ph.D.

Publication Year: 1999.

Source: Psychological Assessment Resources, Inc., P.O. Box 998, Odessa, FL 33556, Call: 1-800-331-TEST/ www.parinc.com

Fee: Yes.

ADDITIONAL INFORMATION/REFERENCES

Eyberg, S. & Pincus, D. (1999). *Eyberg Child Behavior Inventory/Sutter-Eyberg Student Behavior Inventory-Revised: Professional Manual.* Odessa, FL: Psychological Assessment Resources, Inc.

Reed, M. L. (1985). Review of Eyberg Child Behavior Inventory. In *Mental Measurement Yearbook, Vol. 9* pp. 567–568.

Watson, T. S. (1985). Review of Sutter-Eyberg Student Behavior Inventory. In *Mental Measurement Yearbook, Vol. 9* pp. 910–912.

FUNCTIONAL ASSESSMENT AND INTERVENTION PROGRAM

Reviewed by: Kristin A. Gansle & George H. Noell

Purpose

To assist school personnel in conducting and interpreting functional assessments for students' problem behaviors.

Population

The program is designed to be used by school personnel for students. No specific age range for target students is specified in the manual.

Description

This computer program uses a question and answer format to amass many different kinds of information that may be relevant to student misbehavior. It asks questions related to the student's current school situation, including demographic data, a variety of information related to the behavior, and information related to the environment(s) in which the behavior occur(s). The program then identifies possible factors that may influence the student's behavior, which the respondent is free to confirm or discard. Hypotheses regarding factors assumed to maintain the behavior are presented, as well as strategies and intervention suggestions for dealing with those behaviors. The respondent is also free to confirm or discard them. According to the manual, "professional judgment" is what drives the system, and the primary goal of the program is to improve positive learning outcomes for students with disabilities. The manual assumes that the respondent "consider" each question it asks carefully and answer as accurately as possible.

Administration

Answering all of the questions posed by the software can be accomplished relatively quickly, 15 to 30. However, this presumes that the respondent is prepared to answer questions regarding the temporal distribution, antecedents, and consequences of the behavior.

Scoring

There is no scoring for this instrument. The respondent answers the questions provided on-screen by the program, and functional hypotheses and intervention suggestions are proposed by the program. The respondent may then accept or reject the hypotheses and interventions that were derived from their own responses.

Psychometric Properties

Norms: No data were reported in the manual.

Reliability: No information regarding the reliability of the instrument is provided.

Validity: No information is provided by the authors regarding the validity or treatment utility of the hypotheses derived through this program.

Clinical Utility

Limited. It should be noted that the intervention recommendations generated by *FAIP* are very global in nature (e.g., behavioral contracting, compliance training). Taking these global treatment strategies and developing them into a procedurally stated plan that is linked to the assessment data, likely to be effective, and educationally appropriate, will require a high level of skill.

Strengths/Limitations

FAIP could be described as a structured interview format that primarily serves to record the respondent's assumptions and impressions regarding a student. As a result, the accuracy and utility of the *FAIP* will be determined by the clinical/educational skills of and the data available to the respondent.

Authors: William R. Jenson, Marilyn Likins, R. Brad Althouse, Alan M. Hofmeister, Daniel P. Morgan, H. Kenton Reavis, Ginger Rhode, Mae Taylor-Sweeten.

Publication Year: 1999.

Source: Sopris West, 4093 Specialty Place, Longmont, CO 80504, (303) 651-2829, www.sopriswest.com

Fee: Yes.

HOME SITUATIONS QUESTIONNAIRE—ORIGINAL AND REVISED, SCHOOL SITUATIONS QUESTIONNAIRE—ORIGINAL AND REVISED

Reviewed by: Aaron Clendenin & Mary Lou Kelley

Purpose

To aid clinicians in the identification of different situations that may present difficulties for children with behavior problems.

Population

HSQ: 4–16 years, HSQ-R: 6–12 years; SSQ: 4–11 years, SSQ-R: 6–12 years.

Description

The Home Situations Questionnaire and School Situations Questionnaire come in original (HSQ & SSQ) and revised (HSQ-R & SSQ-R) versions. These instruments are designed for the rater to give a "Yes" or "No" response indicating if the situation under consideration poses a problem for the child. If endorsed "Yes", a nine-point Likert-type scale is used to specify the severity (1 = Mild, 9 = Severe). The number of items that comprises each form is 1) HSQ: 16, 2) SSQ: 12, 3) HSQ-R: 14, and 4) SSQ-R: 8. The author's stated purpose of the original versions refers to gathering information regarding defiant, aggressive, and oppositional behavior. The revised forms are tailored more towards attention problems and, therefore, most useful with assessment regarding this aspect of ADHD.

Administration

All instruments are administered via paper-and-pencil format to a primary caregiver or teacher. These measures could be completed in about 5 minutes.

Scoring

The scoring for the original versions is done by summing all severity scores and dividing by the number of problem settings. This yields a mean severity score that is compared to norms tables in the manual. The revised versions also follow this scoring procedure, but with the addition of two factor scores on the HSQ-R (Factor 1: Compliance Situations and Factor 2: Leisure Situations). These subscales are composed of select items and are also compared to norms tables.

Psychometric Properties

Norms: These measures appear to be standardized on an adequate number of participants with an acceptable distribution of age and gender. Other demographic characteristics, however, were unclear from the manual.

Reliability: These instruments were shown to have good internal consistency and test-retest reliability.

Validity: These instruments are sensitive to treatment effects, discriminate between clinical and non-clinical groups, predict future conflict, and correlate significantly with other well-known measures of the same construct.

Clinical Utility

High. These instruments may be helpful when seeking to identify specific problem settings with behaviorally disordered children.

Strengths/Limitations

These measures are easy to administer and score. Their ample psychometric support makes them useful for a variety of clinical and research purposes. Caution is urged when using norms tables for traditionally underrepresented groups.

Author: Russell A. Barkley.

Publication Year: 1991.

Source: The Guilford Press, 72 Spring Street, New York, NY 10012.

Fee: Yes.

INDIVIDUALIZED CLASSROOM EDUCATION QUESTIONNAIRE: ACTUAL CLASSROOM—LONG AND SHORT FORMS, PREFERRED CLASSROOM—LONG AND SHORT FORMS

Reviewed by: Nicole Francingues Lanclos and Mary Lou Kelley

Purpose

To measure perceptions of the classroom environment among secondary school students and their teachers.

Population

Teachers and Junior and Senior High School Students.

Description

The ICEQ evaluates students' and teachers' perceptions of the Actual Classroom environment. In addition, the ICEQ has a form that assesses the Preferred Classroom environment. There are long and short forms for assessing the Actual and Preferred Classroom environments. The ICEQ-Long and Short forms consist of 50 and 25 items, respectively. Thus, the four versions of the ICEQ include the Actual Classroom-Long Form, Actual Classroom-Short Form, Preferred Classroom-Long Form, and the Preferred Classroom-Short Form. The wording between the Actual and Preferred Forms is almost identical except for the use of the word "would" in the Preferred Form to indicate that the rater is evaluating a preferred environment.

The ICEQ instructions are clear, concise, and easy to understand. The items on the ICEQ describe specific behaviors of the teacher as well as the students. Respondents rate items on a 5-point Likert scale by frequency of occurrence with 1 = Almost Never, 3 = Sometimes, and 5 = Very Often. The 50-item Long Forms and the 25-item Short Forms of the ICEQ both contain five subscales: Personalization, Participation, Independence, Investigation, and Differentiation. The ICEQ Long Forms contain 10 items per subscale, and the Short Forms contains 5 items per subscale.

Administration

The ICEQ can be completed by high school students and teachers. The estimated completion time for the long form is 15 to 30 minutes, whereas the short form takes between 10 to 15 minutes to complete.

Scoring

Scoring the ICEQ is fairly simple. Responses are tallied for subscales which can be compared to norms tables or summed for a Total score which also may be compared to norms.

Psychometric Properties

Norms: The ICEQ was normed on 3707 students from two separate samples in Australia. However, the data from the two nonrandom samples were combined to generate overall statistical information for the ICEQ without mention of analyses of significant differences between groups prior to combining the samples. Means and standard deviations of the demographic variables such as gender, grade level, or SES for the separate samples are not provided. The author indicates the two samples "were carefully selected to be as representative as possible of the population of school in New South Wales and Tasmania". However, no statistics of the standardization sample as compared to the national census are provided. Additionally, no information is provided regarding individual teacher characteristics in sample two, such as years of teaching experience.

Reliability: Internal consistency estimates for the ICEQ were adequate with alpha coefficients ranging from .67 to .92 and .63 to .85 for the subscales of the long and short forms, respectively. Test-retest reliability was only conducted on the ICEQ-Actual Classroom, Long Form with coefficients ranging from .67 to .83 for the five subscales.

Validity: To assure appropriate content validity, the author selected items following extensive literature reviews and interviews with teachers and students to ensure adequate representation of the classroom environment. However, the construct validity of the ICEQ is not clearly delineated in the manual. The manual provides mean correlations of a subscale with the other four subscales as an index of scale independence, i.e., individual subscale-subscale correlations are not provided to estimate independence of the subscales. Additionally, item/total score correlations for each of the five subscales are not provided in the manual; therefore, the statistical loading of individual items to a particular subscale cannot be evaluated by the consumer. The author reported the ability of the ICEQ to differentiate between the perception of students in different classrooms.

Clinical Utility

Limited. There are concerns regarding the selection of the sample and the lack of adequate construct validity data presented. However, the ICEQ may serve as a useful descriptive tool for teachers to evaluate their students' perceptions of the actual as well as desired classroom environment.

Strengths/Limitations

The ICEQ is unique in its evaluation of students' perceptions of their classroom environment. The instrument has good face validity, but additional psychometric properties are either limited or not presented in the manual. Also, it is not clearly described how the measure would foster classroom learning or performance.

Author: Barry J. Fraser.

Publication Year: 1990.

Source: Australian Council for Educational Research.

Fee: Yes.

INTERVIEW SCHEDULE FOR CHILDREN AND ADOLESCENTS

Reviewed by: Patrick M. O'Callaghan and David Reitman

Purpose

To assess childhood-onset affective disorders using a semi-structured, symptom-oriented psychiatric interview format.

Population

The Interview Schedule for Children and Adolescents (ISCA) is intended for use with children and adolescents aged 8 to 17.

Description

The ISCA was developed as part of a longitudinal study of the presentation, course, and outcome of affective disorders in children. The instrument is comprised of two versions: the "intake" ISCA for primary assessment and the follow-up ISCA for reevaluation.

The ISCA and follow-up version each contain 5 sections and additional items pertaining to the overall global functioning of the child. The first section, symptoms and signs, contains 69 items related to mood, anxiety, cognitive problems, problems in neurovegetative functioning, dysregulated behavior and conduct, and developmental difficulties. The second section, mental status, is comprised of 10 items regarding orientation, delusions, hallucinations, and other subsidiary relevant items. The behavioral observation section contains 17 items that examines the verbal, nonverbal, and motor expression of the child during the interview. The 6-item clinician's impressions section appraises the interviewer's impressions of the subject's social maturity. The final section, developmental milestones, contains an item on sexual behavior and an item concerning dating.

Administration

The ISCA is intended to be administered by an experienced clinician with training in semi-structured psychiatric interviews. The initial evaluation requires 2 to 2.5 hours with the parent and 45 minutes to 90 minutes with the child. The follow-up interview administration time may vary depending on comorbidity and the interim symptomatology.

The assessment consists of a series of standardized inquiries and prompts. The ICSA assessment begins with open-ended questions. The parent is typically interviewed first, followed by a separate interview with the child by the same rater. Separate sets of ratings for parent and child are entered during the interview. A third set of ratings, completed by the clinician, incorporates parent and child information.

Scoring

Most items of the ISCA are rated on a scale ranging from 0 (absence of a symptom) to 8 (severe symptom). A score greater than or equal to 3 has been defined as "clinically significant". Some items are rated on a 0- to 3-point scale where a score greater than or equal to two is "clinically significant". Categorical and subsidiary items are rated "yes" or "no" and mental status and clinician's impressions are rated on content-specific scales. Additional items are rated on a dichotomous scale designed to verify the presence or absence of significant symptoms. A single rating is derived for clinical impressions and behavioral observations. Diagnostic decisions are based on the rater's overall or single ratings for an item, which are applied to the relevant operational criteria.

Psychometric Properties

Norms: The ISCA was evaluated in 2 separate studies of 76 patients selected from a child outpatient service and a longitudinal study of diabetes. Participants ranged from 8 to 15-years-old and were predominantly Caucasian (60%) or African-American (30%). Raters included 2 psychiatric social workers and a master's level psychologist, who were paired randomly and alternated as an interviewer and observer.

Reliability: The large majority of the items had inter-rater reliability coefficients of .80 or greater. Parent and child reports were significantly related. Inter-rater agreement across two raters ranged from .64 to 1.00. Reports of internalizing and externalizing symptoms were equally reliable.

Validity: The construct validity of diagnoses generated from the ICSA were supported by data on psychosocial concomitants. ISCA-based diagnoses have also been reported to predict subsequent biomedical complications, supporting the predictive validity of these diagnoses.

Clinical Utility

Adequate. The lengthy administration time greatly detracts from the clinical utility of the instrument, but produces a large amount of clinical data.

Strengths/Limitations

The ISCA is structured around symptom reports, rather than a nosological system, which may aid in diagnostic decisions and could be used to explore alternative ways of defining disorders. The ISCA has been used in diverse medical and psychiatric populations. However, the instrument requires more psychometric support and is lengthy, which may limit its utility in typical outpatient practice.

Author: Maria Kovacs, Ph.D.

Publication Year: 2000.

Source: Psychiatric Institute and Clinic, 3811 O'Hara Street, Pittsburgh, PA 15213.

Fee: Yes.

ADDITIONAL INFORMATION/REFERENCES

McClellan, J. M., & Werry, J. S. (2000). Research Psychiatric Diagnostic Interviews for Children and Adolescents. *Journal of the American Academy of Child and Adolescent Psychiatry, 39,* 19–27.

Sherrill, J. T., & Kovacs, M. (2000). Interview Schedule for Children and Adolescents. *Journal of the American Academy of Child and Adolescent Psychiatry, 39,* 67–75.

LOUISVILLE BEHAVIOR CHECKLIST

Reviewed by: Aaron Clendenin & Mary Lou Kelley

Purpose

To aid caretakers in the conceptualization of behavior and communication of concerns regarding their children.

Population

School children from 4–17 years old.

Description

The Louisville Behavior Checklist (LBC) is designated into 3 separate forms, E1 E2, and E3, which are for ages 4–6, 7–12, and 13–17, respectively. Each form contains 164 items of prosocial and deviant behaviors divided into 20 scales for E1, 19 scales for E2, and 13 scales for E3. Each item is a declarative statement to be answered as true (T) or false (F) by a parent or guardian. E2 consists of all the scales for E1 except that Academic Disability replaces Intellectual Deficit, Learning Disability replaces Cognitive Disability, and the School Disturbance Predictor scale is discarded. The remaining scales are Infantile Aggression, Hyperactivity, Antisocial Behavior, Aggression, Social Withdrawal, Sensitivity, Fear, Inhibition, Intellectual Deficit, Academic Disability, Immaturity, Cognitive Disability, Learning Disability, Normal Irritability, Severity Level, Prosocial Deficit, Rare Deviance, Neurotic Behavior, Psychotic Behavior, Somatic Behavior, Sexual Behavior, and School Disturbance Predictor. The 13 scales of form E3 are Egocentric-Exploitive, Destructive-Assaultive, Social Delinquency, Adolescent Turmoil, Apathetic Isolation, Neuroticism, Dependent-Inhibited, Academic Disability, Neurological or Psychotic Abnormality, General Pathology, Longitudinal, Severity Level, and Total Pathology. The same checklist is used for boys and girls with sex-specific items labeled "For Boys Only" and "For Girls Only".

Administration

Approximately 20 to 30 minutes to a parent or guardian.

Scoring

There are several ways to score the LBC. For the paper-and-pencil version, a set of scoring keys is provided in the form of templates, which overlay the Answer-Profile Sheet for easy tabulation of raw scores. The raw scores for each scale are compared to general or clinical population norms given in the manual.

Alternatively, two versions of computerized scoring are available. An examiner can either use machine-scannable Answer Sheets to mail in to the Western Psychological Services (WPS) Test Report service or obtain computer disks for direct computerized administration or entry of item responses from an Answer Sheet for a printed report from the administrator's computer. The WPS Test Report covers all the needed information for analysis of scores and comparison to norms. Generally, it provides: profile of scores, validity of responses, description of elevated scales, and profile analysis of high and low scores.

Psychometric Properties

Norms: For standardization of general population norms, form E1 of the LBC was given to a sample of 287 male and female children ages 4–6 in various school settings in Louisville, KY. This sample was balanced for family income and race to represent the general population. Similarly, E2 was given to 236 children ages 7–12 from the same community.

For clinical population, norms were based on data obtained from children receiving psychological services.

Reliability: Generally, reliability scores were comparable for different age groups and populations. In forms E1 and E2, coefficients on the broad-band factor scales ranged from .80–.92, while narrow-band ranged from .70–.88 and special scales ranged from .85–.97. When combined into the Severity Level scale, a high reliability resulted ($r = .97$). For form E3, reliability coefficients ranged from .63–.94. All scales were acceptable except Adolescent Turmoil and Neurological or Psychotic Abnormality. Test-retest reliability for form E2 ranged from .45–.92

Validity: Validity data are limited and consist primarily of studies showing the LBC differentiates children with pathological disorders from those in the general population.

Clinical Utility

Limited. This measure is inconsistent and convoluted across forms. Furthermore, its inadequate psychometric properties make it undesirable as a clinical tool.

Strengths/Limitations

Given the small standardization sample and lack of reliability and studies showing validity, the clinical utility of the scale is poor. Also, factor scale names and items are outdated and negative with regard to contemporary practice.

Author: Lovick C. Miller.

Publication Year: 1984.

Source: Western Psychological Services, 12031 Wilshire Blvd. Los Angeles, CA 90025.

Fee: Yes.

MANIFESTATION OF SYMPTOMATOLOGY SCALE

Reviewed by: Nicole Francingues Lanclos and Mary Lou Kelley

Purpose

To assess self-reported behavioral and emotional problems in adolescents.

Population

The MOSS was developed for use with adolescents between the ages of 11 and 18 years.

Description

The MOSS is a 124-item adolescent self-report questionnaire consisting of brief statements describing an array of behaviors and emotional states. The MOSS utilizes a True-False response format with items both positively and negatively keyed, 66 and 58 items respectively. Although several items are written at the fourth grade reading level, most items are written on a first through third grade level. There are thirteen content scales, four validity scores, and three summary indexes that can be obtained from the MOSS. Content scales include Sexual Abuse, Alcohol and Drugs, Suspiciousness, Thought Process, Self-Esteem, Depression, Anxiety, Mother, Father, Home Environment, Impulsivity, School, and Compliance. The validity scores include the following: Inconsistent Responding, Random Responding, Faking Good, and Faking Bad.

The "Affective State" summary index is based on the sum the Depression, Anxiety, and Self-Esteem content scales with higher scores indicating greater emotional instability. Items on the "Home" summary index are summed from the Mother, Father, and Home Environment content scales and serves as a measure of the respondent's overall feelings about his or her parents and home life. The "Acting Out" summary index represents the respondent's potential to exhibit problematic behavior and reflects items from the Impulsivity, School, and Compliance content scales.

Administration

The MOSS is a self-report measure completed by the adolescent in 15–20 minutes.

Scoring

Scores from the MOSS yield four validity scores, thirteen content scale, and three summary indexes with higher scores representing increased symptomatology.

Psychometric Properties

Norms: The MOSS scales were normed on 713 adolescents. The author attempted to obtain a normative sample corresponding to 1990 national census with regard to ethnicity and geographic representation. Separate norms are available for males and females.

Reliability: Internal consistency estimates for the MOSS were adequate with alpha coefficients ranging from .64 to .85 for the content scales. Summary index internal consistency scores were somewhat higher ranging from .85 to .92 for the three indexes. Test-retest reliability ranged from .67 to .92 for the content scales and .88 to .95 for summary indexes.

Validity: Content, construct, and criterion validity was evaluated for the MOSS. The relationships between the MOSS and other measures of personality as well as internalizing disorders were examined with estimates of construct validity being in the high range. Predictive validity has been shown for several of the scaled scores including adolescents with "Home

Problems," "Alcohol and Drug Problems," "Sexual Abuse," "School Problems," and an "Unruly" group with relevant, sensitive scores being elevated as expected. Overall, the validity data support the usefulness of the instrument.

Clinical Utility

Adequate. The MOSS can be administered in less than thirty minutes and can provide a screening measure of internalizing and externalizing problems for adolescents.

Strengths/Limitations

The MOSS is a user-friendly, self-report screening instrument for adolescents that provides a useful array of psychopathology and personality scales. However, the standardization and reliability data were limited.

Author: Neil L. Mogge, Ph.D.

Publication Year: 1999.

Source: Western Psychological Services, 12031 Wilshire Boulevard, Los Angeles, California 90025–1251.

Fee: Yes.

THE MATSON EVALUATION OF SOCIAL SKILLS WITH YOUNGSTERS: SELF REPORT VERSION, TEACHER REPORT VERSION

Reviewed by: Patrick M. O'Callaghan and David Reitman

Purpose

To provide a measure of social skills, identify potential problem behaviors, and provide a measure of treatment outcome.

Population

The Matson Evaluation of Social Skills with Youngsters (MESSY) can be used with children ages 4 to 18, and has also been used with deaf children.

Description

The MESSY consists of teacher and self ratings. The teacher report version consists of a 64-item checklist of social behaviors that are rated by teachers on 5-point Likert Scale which ranges from 1 = Not At All to 5 = Very Much True. The self-report version is identical in format, but contains a 62- item checklist. These two scales may be used to determine the child's perception of their behavior compared to that of the teacher. Items on the MESSY are concrete and observable making the skills listed easily identifiable and face valid. Items on the self-report scale yield five factors: Appropriate Social Skills, Inappropriate Assertiveness, Impulsive/Recalcitrant, Overconfident, and Jealousy/Withdrawal. Items on the teacher-report scale yield two factors: Appropriate Social Skills and Inappropriate Assertiveness.

Administration

The teacher form can be completed in approximately 15–30 minutes. Teachers should wait approximately one-month before completing the MESSY to facilitate more accurate rating. Teacher judgment is required to determine if a student is capable of completing the self -report.

Scoring

Items are grouped by factor and are individually calculated. Factors II-V are combined to form the Negative Score. Factor I is subtracted from a constant to form the Positive Score. The Positive and Negative score are combined to determine the Total Score. MESSY scoring software is also available.

Psychometric Properties

Norms: A sample of 722, primarily Caucasian, Catholic and public school children from urban areas of Illinois were divided into two groups. The self-report group consisted of 422 children between the ages of four and eighteen with a mean age of 12 years. The remaining 322 children were rated by their teachers.

Reliability: Coefficient alpha was .93 for the teacher report and .80 for the self-report. Split-half reliability was .87 for the teacher report and .78 for the self-report.

Validity: The MESSY is correlated with other measures of social skills, such as the Child Behavior Checklist. The MESSY has also been correlated with teacher ratings of child popularity and social skills.

Clinical Utility

High. The MESSY is easy to administer and score. Items are specific and yield useful information about observable social behaviors. The self- report form may be inappropriate for children below the fourth grade level and children with severe developmental disabilities.

Strengths/Limitations

Factor structure and norms are tentative and require further investigation. However, the instrument is brief and easy to administer and score. The MESSY has also been used in a variety of populations and has been successfully translated into another language; yielding high reliability (Chou, 1997).

Authors: Johnny L. Matson, Anthony F. Rotatori and William Helsel.

Publication Year: 1985.

Source: International Diagnostic Systems, 15127 South 73rd Avenue, Suite H-2, Orland Park, IL 60462.

Fee: Yes.

ADDITIONAL INFORMATION/REFERENCES

Bell-Dolan, D. J., & Allan, W. D. (1998). Assessing elementary school children's social skills: Evaluation of the parent version of the Matson Evaluation of Social Skills with Youngsters. *Psychological Assessment, 10,* 140–148.

Chou, K. L. (1997). The Matson Evaluation of Social Skills with Youngsters. *Personality and Individual Differences, 22,* 123–125.

Matson, J. L., Macklin, G. F., & Helsel, W. J. (1985). Psychometric properties of the Matson Evaluation of Social kills With Youngsters (MESSY) with emotional problems and self concept in deaf children. *Journal of Behavioral Therapy and Experimental Psychiatry, 16,* 117–123.

Kazdin, A. E., Matson, J. L., & Esveldt-Dawson, K. (1984). The relationship of role play assessment of children's social skills to multiple measures of social competencies. *Behavior Research and Therapy, 22,* 129–140.

MULTIDIMENSIONAL SELF CONCEPT SCALE

By: Shannon Self-Brown & Mary Lou Kelley

Purpose

To serve as a comprehensive assessment of self-concept in youth.

Population

Youth aged 9–19 years in grades 5–12.

Description

The author of the Multidimensional Self Concept Scale (MSCS) defines self-concept as a multidimensional and context-dependent learned behavioral pattern that reflects a person's evaluation of past behaviors and experiences, influences current behavior, and predicts future behaviors. The MSCS consists of 150 behaviorally worded items, which are rated on a 4-choice scale that ranges from Strongly Agree to Strongly Disagree. The MSCS presumes that self-concept is a learned behavioral pattern controlled by context-specific environments that are moderately intercorrelated. To reflect this idea, the MSCS contains six scales that represent the six environmental contexts in which youth spend the majority of their waking hours. The environmental context scales are as follows: Social; Competence; Affect; Academic; Family; Physical. The Total Score for the MSCS is derived from the combination of these scales and is reflective of the idea that self-concept is at the center of the various environmental contexts.

The MSCS is fairly easy to score. Each page in the MSCS record booklet consists of one of the six environmental context scales. Positively worded items and negatively worded items on each page are summed separately and then combined to create the raw score for each scale and Total Scale raw score is determined by adding the raw score sums for each of the six scales. Standard scores and percentile ranks for each of the MSCS scales and the Total Scale are located in the Examiner's manual.

Administration

The MSCS can be administered by anyone with training in test administration and can be completed in 20–30 minutes in most circumstances.

Scoring

The MSCS contains positively and negatively worded items which are scored oppositely, where "strongly agreeing" with a positive item and "strongly disagreeing" with a negative item both earn the examinee 4 points. Raw scores for the individual subscales are obtained by summing the respective items. These can be compared to standard scores or added for a Total score which is also compared to standard scores. A procedure for prorating Total scores when certain subscales are not used is also described in the manual.

Psychometric Properties

Norms: The MSCS was standardized on 2501 children from nine different states who were enrolled in Grades 5–12. The children ranged in age from 9–19 years and were representative of the U.S. population.

Reliability: Internal consistency for the Total scale was high, ranging from .97–.99. For the six MSCS scales, internal consistency ranged from .87 to .97. Test-retest correlations for the six scales and the Total scale were moderately strong and ranged from .73–.90, with no significant changes found between pretest and posttest scores.

Validity: To ensure content validity, the author conducted a thorough review of the self-concept literature and available assessment measures. The six domains represented in the MSCS were well supported in the literature. Concurrent validity was established by correlating scores from the MSCS with corresponding measures of self-esteem and self-concept including: Coopersmith Self-Esteem Inventory, Piers Harris Children's Self-Concept Scale, SDQ-I and SDQ-II. The correlations obtained between the MSCS and these measures varied considerably. Divergent validity was assessed by comparing the MSCS to the Assessment of Interpersonal Relations. The correlations obtained between these instruments suggested that different constructs are measured by each measure.

Clinical Utility

High. The MSCS provides an objective, clinical diagnostic tool or screening tool of self-concept.

Strengths/Limitations

The MSCS has a sound theoretical base, is easy to administer and score, and has good psychometric properties, which places this instrument above other currently available self-concept scales. One possible limitation of the MSCS is that preteens or youth with attentional problems may find it difficult to complete due to the length of the measure (150 questions). Overall, the MSCS should be considered an appropriate scale for measuring self-concept.

Author: Bruce A. Bracken.

Publication Year: 1992.

Source: Pro-Ed, Inc. 8700 Shoal Creek Blvd., Austin, TX 78757-6897, (800) 897-3202.

Fee: Yes.

ADDITIONAL INFORMATION/REFERENCES

Archambault, F. X. (1995). Review of the Multidimensional Self Concept Scale. In: *Mental Measurement Yearbook: Volume 12,* pp. 647–648.

Willis, W. G. (1995). Review of the Multidimensional Self Concept Scale. In: *Mental Measurement Yearbook: Volume 12,* pp. 649–650.

PERSONALITY INVENTORY FOR CHILDREN

Reviewed by: Shannon Self-Brown & Mary Lou Kelley

Purpose

To provide comprehensive and clinically relevant descriptions of behavior, affect, and cognitive status, as well as family characteristics for children and adolescents.

Population

Children and adolescents ranging in age from 3–16 years.

Description

The current revised version of the Personality Inventory for Children (PIC) contains 420 items with three sections that can be completed separately or conjunctively. Parents rate each item as "True" or "False" concerning their child's behavior. Responses to the PIC items are recorded on a Profile Form. Separate Profile Forms are available for boys and girls for two age groupings (3–5 years and 6–16 years).

The PIC contains four factor scales (Discipline/Self-Control, Social Incompetence, Internalization/Somatic Symptoms, and Cognitive Development) and 16 profile scales (Lie, F, Defensiveness, Adjustment, Achievement, Intellectual Screening, Development, Somatic Concern, Depression, Family Relations, Delinquency, Withdrawal, Anxiety, Psychosis, Hyperactivity, Social Skills). These scales were derived rationally rather than through empirical methods. Parents have the option of completing sections of the PIC or the entire scale. Parents completing Part I of the PIC answer 131 questions that provide information on the four factor scales and the Lie profile scale. Parents completing Part I and II of the PIC will complete an additional 140 questions which consist of abbreviated versions of the14 profile scales. Parents completing all three parts of the PIC will complete the entire measure which will provide information on the four factor scales, 16 profile scales, and the complete critical item set.

Administration

The time to complete the PIC varies according to how many parts the responder completes.

Scoring

Explicit instructions for hand scoring and computerized administration and scoring are provided in the PIC manual. Total raw scores for each scale are copied onto a Profile form and a profile line is drawn to connect the 12 clinical scales, the 4 validity and screening indicators, and the 4 factor scales. Instructions for interpreting the PIC profile are provided in the manual. Raw scores may also be converted to T-scores to allow for a more accurate form of interpretation. The more elevated the T-score, the increased probability the child has of psychopathology or deficit.

Psychometric Properties

Norms: The PIC was standardized for ages 6 through 16 years on 2390 children and adolescents from Minnesota public schools, medical centers, cooperating organizations, and door-to-door canvasing. The PIC was standardized for preschool age children on 102 boys and 90 girls.

Reliability: Test-retest reliability was completed for the 16 PIC profile scales, which had an average reliability coefficient of .86, and for the PIC factor scales, on which the majority of correlations fell between .82 and .97. Internal consistency was computed on 13 of the 16 profile scales. On these scales, which are assumed to be important for clinical populations, internal consistency estimates ranged from .57 to .86, with an average of .74. Studies on the same 13 profile scales were conducted to compare the degree of interrater reliability between mothers and fathers descriptions of their children using the PIC. Average correlations ranged from .57 to .69.

Validity: Construct validity was assessed in studies conducted to determine if factor scales would differentiate among homogeneous samples of problem children in a meaningful and predictable way. Significant differences were found between the homogenous groups indicating that the PIC could aid in child and adolescent diagnosis. Predictive validity was supported by a study showing a strong relationship between scale elevation and external child descriptors obtained from parents, educators, and clinicians. Validity studies were also completed on the 16 profile scales but the discussion of this data is beyond the scope of this review.

Clinical Utility

Adequate. The PIC can assist the clinician in gathering information from parents on their child's behavioral strengths/weaknesses and in establishing a focus for treatment. Additionally the PIC may be used to assess changes in psychological status over time.

Strengths/Limitations

The PIC provides a systematic inventory that can provide pertinent information about a specific child's current behavior. It is well researched and has strong psychometric properties. Limitations of the PIC include the True/False format, which may force parents to endorse behaviors that are rarely a problem for their child, the length of the PIC, and the technical manual which was very difficult to decipher.

Authors: Robert Wirt, David Lachar, James Klinedinst, Philip Seat.

Publication Year: 1990 (most recent version).

Source: Western Psychological Services, 12031 Wilshire Blvd. Los Angeles, CA 90025.

Fee: Yes.

PIERS-HARRIS CHILDREN'S SELF-CONCEPT SCALE— (THE WAY I FEEL ABOUT MYSELF)

Reviewed by: Joy H. Wymer & Mary Lou Kelley

Purpose

To assess self-concept of children and adolescents based on self-report. The measure focuses on the child's conscious self-perceptions, or self-esteem.

Population

The Piers-Harris is designed for use with children and adolescents ages 8 to 18 years.

Description

The Piers-Harris is an 80-item, self-report questionnaire consisting of statements describing people's feelings about themselves. Children are asked to decide whether each statement applies to them by indicating "yes" or "no". The Piers-Harris yields an overall assessment of self-concept and is broken down into six "cluster scales": Behavior, Intellectual and School Status, Physical Appearance/Attributes, Anxiety, Popularity, and Happiness/Satisfaction. The Piers-Harris also has two validity scales: Response Bias Index and Inconsistency Index. Raw scores are converted to T-scores, percentile ranks, and stanines. Total and subscale scores are figured such that lower scores indicated increased symptomatology.

The Piers-Harris instructions and scoring procedures are clear and concise. The authors discuss in detail the measure's guidelines for use and limitations. The Piers-Harris is accompanied by a user friendly manual, revised in 1984, that describes its purpose, interpretation and use, and reliability and validity.

Administration

The Piers-Harris may be administered either individually or in a small group. It is permissible to read the individual items to a child or to define words. Time to complete is 15–20 minutes. The Piers-Harris may be administered by a trained technician or paraprofessional under the supervision of a qualified psychologist.

Scoring

This measure can be hand scored or computer scored with the option of online administration and immediate scoring.

Psychometric Properties

Norms: For the total self-concept score, the Piers-Harris was standardized in 1960 on 1183 fourth through eleventh graders in one school district in Pennsylvania. Limitations of using the measure with other populations is discussed. Norms for the cluster scales were based on a sample of 485 public school children.

Reliability: With a retest interval of less than 4 months, test-retest reliability was generally .70 or above with a high of .92 for a retest interval of 3–4 weeks. The manual also cites studies of test-retest reliability in special populations. Various studies of internal consistency yielded coefficients of .88 to .93.

Validity: The authors seem to have put sufficient effort into ensuring content validity, but the manual provides few details as to their methods. Relationships between the Piers-Harris and other measures of self-concept as well as measures of personality and behavior were examined. Moderate concurrent validity was reported when the Piers-Harris was compared with corresponding measures; relationships with personality and behavior were reported to be in the expected direction. Intercorrelations between the cluster scores ranged from .21 to .59; items within a cluster were more related. Diagnostic validity was established by comparing nonclinical groups to mentally retarded, physically abused, and other clinical groups. Other studies have replicated all of the factors identified in the original study, identified additional factors, identified fewer factors, or found factor instability. Care should be used when interpreting cluster scores.

Clinical Utility

High. The Piers-Harris can be administered and scored in under 30 minutes and is cost efficient. Psychometrics are acceptable, but, as the manual suggests, the measure is intended as a screening instrument only; it is not to be used in isolation.

Strengths/Limitations

The Piers-Harris has good clinical utility and may aid in diagnosis and treatment. The measure's limitations are discussed candidly by its authors in the manual. They suggest cautionary interpretation due to the specific standardization sample and recommend not placing too much interpretative value on any individual responses.

Authors: Ellen V. Piers, Ph.D and Dale B. Harris, Ph.D.

Publication Year: 1996.

Source: Western Psychological Services, 12031 Wilshire Blvd., Los Angeles, CA 90025; Call: (1-800-648-8857).

Fee: Yes.

ADDITIONAL INFORMATION/REFERENCES

Epstein, J. H. (1985). Review of Piers-Harris Children's Self-Concept Scale (The Way I Feel About Myself). In *Mental Measurement Yearbook, Volume 9,* pp. 1167–1169.

Jeske, P. J. (1985). Review of Piers-Harris Children's Self-Concept Scale (The Way I Feel About Myself). In *Mental Measurement Yearbook, Volume 9,* pp. 1169–1170.

Piers, E. V. (1984). *Piers-Harris Children's Self-Concept Scale: Revised Manual 1984* (Rev. ed.). Western Psychological Services: Los Angeles, CA.

THE PORTLAND PROBLEM BEHAVIOR CHECKLIST—REVISED

Reviewed by: Shannon Self-Brown & Mary Lou Kelley

Purpose

To aid school and mental health personnel in identifying problem behaviors, making classification or diagnostic decisions, and evaluating counseling, intervention, or behavioral consultation procedures.

Population

The PPBC—R is intended for use with children and adolescents in grades K-12.

Description

The Portland Behavior Checklist-Revised (PPBC—R) is a rating scale designed to identify and rate specific problems that classroom teachers perceive of students in the classroom. The PPBC—R contains 29 items, which each describes an inappropriate behavior. The PPBC-R instructions are somewhat ambiguous. The choices for rating a behavior are No Problems, Minor, Moderate, or Severe. The scale includes no definitive explanation for what differentiates one rating from another, i.e. what makes a certain behavior minor versus moderate. An additional difficulty is that the items are not all observable behaviors. For example, the first item is "Negative self statements". It is likely that a teacher will have difficulty rating the frequency of this item.

The PPBC—R is accompanied by an easy to read technical manual. The manual describes the purpose of the test, normative data, and data on the measures of reliability and validity. Suggested uses of the PPBC—R are also included in the manual.

Administration

The PPBC—R should be completed by teachers who have daily contact with the student. The instrument can be completed within 15–20 minutes.

Scoring

The PPBC—R total score is computed by summing all items. The percentiles for total scores are presented in tables in the technical manual. Each item on the PPBC-R falls into a factor analytically determined subscale: Conduct Problems, Academic Problems, Anxiety Problems, and Peer Problems. Scores for each subscale are computed by summing the items in the subscale and percentiles are listed on the rating scale form.

Psychometric Properties

Norms: The PPBC—R was normed on 306 children and youth from 10 schools in Portland, Oregon and included only children in regular education. The norms were separated into males and females grades K–6, and males and females grades 7–12. The manual reported that the sample included representatives from different racial, ethnic, and socioeconomic groups, however, no adequate description of the demographic characteristics were provided.

Reliability: Internal consistency and test-retest reliability for the PPBC-R were adequate. Internal consistency was above .90. Test-retest reliability generally was above .78 for each of the age and gender groups. Inter-rater reliability and item reliability were not as adequate. Interrater reliability for the total score was estimated to be .54 and the item reliabilities ranged from .34 to 1.00.

Validity: To ensure content validity on the PPBC—R, the author included the top 29 most frequently identified problem behaviors among students referred to a community health program by school personnel. Construct validity for the PPBC—R was established by correlating scores with corresponding measures with good psychometric properties (e.g. AML Checklist, Walker Problem Behavior Identification Checklist, Piers-Harris Children's Self-Concept Scale, Waksman Social Skills Rating Scale). The correlations obtained were somewhat low ranging from .49 to .66. An attempt was made to measure changes on the PPBC—R following psychological treatment. The ratings for this group did show more improvement than a control group. Finally, a comparison of a group of emotionally disturbed children to a corresponding group from the normative sample was made to offer further support for construct validity. Significant differences between the two groups were obtained.

Clinical Utility

Limited. The PPBC—R is a scale containing items that are not worded behaviorally and are evaluated based on the rater's subjective opinion for what determines minor problems from major problems. The normative data are based on a small, regionalized sample which further limits the usefulness of this scale. These problems limit the clinical usefulness of this scale and indicate that instrument should not be used in a diagnostic manner.

Strengths/Limitations

The PPBC—R may be used for descriptive or screening purposes. However, the usefulness as a behavior rating scale is limited, mainly due to the lack of adequate psychometric and normative data. Overall, the PPBC—R should not be considered an appropriate instrument for assessing problem behavior.

Author: Stephen A. Waksman, Ph.D.

Publication Year: 1984.

Source: Enrichment Press, 54441 SW Macadam Ave., Suite 206, Portland, OR 97201.

Fee: Yes.

ADDITIONAL INFORMATION/REFERENCES

Stinnett, T. A. (1989). Review of the Portland Problem Behavior Checklist. In: *Mental Measurement Yearbook: Volume 10,* pp. 647–650.

Svinicki, J. G. (1989). Review of the Portland Problem Behavior Checklist. In: *Mental Measurement Yearbook: Volume 10,* pp. 650–651.

PRESCHOOL AND KINDERGARTEN BEHAVIOR SCALES: SOCIAL SKILLS SCALE, PROBLEM BEHAVIOR SCALE

Reviewed by: Kellie A. Hilker & Mary Lou Kelley

Purpose

The Preschool and Kindergarten Behavior Scales (PKBS) was developed to identify young children at risk for developing behavior or social problems. The author states that the scale can be a component of a full assessment on social and behavior problems and can guide the development of interventions. Lastly, this instrument was developed for future research on social skills and behavior of children age 3 to 6.

Population

The Preschool and Kindergarten Behavior Scales is an assessment instrument for children aged 3 through 6 years of age.

Description

The PKBS is divided into two scales. The Social Skills scale measures both peer-related and adult-related social behaviors. This scale has 34 items presented as a 4-point scale from 0 never to 3 often. Three subscales comprise the first scale: Social Cooperation, Social Interaction, and Social Independence. The Problem Behavior scale is divided into two Area scales of Internalizing Problems and Externalizing Problems. There are 42 questions on the Problem

Behavior scale, which are presented in the same format as the first scale. This scale has 5 subscales: Self-Centered/Explosive, Attention Problems/ Overactive, Antisocial/ Aggressive, Social Withdrawal, and Anxiety/ Somatic Problems.

Administration

The PKBS can be completed by teachers, parents, or other adults familiar with the child. Completion of the measure will take approximately 8 to 12 minutes.

Scoring

Raw scores are summed for subscale, area, and total scores. These are then converted into percentile ranks, standard scores, and functional levels using the tables provided in the manual. Functional levels are identified by percentile ranks. For the Social Skills scale functional levels fall into one of 4 categories including high functioning, average, moderate deficit, and significant deficit. The Problem Behavior scale has five possible functional levels including high functioning, average, moderate problem, and significant problem.

Psychometric Properties

Norms: The PKBS was developed using 2855 children, which represented a heterogeneous sample. The variables of sex, age, ethnicity, parent occupation, and socioeconomic status were evaluated during the standardization process. Children aged 3 were underrepresented in the sample when compared to children in the other age groups. Occupation of parents was categorized into 7 nominal groups. The sample of children with parents working as operators, fabricators, and laborers (category VI) was overrepresented, while the sample of children with parents not currently in labor force (category VII) was underrepresented.

Reliability: Internal reliability was high. Test-retest reliability was reported for 3 weeks and 3 months and was moderate to high. Inter-rater reliability was low to moderate.

Validity: Validity of the PKBS appears to be adequate. Content, construct, convergent, and divergent validity appear to be in the moderate to high range. The factor structure of the Problem Behavior scale is not as clear at the subscale level; however, factor analysis supported the two area scores (Internalizing, Externalizing) of the Problem Behavior scale and the Social Skills scale.

Clinical Utility

Limited. Additional research is needed to further support the utility of the PKBS.

Strengths/Limitations

The PKBS is a brief measure making it useful for screening young children. Limitations include weak inter-rater reliability, minor problems with the standardization sample, and the inability of the instrument to contribute to treatment planning.

Authors: Kenneth W. Merrell.

Publication Year: 1994.

Source: PRO-ED, 8700 Shoal Creek Blvd., Austin, TX 78757-6869, (800) 897-3202.

Fee: Yes.

ADDITIONAL INFORMATION/REFERENCES

Macphee, D. (1998). Review of the Preschool and Kindergarten Behavior Scales. In J. C. Impara & B. S. Plake (Eds.), *The Thirteenth Mental Measurements Yearbook* (pp. 964–969). Lincoln, NE: Buros Institute of Measurements, University of Nebraska.

Watson, T. S. (1998). Review of the Preschool and Kindergarten Behavior Scales. In J. C. Impara & B. S. Plake (Eds.), *The Thirteenth Mental Measurements Yearbook* (pp. 771–773). Lincoln, NE: Buros Institute of Measurements, University of Nebraska.

REVISED BEHAVIOR PROBLEM CHECKLIST: PARENT FORM, TEACHER FORM

Reviewed by: Molly A. Murphy and David Reitman

Purpose

This instrument is intended to screen for common school-based behavior problems. It may serve to clarify differential diagnosis of the various disorders associated with these child behavior problems and can be used as a criterion measure for interventions.

Population

The Revised Behavior Problem Checklist (RBPC) is intended for use with children ages 5–18 years.

Description

The Revised Behavior Problem Checklist appears in teacher and parent forms. It consists of 89 questions on a three point scale ranging from 0 = not a problem, 1 = a mild problem, 2 = a severe problem. The parent or teacher answer questions from six subscales; Conduct Disorder (CD), Socialized Aggression (SA), Attention Problems-Immaturity (API), Anxiety-Withdrawal (AW), Psychotic Behavior (PB), and Motor-Tension Excess (ME). The questions were derived from a review of factors indicative of clinical child problems from over 40 published studies (Dezolt, 1992).

Administration

The RBPC can be administered by individuals with at least a Master's Degree. It can be completed by either a parent or teacher in approximately 10 minutes.

Scoring

The scale can be scored manually. Tables are provided for conversion of the raw score to T-scores. Of the 89 questions, twelve do not load on a specific factor and contribute only to the full scale score.

Psychometric Properties

Norms: The norms for the RBPC only allow for the generation of a T-score from similar comparison groups within the manual. Comparison norm groups were obtained from various settings, clinical and non-clinical. Samples included children from private psychiatric facilities, outpatient and inpatient clinics, a private school for learning disabilities, another school specializing in learning disabilities sponsored by the community, and a summer camp for children in grades 1 through 8 with diabetes (Shapiro, 1992). The norms reported in the manual are not gender or grade specific. No national norms are reported and the development of local norms is recommended.

Reliability: Overall, internal consistency for the scale and it subscales appear good (range .70 to .95).

Validity: Discriminant validity were reported in the manual contrasting a clinical sample and control group on all six subscales (Dezolt, 1992). High correlations were found between the revised scale and the original Behavior Problem Checklist, as well as the Child Behavior Profile. In other studies using the RBPC however, no relationship was observed between direct observations and the RBPC subscales (Shapiro, 1992). Based upon the mixed validity data, Tryon (1994) reported a need for a more content-valid behavioral measure of child behavior problems.

Clinical Utility

Limited. The scale was intended for use in clinical, research, and educational settings.

Strength/Limitations

Problems with the representativeness of norms should be taken into consideration when using this scale for research. On a positive note, the scale can provide a good framework to identify potential behavior problems in a clinical setting.

Authors: Herbert C. Quay, Ph.D. and Donald R. Peterson, Ph.D.

Publication Year: 1989.

Source: Herbert Quay.

Fee: Yes.

ADDITIONAL INFORMATION/REFERENCES

Dezolt, D. M. (1992). Review of the Revised Behavior Problem Checklist. *MMY Review, 11,* 764–765.

Hogan, A., Quay, H. C., Vaughn, S., Shapiro, S. (1989). Revised Behavior Problem Checklist: Stability, prevalence, and incidence of behavior problems in kindergarten and first-grade children. *Psychological Assessment, 1,* 103–111.

Shapiro, E. S. (1992). Review of the Revised Behavior Problem Checklist. *MMY Review, 11,* 765–766.

Simpson, R. G. (1991). Agreement among teachers of secondary students in using the Revised Behavior Problem Checklist to identify deviant behavior. *Behavioral Disorders, 17,* 66–71.

Tryon, W. W. & Pinto, L. P. (1994). Comparing activity measurements and ratings. *Behavior Modification, 18,* 251–261.

SCHOOL ARCHIVAL RECORDS SEARCH

Reviewed By: Sara E. Sytsma & Mary Lou Kelley

Purpose

To systematically code and quantify archival school records.

Population

Elementary school-aged children.

Description

The School Archival Records Search (SARS) is designed to systematically integrate information available in school records to assist with school-based decision making related to students at risk for behavior disorders and later school dropout. The SARS can also be used in compliance with the P.L. 94–142 requirement for systematic examination of a student's school history and as a fourth stage of screening in conjunction with the Systematic Screening for Behavior Disorders (SSBD; Walker & Severson, 1990).

The School Archival Records Search (SARS) quantifies scores on 11 archival variables, including Demographics, Attendance, Achievement Test Information, School Failure, Disciplinary Contacts, Within-school Referrals, Certification for Special Education, Placement Out of Regular Classroom, Receiving Chapter I Services, Out-of-school Referrals, and Negative Narrative Comments. These variables can be aggregated into 3 domain scores: Disruption, Needs Assistance, and Low Achievement.

The SARS is designed for evaluating records across an entire school year, and is recommended for use either at the end or beginning of the school year, referring to records from the most recently completed school year. The SARS is most beneficial as a screening tool for use by school personnel.

The SARS manual is straightforward and thorough, providing useful information regarding test rationale, administration and scoring procedures, interpretation and application of results, as well as development and standardization of the scale. A valuable feature of the SARS is inclusion of multiple scoring methods derived for various applications, including systematic screening and research.

Administration

The SARS can be completed by school personnel in 15 to 30 minutes.

Scoring

Three methods of scoring the SARS have been developed and validated: 1) scoring individual variables, 2) calculating domain scores, and 3) calculating factor scores for each domain. Using the first method, each of the 11 variables are scored as "yes" or "no" based on criteria listed in the manual. The greater the number of variables scored positive, the greater the risk of school failure and dropout. Students with an externalizing profile are considered at high risk if more than 5 variables are rated "yes"; for those with an internalizing profile, the cutoff is more than 3 variables. The second scoring method aggregates variables into 3 factors. Positive ratings on two or more variables in a domain suggest high risk of a behavior disorder or school dropout. Elevations on individual factors have been shown to discriminate between externalizing and internalizing behavior problems, and may suggest particularly problematic areas. The third scoring method allows conversion of raw scores to standard scores which can be summed to determine factor scores. This is mainly recommended for use in research; although, a student's factor scores can be compared with mean scores for known groups in the normative sample to aid in interpretation.

Psychometric Properties

Norms: The SARS was normed concurrently with the SSBD on over 300 elementary school students in grades 1 through 6 from Oregon, although subsequent samples have included a total of over 800 students in grades 1 through 10 in Oregon and Washington. No information was reported regarding the demographic characteristics of the samples.

Reliability: The SARS was found to have excellent interrater reliability (above .9 for variables and the total form) and test-retest reliability after a one-week interval (mean = .96 overall).

Validity: Factorial and discriminant validity were supported. The SARS demonstrated a stable 3-factor solution. The factors discriminated between externalizing, internalizing, and normal control students, although the method of determining known groups was not described.

Clinical Utility

Adequate. The SARS has utility as a screening device for use in the schools, but its predictive value may be limited by use of dichotomous scoring on each variable.

Strengths/Limitations

The SARS provides a systematic method for aggregating readily available information found in archival school records. Initial psychometric properties have been found to be adequate. However, the measure would benefit from further validation in a geographically diverse sample with its characteristics described in greater detail. Utility of the SARS is limited by agents' access to necessary records, although presence or absence of many of these variables could be determined from interviews and parent records.

Authors: Hill M. Walker, Alice Block-Pedego, Bonnie Todis, & Herbert Severson.

Publication Year: 1991.

Source: Sopris West, 4093 Specialty Place, Longmont, CO, 80504. Phone: (303) 651-2829, Internet: www.sopriswest.com

Fee: Yes.

ADDITIONAL INFORMATION/REFERENCE

Walker, H. M., Block-Pedego, A., Todis, B., & Severson, H. (1991). *School Archival Records Search (SARS) Manual.* Longmont, CO, 80504.

SCHOOL SOCIAL BEHAVIOR SCALES

Reviewed by: Monique LeBlanc & Mary Lou Kelley

Purpose

To provide a screening measure for social skills and antisocial behavior in the academic setting. To be utilized as a part of a multi-method, multi-source assessment for educational placement and treatment planning. To investigate social competence and antisocial behavior in school age children.

Population

This measure is intended for children and adolescents in grades K–12.

Description

The School Social Behavior Scales is a 65-item rating scale for children in grades K–12. The SSBS was designed to be completed by teachers or other educational personnel on a single student. It has a 5-point Likert scale with items ranging from Never to Frequently. It consists of two major scales, Social Competence (Scale A) and Antisocial Behavior (Scale B). Each scale is broken further into three empirically derived subscales. Scale A subscales consists of interpersonal skills, self-management skills, and academic skills, and are positively worded. Scale B subscales consist of hostile-irritable, antisocial-aggressive, and disruptive-demanding, and are negatively worded. Scale A contains 32 items and Scale B contains 33 items. The manual notes that this measure differs from other measures as it focuses upon behaviors relevant to educational setting only. Low frequency, blatantly clinical items were not included.

Administration

The SSBS can be completed by teachers of K–12 students, or any school personnel who knows the child well. The measure was not designed to be completed by parents as the primary focus is upon school behaviors. The manual recommends that the rater must have had opportunity to observe the student for a minimum of six weeks. The scale generally takes about 10 to 15 minutes to complete. All items must be completed in order to score the SSBS. The scale can be used with regular education, special education, clinic, and at-risk children.

Scoring

The instructions for scoring the SSBS are concise and explicit. Standard scores can be obtained for Scale A and Scale B, but only functioning levels can be obtained for the three subscales of each scale. Levels range from Significant deficit to High functioning. For Scale A, higher scores denote greater social competence. For Scale B, higher scores indicate greater levels of problem behavior. Raw score conversion tables are separated into two overall grade ranges, elementary (K-6) and secondary (7–12). Gender and grade level comparisons are available, but the manual states that these should not be used for screening or placement due to the small sample in each cell. One potential scoring problems exists as the rater is instructed to score 1, or never, if the rater has not had the occasion to witness the behavior. Scores may be lowered, underestimating the students' skill.

Psychometric Properties

Norms: Normative data were gathered on 1858 students in grades K–12 from 22 different public school districts. Ratings were obtained from 688 teachers. Sample demographics underrepresented minorities as compared to national census data. Also, the northwestern portion of the United States appeared to be oversampled. Thirdly, socioeconomic status for approximately half of the normative sample was unknown. SES for the remainder was calculated by having the teacher list the occupation of the primary wage earner in the family. The category of Laborer appeared more frequently in this sample than in the U.S. general population. Lastly, SES was calculated by utilizing the primary wage earners occupation only.

Reliability: Internal consistency for the SSBS for both subscales was above .90. Test-retest reliability was calculated at a three-week interval with a sample of 72 teachers. Reliability coefficients for Scale A ranged from .76 to .82, while the coefficients for Scale B ranged from .60 to .73. Inter-rater reliability ranged from .72 to .83 for Scale A and .53 to .71 for Scale B.

Validity: The manual provides a description of the procedures to ensure content validity. Factor analyses were utilized to justify the use of three separate subscales on each of the SSBS scales. Criterion-related validity was established by correlating the SSBS with three other rating scales. These scales included: Wakesman Social Skills Rating Scale (WSSRS), Conners' Teacher Rating Scale (CTRS-39), and the Walker-McConnell Scale of Social Competence and School Adjustment. Moderate to high correlations were obtained. An additional attempt to establish criterion related validity was conducted by comparing the SSBS to a behavioral observation measure, the Child Behavior Checklist- Direct Observation Form, Revised (CBC-DOF). These correlations were low to moderate, ranging from .01 to .52. Finally, two investigations were conducted to examine the discriminant ability of the SSBS. Significant differences between the normative group and students with emotional, behavioral, and other difficulties were obtained.

Clinical Utility

Limited. The SSBS demonstrates potential as a screening tool in the academic setting. More research, especially by independent researchers, may be useful to establish its definitive usefulness.

Strengths/Limitations

The strengths of the SSBS include the ease and simplicity of administration and scoring. Additionally, current psychometrics appear satisfactory. However, limitations included inadequate information about test-retest over longer intervals, low correlations with measures of direct observation, and lack of studies by independent researchers. Furthermore, the usefulness of this measure with minority children is questionable due to the underrepresentation of minority children in the normative sample.

Author: Ken Merrell, Ph.D.

Publication Year: 1993.

Source: PRO-ED, 8700 Shoal Creek Blvd., Austin, TX 78757-6869, (800) 897-3202.

Fee: Yes.

ADDITIONAL INFORMATION/REFERENCES

Demaray, M. K., Ruffalo, S. L., Carlson, J., Busse, R. T., Olson, A. E., McManus, S. M., & Levental, A. (1995). Social skills assessment: A comparative evaluation of six published rating scales. *School Psychology Review, 24,* 648–671.

Hooper, S. R. (1998). Review of School Social Behavior Scales. In *Mental Measurement Yearbook, Vol. 13,* pp. 878–880.

Welsh, L. A. (1998). Review of School Social Behavior Scales. In *Mental Measurement Yearbook, Vol. 13,* pp. 880–882.

SCHOOL SOCIAL SKILLS RATING SCALE

Reviewed by: Mary Lou Kelley

Purpose

To provide a scale that consists of objective, socially valid and positively worded items that encompass social skills important to school functioning. Information gathered from the School Social Skills (S3) is used to determine a student's social skill acquisition in order to develop intervention plans and evaluate intervention effectiveness. The measure is not intended for use in diagnosis or discriminating special education from regular education children.

Population

The S3 is intended for use with children in grades K to 12.

Description

The S3 consists of 40 items that are rated using a 6-point Likert-type scale. Items are rated according to frequency: 1 = No Opportunity to Observe; 2 = Never uses the skill; 3 = Rarely uses the skill; 4 = Occasionally uses the skill and/or uses it an incorrect times; 5 = Often uses the skill under appropriate conditions; or 6 = Always uses the skill under appropriate conditions. The scale is completed by teachers or other school personnel very familiar with the student's behavior.

Initial items for the S3 were obtained by generating a positive alternative to items on a variety of school behavior questionnaires. Items were grouped into four categories: Adult Relations, Peer Relations, School Rules, and Classroom Behaviors. Items were reviewed by teachers and refined according to their suggestions. Examples of items included "Accepts criticism from adults concerning his/her inappropriate behavior", "Apologizes voluntarily to adults after engaging in inappropriate or accidental behavior", "Makes conversation when in the company of peers", and " Volunteers to assist peers when it appears they may need assistance". Items are not summed; rather items with ratings of "2", "3", or "4" are recorded on the form as behaviors targeted for instruction and reinforcement.

The technical manual generally is well written and the psychometric properties of the scale are adequately described. A unique feature of the S3 is that the manual lists component skills for each item.

Administration

The S3 can be completed in approximately 10 minutes.

Scoring

The scale is not scored as it is a criterion referenced rather than norm referenced measure.

Psychometric Properties

Norms: Standardization data are not available.

Reliability: Test-retest, and inter-rater reliability was adequate.

Validity: Minimal validity data are reported. The authors reported some content validity data with regard to item generation and refinement. Other forms of validity data are not reported.

Clinical Utility

Limited. The S3 is easy to administer, has considerable face validity and may be useful for identifying pro-social behaviors to include in an intervention. The lack of validity data limits the confidence with regard to the comprehensiveness of the scale and whether the items truly represent the most important social skills for classroom adjustment.

Strengths/Limitations

The S3 does provide a list of seemingly important prosocial behaviors and the component skills. It is limited by the lack of standardization data and psychometric support.

Authors: Laura J. Brown, Donald D. Black, and John C. Downs.

Publication Year: 1984.

Source: Slosson Educational Publications, Inc. P.O. Box 280 East Aurora, NY 14052-0280, (800) 828-4800.

Fee: Yes.

ADDITIONAL INFORMATION/REFERENCES

Demaray, M. K., Ruffalo, S. L., Carlson, J., Busse, R. T., Olson, A. E. McManus, S. M., Leventhal, A. (1995). Social skills assessment: A comparative evaluation of six published rating scales, *School Psychology Review, 24,* 648–671.

Bader, B. D. (1995). Review of the School Social Rating Scale. *Mental Measurements Yearbook, 12,* 932.

Wilkinson, W. K. (1995). Review of the School Social Rating Scale. *Mental Measurements Yearbook, 12,* 932–933.

SEMISTRUCTURED CLINICAL INTERVIEW FOR CHILDREN AND ADOLESCENTS

Reviewed by: Stephen D. A. Hupp and David Reitman

Purpose

To assess behavioral and emotional problems in children and adolescents. The Semistructured Clinical Interview for Children and Adolescents (SCICA) is one component of an empirically-based multiaxial approach to assessment and corresponds with the Child Behavior Checklist (CBCL; Achenbach, 1991a) and the Teacher's Report Form (TRF; Achenbach, 1991b).

Population

The SCICA is intended for use with children and adolescents aged 6–18.

Description

The SCICA is a standardized interview in which children and adolescents respond to open-ended questions. During the interview the clinician writes down the child's report of his or her own behavior and also makes observations of the child's behavior on the Protocol Form. The interview covers (1) activities, school, job; (2) friends; (3) family relations; (4) fantasies; (5) self-perception, feelings; and (6), parent- or teacher- reported problems. Along with questions covering these topics, the interviewer prompts the child to draw a picture of his or her family, administers mathematics and reading achievement tests (optional), obtains a writing sample, assesses fine and gross motor skills (ages 6 through 12 only), and assesses somatic complaints, alcohol, drugs, and trouble with the law (ages 13 through 18 only). The interviewer uses information from the Protocol Form to complete the Self-Report Form and the

Observation Form. The Self-Report Form contains 114 items for children aged 6 through 12 and 125 items for children aged 13 through 18, and the Observation Form contains 120 items. Items on both forms largely correspond to items on the CBCL and TRF and are scored on a 4-point scale which ranges from 0 = "no occurrence" to 3 = "a definite occurrence with severe intensity or 3 or more minutes duration."

A scoring profile has been developed for ages 6 through 12, and the authors are currently developing a scoring profile for adolescents. Five empirically-based syndrome scales were derived from items on the Observation Form (Anxious, Attention Problems, Resistant, Strange, and Withdrawn), and three scales were derived from the Self-Report Form (Aggressive Behavior, Anxious/Depressed, and Family Problems). Internalizing and Externalizing broad-band scales were derived from the narrow-band scales. A technical manual accompanies the SCICA which describes purposes of the interview, administration, normative data, and psychometrics.

Administration

The interviewer must have graduate training with at least a Master's degree (or two years residency) and supervised experience interviewing children. The open-ended questions take 45–60 minutes to complete, and the optional achievement tests and the fine and gross motor screen adds an additional 15–20 minutes. The additional questions for adolescents add 10–15 minutes to administration time.

Scoring

Scoring is similar to scoring the CBCL and can be done cumbersomely by hand or much more quickly with the computer scoring program. Raw scores are converted into subscale standard T-scores and percentile ranks, and higher scores represent more problems. All children aged 6 through 12 are grouped together and the same normative information is used for males and female. Scoring for adolescents must be done using the normative data for children; although, normative data for adolescents is currently being collected.

Psychometric Properties

Norms: The child interview was normed on 168 (119 boys and 49 girls) children ages 6 through 12. All of the participants were referred to the same clinic for psychoeducational assessments, and they were all Caucasian (except for one). Children were excluded from the sample if they had a full scale IQ below 75 or physical disabilities.

Reliability: Internal consistency for the subscales was above .81, representing moderate to high agreement. Test-retest correlations were .69 for Internalizing scale and .84 for Externalizing scale. Inter-rater reliability was .64 for the Internalizing scale and .72 for the Externalizing scale. All of these correlations were statistically significant ($p < .01$).

Validity: Children in a clinic-referred group scored significantly higher than children in a nonreferred group on all scales, except the Anxious scale. The SCICA also successfully differentiated between children classified with Emotional/Behavioral Disabilities and Learning Disabilities. Significant but modest correlations were found between the SCICA and the CBCL and TRF.

Clinical Utility

High. The SCICA is one component of a multiaxial approach to assessment, corresponding with other well-validated instruments (i.e, CBCL, & TRF). It adds structure to interviewing children and adolescents and addresses limitations of structured interviews. The SCICA has good reliability and validity and has been shown to aid in diagnostic decisions.

Strengths/Limitations

The SCICA has high clinical utility and adds to the other well-established measures of child behavior. There are currently no norms for adolescents and the normative sample for the children was small; however, the authors are currently developing new scoring profiles for children and adolescents.

Author: Stephanie H. McConaughy, Ph.D. and Thomas M. Achenbach, Ph.D.

Publication Year: 1994.

Source: Child Behavior Checklist, 1 South Prospect Street, Burlington, VT 05401, Web: http://Checklist.uvm.edu

Fee: Yes.

ADDITIONAL INFORMATION/REFERENCES

McConaughy, S. H., & Achenbach, T. M. (1994). *Manual for the Semistructured Clinical Interview for Children and Adolescents.* Burlington, VT: University of Vermont Department of Psychiatry.

McConaughy, S. H. (1996). The interview process. In M. Breen & C. Fielder (Eds). *Behavioral approach to assessment of youth with emotional/behavioral disorders* (pp. 181–241), Austin, TX: PRO-ED.

SOCIAL BEHAVIOR ASSESSMENT INVENTORY

Reviewed by: Mary Lou Kelley

Purpose

To assess performance level of social behaviors exhibited in the classroom.

Population

Children grades Kindergarten to 9th.

Description

The SBAI is a 136-item curriculum based measure of social skills intended to be used in conjunction the *Social Skills in the Classroom* (Stephens, 1992) curriculum. The measure is completed by teachers or other professionals familiar with the child's behavior in the relevant settings. It can be used as a direct observation measure or completed by the teacher based on his/her past observations of the student. The measure is intended for screening for social skill weaknesses or for intervention planning. Items are grouped into 30 subscales which are further grouped into four areas: Environmental Behavior, Interpersonal Behavior, Self-Related Behavior, and Task -Related Behavior. Items are positively worded and evaluated on a scale of 0–3. Environmental Behavior items deal with caring for the environment, dealing with emergencies, lunchroom manners, and moving about without disrupting others. Interpersonal Behavior items comprise the majority of the instrument and include an array of social behaviors such as accepting criticism, making conversations, and helping others. Self-related Behavior items tap accepting consequences, truthfulness, and positive self-evaluative actions. Task Related Behavior deal with academic performance.

Administration

The SBAI can be completed in approximately 30–45 minutes.

Scoring

Items are summed for each subscale and plotted on a profile grid. There are no norms and it is not clear how the authors determined whether a score is the elevated range or within the expected range.

Psychometric Properties

Norms: Standardization data are not available.

Reliability: Internal consistency and inter-rater reliability was good. Test–retest reliability was not reported.

Validity: Content validity was determined by asking teachers to evaluate item importance. Other validity data are limited but support the instrument.

Clinical Utility

Limited. The lack of standardization data, and psychometric support greatly limits the utility of the scale.

Strengths/Limitations

The SBAI has good face validity and would be useful when used in conjunction with the curriculum.

Authors: Thomas M. Stephens and Kevin D. Arnold.

Publication Year: 1992.

Source: Psychological Assessment Resources, Inc. P.O. Box 998, Odessa, FL 33556.

Fee: Yes.

SOCIAL COMPETENCE AND BEHAVIOR EVALUATION—PRESCHOOL EDITION

Reviewed by: Aaron Clendenin & Mary Lou Kelley

Purpose

To aid clinicians in the assessment of patterns of social competence, affective expression, and adjustment difficulties in preschoolers.

Population

Children from 30 to 78 months old.

Description

The Social Competence and Behavior Evaluation-Preschool Edition (SCBE), formerly called the Preschool-Socio-Affective Profile (PSP), is an 80-item questionnaire that consists of eight basic scales and four summary scales. The measure evaluates children's emotional, behavioral, and relational strengths and difficulties. The eight basic scales are comprised of 10 items each, half of which pertain to successful adjustment and half of which pertain to difficulties with adjustment. The first three basic scales describe a child's typical pattern of emotional response. These are Depressive-Joyful, Anxious-Secure, and Angry-Tolerant. The next three scales assess peer interaction. These are Isolated-Integrated, Aggressive-Calm, and Egotistical-Prosocial. The two remaining scales were designed to describe teacher-child relations. These are Oppositional-Cooperative and Dependent-Autonomous.

Four summary scales are derived from the eight basic scales. The Social Competence summary scale comprises 40 items and examines positive adaptive social behaviors. The Internalizing Problems summary scale consists of 20 items and represents behaviors that are typically associated with anxiety and depression. The remaining 20 items are found in the Externalizing Problems scale. This scale is an indicator of difficulties with behaviors in areas such as anger, aggression, and opposition. The General Adaptation summary scale is reflected in the totality of items and is intended for use as an overall index of functioning.

Administration

Approximately 15 minutes to a teacher.

Scoring

The scoring procedure for the SCBE is simple and can be completed in approximately 10 minutes. Each circled value is transferred to the scoring grid based on item number. Rows of five items are added for a subtotal score and two subtotal scores are added to form a Basic Scale raw score. Basic Scale raw scores are then transferred to designated positions and tallied to obtain Summary Scale scores. All appropriate scores are plotted on a profile sheet where they can be compared to percentiles and T-scores.

Psychometric Properties

Norms: Initial development of the SCBE was conducted on French-speaking Canadian children. After being translated into English in the early 1990s, standardization data was collected on 1263 American children ranging in age from 30 to 78 months. This was done with approximately 100 preschool classrooms at six sites from Indiana and Colorado. There were 824 preschool children (419 girls, 405 boys) in the Indiana sample and 439 preschool children (212 girls, 227 boys) in the Colorado sample. The demographics of this combined sample closely approximated the national averages, but with a slight underrepresentation of Caucasians and Hispanics and a slight overrepresentation of African-Americans and Asian-Americans.

Reliability: For the Indiana sample, interrater reliability for separate teacher ratings ranged from .72 to.89. Each of the eight scales was found to have an acceptable degree of internal consistency with correlations ranging from .80 to .89.

Validity: Evidence of convergent and discriminant validity was found through correlations between scales of the SCBE and Child Behavior Checklist (CBCL; Edelbrock & Achenbach, 1984). Criterion validity was established through peer sociometric ratings and direct observations.

Clinical Utility

Adequate. The SCBE is fairly comprehensive and useful in treatment planning with regard to interpersonal relationships.

Strengths/Limitations

The SCBE addresses competencies as well as deficiencies in a child's behavior. The six-point scale to assess the frequency of a behavior requires careful observation on the part of raters. Caution is urged due to the geographic limitations of the standardization sample.

Author: Peter J. LaFreniere & Jean E. Dumas.

Publication Year: 1995.

Source: Western Psychological Services, 12031 Wilshire Blvd. Los Angeles, CA 90025.

Fee: Yes.

ADDITIONAL INFORMATION/REFERENCE

Edelbrock, C. & Achenbach, T. M. (1984). The teacher version of the child behavior profile: I. Boys aged 6–11. *Journal of Consulting and Clinical Psychology.*

SOCIAL SKILLS RATING SYSTEM: PARENT RATING FORM—PRESCHOOL, ELEMENTARY, & MIDDLE/HIGH SCHOOL VERSIONS, SELF RATING FORM—GRADES 3–6 & 7–12 VERSIONS TEACHER RATING FORM—PRESCHOOL, ELEMENTARY, & MIDDLE/HIGH SCHOOL VERSIONS

Reviewed by: Mary Lou Kelley

Purpose

To assess student social behavior that can affect teacher-student relations, peer acceptance, and academic performance utilizing multiple informants. The Social Skills Rating System (SSRS) is designed to assist professionals in screening and classifying children suspected of having social behavior problems and aid in the development of appropriate interventions.

Population

The SSRS is intended for use for children in grades Pre-K–12.

Description

The SSRS consists of teacher, parent, and student rating scales for sampling the behavior domains of social skills, problem behaviors, and academic competencies. Teacher and parent forms are available at three developmental levels: preschool, elementary school, and middle/high school. Self-rating forms are available for students at two different grade levels (3–6 and 7–12). The various forms contain norms at each developmental level. Although social behavior is examined most comprehensively, the scale measures problem behavior and academic skills due to the relationship between these problems and social behavior deficits.

The Social Skills Subscale varies across the different versions, but each subscale consists of between 30–40 items. All items on the Social Skill Subscale of the SSRS are positively worded. The items are rated with regard to frequency (Never, Sometimes, or Very Often) and Importance (Not Important, Important, or Critical). Only students at the high school level rate importance.

The Social Skills Subscale for the teacher, parent, and student versions assesses social skills in three areas: Cooperation, Assertion, and Self-control. Additionally, the parent form assesses "Responsibility" behavior and the student version measures "Empathetic" behavior. Items on the " Cooperative" subdomain cover helping, sharing, and complying with rules and directions. Items on the "Assertiveness" subdomain assess initiating interactions such as asking for help and responding appropriately to the actions of others such as peer pressure. The "Self-Control" items are concerned with behaviors evident in conflict situations such as responding to teasing. The "Responsibility" items demonstrate an ability to communicate with adults regarding property or work. The "Empathy" items tap behaviors reflecting respect for the views of others and appreciation of the feelings of others.

The Problem Behavior Subscale measures Externalizing and Internalizing Problems, and Hyperactivity. Only the Teacher and Parent versions of the SSRS contain the Problem Behavior Subscale. The number of items ranges from 10–18 depending on the form. Problem behaviors are rated with regard to frequency (Never, Sometimes, Very Often).

The Academic Competence domain assesses student academic functioning in reading and mathematics and is completed by the teacher only. It consists of a == behaviors that are rated by the teacher on a 5-point scale in which the target child is compared to the other students (1 = lowest 10%, 5 = highest 10%).

The technical manual is very well written, clear, and thorough. The manual describes test rationale, test development, administration and scoring procedures, and presents the psychometric data supporting the reliability and validity of the SSRS. In addition, the manual presents a very thorough and useful discussion on the measurement of social competency and a guideline for selecting and a review of empirically based intervention methods. A unique feature of the SSRS is the Assessment-Intervention Record (AIR). The AIR is used to summarize and integrate data from the various informants, analyzing student strengths and weaknesses, functionally analyzing the functions served by the behavior, and developing an intervention plan.

Administration

Completion of the SSRS should take no longer than 25 minutes.

Scoring

The eight versions of the SSRS are scored in the same manner. The SSRS yields scores for each of the areas assessed as well as total scale scores for the Social Skills Subscale and the Problem Behavior Subscale. Raw scores are tallied within each area (e.g., cooperation, internalizing behavior problems) and summed together to form a total Social Skills and Problem Behaviors Subscale score. These raw scores are converted to standard scores and percentile rankings. Behavioral levels that compare the child's score for each area of competency are provided as well. Norms are available for the teacher, parent, and self-report versions at each developmental level. Additionally, norms for handicapped children are also available given the importance of social competency to integrating handicapped children into the regular classroom.

Psychometric Properties

Norms: The SSRS scales were developed and normed on a large heterogeneous sample. Attempts were made to obtain a normative sample that approximated the national distribution with regard to ethnicity, geographic representation, and community size. However, the sample slightly over-represented Blacks and Whites and under-represented Hispanics and other groups. Separate norms are available at each level (preschool, elementary school) each gender, and each informant (teacher, parent, self) as well as for handicapped children rated by their teachers.

Reliability: Internal consistency, test-retest, and inter-rater reliability was adequate to very good for almost all versions of the SSRS. The reliability data were more limited for the student self-report scale as would be expected.

Validity: Considerable validity data were obtained in support of the SSRS. Social, content, criterion related and construct validity were described in detail. The validity data supported the utility of the instrument.

Clinical Utility

High. The SSRS scales are easy to administer and score and allow for comparisons across informants. The AIRS greatly enhances the usefulness of the SSRS for intervention planning.

Strengths/Limitations

The SSRS is psychometrically sound, user friendly, and links assessment data to intervention.

Authors: Frank M. Gresham, Ph.D. & Stephen N. Elliott, Ph.D.

Publication Year: 1990.

Source: American Guidance Service, Circle Pines, MN 55014-1796. 1-(800) 328-2560.

Fee: Yes.

ADDITIONAL INFORMATION/REFERENCES

Demaray, M. K., Ruffalo, S. L., Carlson, J., Busse, R. T., Olson, A. E. McManus, S. M., Leventhal, A. (1995). Social skills assessment: A comparative evaluation of six published rating scales, *School Psychology Review, 24,* 648–671.

Benes, K. M. (1995). Review of the Social Skills Rating System. *Mental Measurements Yearbook, 12,* 964–969.

STRENGTHS AND DIFFICULTIES QUESTIONNAIRE

Reviewed by: Kellie Hilker & Mary Lou Kelley

Purpose

The Strengths and Difficulties Questionnaire (SDQ) is a brief screening instrument evaluating behavioral and emotional concerns.

Population

Children and adolescents 4 to 17 years old.

Description

The SDQ can be obtained from the Youth in Mind website. The proposed uses of the SDQ include clinical assessment, treatment outcome evaluation, epidemiological studies, general research, and screening. The SDQ consists of 25 questions, which are broken down into 5 scales: Emotional Symptoms; Conduct Problems; Hyperactivity; Peer Problems; and Prosocial Behaviour. A Total Difficulties score also is calculated. Examples of items on the Emotional Symptoms scale include "many worries, often seems worried" and "often unhappy, downhearted or tearful". The Conduct Problems Scale includes items such as "often has temper tantrums" and "often lies or cheats". Items on the Hyperactivity Scale include "constantly fidgeting or squirming" and "easily distracted, concentration wanders". The Peer Problems Scale includes items such as "rather solitary, tends to play alone" and "picked on bullied by other children". Finally, examples of items on the Prosocial Behaviour Scale include "considerate of other people's feelings" and "kind to younger children". Extended versions of the SDQ include an impact supplement to evaluate how much difficulties interfere with functioning in different areas (home life, friendships, classroom learning, and leisure activities). Another extended version has a follow-up version to evaluate the impact of an intervention by asking to what degree the intervention has been helpful and following up on problem areas.

The SDQ can be completed by parents, teachers, and a self-report version is available for adolescents aged 11 to 17. For the parent and teacher questionnaires, there are two versions, one for children aged 4 to 10 and the second for children aged 11 to 17. Each item on the SDQ is rated on a three-point scale with the choices being "not true", "somewhat true", and "certainly true".

Administration

The SDQ can be administered in approximately 5 minutes to a Parent, Teacher, or to the Adolescent being screened.

Scoring

A scoring template can be printed from the website onto transparency paper. Each item is given a score of 0 through 2. Each of the five scales is summed for scale totals. A total score is derived by summing all of the items except for those on the Prosocial Behaviour Scale. A record sheet also is available online to chart totals of the scales. The scores fall into three categories: Normal, Borderline, and Abnormal. The Impact Scores are calculated by summing the scores for each of the impact items. Impact Scores are classified as Normal = 0, Borderline = 1, and 2 or more is Abnormal. A predictive algorithm is found on the website, which predicts child psychiatric diagnoses from the scores derived on the SDQ. The predictive algorithm use four broad categories (conduct disorders, emotional disorders, hyperactivity disorders, and any psychiatric disorder). The algorithm calculates how likely the child has a psychiatric diagnosis with ratings of "unlikely", "possible", or "probable".

Psychometric Properties

Norms: A large group of parents (10,298), teachers (8208), and adolescents (4228) were recruited to obtain normative data. Normative information for Britain is available from the website. The normative information provided includes means, standard deviations, and frequency distributions by age band and gender. Limited normative information is presented for Finland, Germany, and Sweden.

Reliability: No explicit information regarding reliability of the SDQ is presented on the webpage, however, limited information can be obtained from the abstracts listed. In one study, an internal consistency coefficient of .71 was calculated with the Finnish version of the SDQ. A study evaluating the English version evaluated test-retest reliability after two weeks with the extended version with the impact supplement of the SDQ. Coefficients varied from .44 for an individual question assessing the burden of difficulties on the family to .85 for the Total Difficulties score. In general, there is initial support for adequate temporal stability for the SDQ and for the perceived difficulties questions found on the impact supplement.

Validity: As with reliability data, limited data about validity is presented on the webpage in the form of abstracts of articles assessing this variable. Concurrent validity with other measures of childhood psychopathology, like the Child Behavior Checklist, the Rutter questionnaire, and the Youth Self Report, resulted in moderately strong correlations. Additionally, the SDQ has been shown to be able to discriminate between psychiatric and dental clinic patients. Finally, the Swedish version of the SDQ utilized factor analysis to confirm the structure of the SDQ scales. Overall, initial support for validity of the SDQ is provided.

Clinical Utility

Adequate. The best use of this instrument appears to be for screening purposes. The author also suggests that the SDQ can be a valuable part of a clinical assessment, however, many alternative measures have more solid psychometric data and may provide a more thorough assessment.

Strengths/Limitations

The SDQ is a brief screening instrument that can be used to evaluate emotional problems, behavioral difficulties, and social concerns. In addition to focusing on problem behavior, the SDQ briefly screens for prosocial behavior exhibited by the child or adolescent. Due to the brevity of the measure and the inclusion of questions assessing prosocial behavior, this may be an acceptable instrument for parents, teachers, and adolescents. The SDQ has over 40 translations available for downloading from the website, however, normative data has been gathered for a limited number of versions. Due to the presentation of the measure online, a complete discussion of the standardization process, reliability, and validity is lacking. Abstracts are presented to provide summaries of validity data, however, these brief descriptions do not allow for a thorough presentation of the data. Without this information, researchers and clinicians may have a difficult time deciding if the SDQ can serve their purposes. On closer examination, the articles that are referenced do have some initial support for both reliability and validity.

Authors: Robert Goodman.

Publication Year: 2000.

Source: www.youthinmind.uklinux.net

Fee: No.

STUDENT ADJUSTMENT INVENTORY

Reviewed by: Aaron Clendenin & Mary Lou Kelley

Purpose

To assess emotional and social problems in adolescents and young adults.

Population

Upper elementary, middle and high school, and beginning college students.

Description

The Student Adjustment Inventory (SAI) is a 78-item questionnaire that assesses problems in the following areas: (1) self-competency/self-esteem, (2) group interaction and social processes, (3) self-discipline, (4) communication skills, (5) energy/effort, (6) learning/studying, and (7) attitudes toward the learning environment. The SAI's stated purpose is to help students better understand personal functioning in the aforementioned areas.

Administration

The SAI is administered via traditional paper-and-pencil format or IBM-compatible personal computer. It is unclear how long this process is expected to take.

Scoring

The measure may be mailed in or computer-scored, depending on the method of administration. A profile report of problem areas is obtained from these two outlets.

Psychometric Properties

Norms: The SAI was normed on 781 males and 691 females. The demographic characteristics of this sample were unclear.

Reliability: Estimates of internal consistency are above .80 with an average coefficient of approximately .84 for males and females.

Validity: The SAI correlates with GPA, reading comprehension, and several aspects of personality.

Clinical Utility

Adequate. The SAI may be a valuable source of information for the clinician regarding target behaviors.

Strengths/Limitations

The SAI appears to be easy to administer. It offers a classroom-based look at self-efficacy and corollary behaviors. The manual has an appendix that is intended as an aid to test interpretation. The standardization sample, however, is not representative of national or regional characteristics and limits the measure's value.

Author: James R. Barclay, Ph.D.

Publication Year: 1989.

Source: MetriTech, Inc. 111 North Market St., Champaign, IL 61820, (800) 747-4868, fax: (217) 3985798.

Fee: Yes.

STUDENT SELF-CONCEPT SCALE

Reviewed by: Sara E. Sytsma & Mary Lou Kelley

Purpose

To measure self-concept and related psychological constructs. The Student Self-Concept Scale (SSCS) is designed for use as a screening instrument or pre-referral assessment of behavior and/or emotional problems, or as a follow-up measure of changes in self-concept resulting from special education placement or related services.

Population

There are separate forms available for children in grades 3 to 6 and for adolescents in grades 7 to 12, and items are written at approximately the third grade reading level.

Description

The Student Self-Concept Scale (SSCS) is a 72-item self-report measure of self-concept and related constructs. The SSCS measures self-concept in three content domains: Self-Image, Academic, and Social. The Self-Image domain taps students' perceptions of self-esteem, such as culturally valued behaviors (e.g., athletic ability) or personal attributes (e.g., physical attractiveness). The Academic domain assesses self-efficacy, or confidence in students' ability to perform behaviors related to academic success. The Social domain measures confidence in students' ability to interact socially.

The SSCS is rated in three dimensions: Self-Confidence, Importance, and Outcome Confidence. The first 50 items are rated in terms of Self-Confidence and Importance. The Self-Confidence scale is a measure of self-efficacy or self-esteem, measuring confidence in ones ability to perform certain behaviors or to have culturally valued attributes. On the Importance scale, children and adolescents report the subjective value of each behavior or attribute. The next 15 items measure Outcome Confidence, or the student's confidence that a certain behavior or attribute will result in specific outcomes. The final 7 items comprise the Lie scale, designed to detect highly socially desirable response sets or "faking good". All scales consist of Likert-style ratings ranging from 0 to 2.

Raw subscale scores are calculated for the three main content domains (i.e., Self-Image, Academic, and Social) across the three main rating dimensions described above, and composite scores are calculated for the Self-Confidence and Outcome Confidence ratings. Raw scores can be converted to standard scores, percentile ranks, and descriptive behavior levels for norm-referenced interpretation.

The technical manual is clearly written and thorough, detailing test rationale, administration and scoring procedures, interpretation and recommended intervention strategies, as well as development and standardization of the scale. A unique feature of the SSCS is the attempt to link assessment results with intervention strategies. The manual provides case studies and sample interventions as well as a brief conceptual framework for the design and implementation of specific intervention methods designed to modify behaviors associated with poor self-concept, greatly enhancing the utility of the instrument.

Administration

The SSCS has been developed for use with children and adolescents in grades 3 to 12 from a variety of ethnic and socioeconomic backgrounds. The SSCS can be administered to students individually, in small groups, or in classroom settings, and can be completed in 20 to 30 minutes.

Scoring

The multilayered, perforated, carbonless protocol can be hand scored in about 5 minutes and plotted according to gender norms using profiles printed inside the protocol.

Psychometric Properties

Norms: The SSCS was normed concurrently with the Social Skills Rating System (SSRS, Gresham & Elliott, 1990) on 3586 elementary and secondary school students from 19 states. Attempts were made to approximate the national distribution with respect to gender, race/ethnicity, geographic region and community size. Special efforts were made to ensure adequate sampling of students with disabilities. Therefore, the SSCS normative sample slightly over-represented children with learning disabilities and behavior disorders. In addition, the SSCS sample slightly over-represented blacks and whites while slightly under-representing Hispanics and other ethnic groups.

Reliability: The SSCS was found to have very good internal consistency, and generally adequate test-retest reliability after a four-week interval. Not surprisingly, secondary students generally had more stable coefficients than elementary students, and composite ratings were more stable than individual subscale ratings. Although Outcome Confidence Subscale ratings showed poor to fair stability across age levels.

Validity: Several indices of validity were reported and found to be adequate. Social, content, criterion-related, and construct validity were described in detail and supported the utility of the SSCS.

Clinical Utility

High. The utility of the SSCS as a screening device for use in the schools is greatly enhanced by its treatment validity. The SSCS can be used in the planning, implementation, and evaluation of treatments for improving self-confidence.

Strengths/Limitations

The SSCS has been found to have adequate psychometric properties, is easy to administer and score, and can be used directly for intervention planning and treatment outcome evaluation.

Authors: Frank M. Gresham, Ph.D., Stephen N. Elliott, Ph.D., & Sally E. Evans-Fernandez, M. A.

Publication Year: 1993.

Source: American Guidance Service, Inc., 4201 Woodland Road, Circle Pines, MN 55014-1796. In the U.S., call 1-800-328-2560. In Canada, call 1-800-263-3558.

Fee: Yes.

ADDITIONAL INFORMATION/REFERENCE

Gresham, F. M., Elliott, S. N., & Evans-Fernandez, S. E. (1993). *Student Self-Concept Scale Manual.* Circle Pines, MN: American Guidance Service, Inc.

SYSTEMATIC SCREENING FOR BEHAVIOR DISORDERS

Reviewed by: Gary Duhon and George H. Noell

Purpose

To screen and identify elementary-aged students who are at risk for school dropout and behavior disorders. The instrument examines both externalizing and internalizing behavior problems and provides links to treatment options.

Population

The Systematic Screening for Behavior Disorders is intended for use with elementary school aged children (grades kindergarten to 6) enrolled in general education. The instrument is appropriate for the assessment of children who are exhibiting internalizing and/or externalizing behavior problems.

Description

The Systematic Screening for Behavior Disorders is a three-stage, multiple-gated screening system for the identification of students with severe behavior disorders. Students are assessed for internalizing and externalizing behavior problems through the use of rankings, ratings, and observations.

In Stage I students are ranked based on the teachers perception of which students most exemplify either internalizing or externalizing behaviors with the top three within each group being assessed in Stage II. In this stage the students are rated on a Critical Events Index and a Combined Frequency Index for Adaptive and Maladaptive behavior. These scores are compared to normative standards to determine if Stage III assessment is warranted. In the final stage direct observations are conducted by someone other than the teacher during classroom and recess activities with at least two observations in each setting recommended. The classroom observations are completed in order to provide a direct measure of the student's behavior in relation to what is expected in this academic setting and to the teacher's behavioral expectations. The observation during recess is completed to provide a measure of the student's social adjustment and interaction with peers in a less structured environment. Depending on the outcome of the completed SSBD specific recommendations for interventions based on either internalizing or externalizing are offered.

Administration

Stage I—approximately 30–45 minutes by the classroom teacher.
Stage II—approximately 30–45 minutes by the classroom teacher.
Stage III—approximately 60 minutes by the trained observer.

Scoring

Stage I data consist of the classroom teacher's rankings of the extent to which students exhibit internalizing and externalizing behavior concerns. As a result no additional scoring is necessary.

Stage II assessment returns scores for the Critical Events Index, the Adaptive Score of the Combined Frequency Index, and the Maladaptive Score of the Combined Frequency Index. The reporting form is clearly and simply structured to permit the instrument to scored very quickly (i.e., less than 5 minutes). The results Stage II screening are then compared to decision guides that were developed based on the standardization sample. The procedure is multidimensional in the sense that it incorporates data from all three scales used with in Stage II, but is straight forward and clearly explained in the manual.

Scoring for Stage III of the assessment consists of summarizing the data from the standardized observational protocol and comparing it to standards developed based on the standardization sample. Scoring consists of simple arithmetic operations to calculate percentage of time academically engaged, social engagement, participation, parallel play, alone, social interaction, negative interactions, and positive interactions. These summaries are then compared to decision making criteria developed through the normative sample and the associated studies. Decision-making is focused on determining whether or not the student's behavior problems are sufficiently severe that the warrant further investigation by a child study team or equivalent organization within the school. Child study teams are typically charged with the responsibility to determine whether or not a child is protected by and entitled to services under the Individuals with Disabilities Education Act.

Psychometric Properties

Norms: There was no standardization data for Stage I of the SSBD, however, Stage II standardization was conducted on 4463 students and Stage III was conducted on 1275 students. Students were drawn from eight states and 18 school districts across the United States with a slight over representation of students from the western states.

Reliability: Test-retest reliability of Stage I and Stage II were conducted. Stage I internalizing and externalizing were low at .72 and .79 respectively, but Stage II test-retest reliability was higher for Critical Events Index at .81 and Maladaptive Behavior Rating Scale at .87. Internal consistency was calculated for the Combined Frequency Index for Adaptive and Maladaptive behaviors. The coefficient alphas averaged .86 on the adaptive scale and .84 on the maladaptive scale. Interrater reliability for Stage III were consistently within .80 to .90 range.

Validity: The authors devote a large section of the technical manual for reporting studies that have been conducted on the validity of the SSBD. Overall adequate levels of discriminate, criterion related, predictive, and concurrent validity are supported by these studies.

Clinical Utility

High. The SSBD shows evidence of sound psychometrics adequate for the purpose of screening. The authors have taken care to design the training manual so that it should be readily accessible for clinicians and educators. The SSBD provides an empirically based means for identifying students with behavior disorders.

Strengths/Limitations

The SSBD should help reduce the subjectivity that typically underlies this type of assessment. Additionally, the SSBD provides some intervention suggestions and sources for additional information that are linked to the assessment's outcome. The assessment's limitations lie in its moderate levels of reliability and validity, but overall are sufficient for the purpose the test was designed.

Authors: Hill M. Walker, Ph.D. and Herbert H. Severson, Ph.D.

Publication Year: 1988.

Source: Sopris West, 1140 Boston Avenue, Longmont, Colorado 80501, (303) 651-2829).

Fee: No.

ADDITIONAL INFORMATION/REFERENCE

Kelley, M. L. (1998). Systematic Screening for Behavior Disorders. In J. C. Impara & B. S. Plake (Eds), *Mental Measurement Yearbook (13)* (pp. 993–996). Lincoln: University of Nebraska Press.

TEACHER–CHILD RATING SCALE 2.1

Reviewed By: Shannon Self-Brown & Mary Lou Kelley

Purpose

To assess children's school problem behaviors and competencies.

Population

Children in grades prekindergarten through eighth.

Description

The Teacher-Child Rating Scale 2.1 (T-CRS 2.1) is a revised version of the T-CRS 1.0. The T-CRS 2.1 consists of 32 items assessing four primary and eight secondary domains of children's adjustment. The four primary domains include: Task Orientation; Behavior Control; Assertiveness; and Peer Social Skills. The Task Orientation domain assesses a child's ability to focus on school related tasks. Items include statements such as "Functions well even with distractions" and "Has poor concentration, limited attention span". The Behavior Control domain asses a child's skill in tolerating and adapting to his/her own limitations or limits imposed by the school environment. Examples of Behavior Control items include "Copes well with failure" and "Disruptive in class". The Assertiveness domain was developed to measure a child's interpersonal functioning and confidence in dealing with peers. Items developed to assess assertiveness include "Defends own views under group pressure" and "Withdrawn". The Peer Social Skills domain measures the child's likeability and popularity among peers and includes items such as "Well liked by peers" and "Has trouble interacting with peers". Each of the primary domains can be divided into two, four-item secondary scales which measures either positive, competency behaviors or behavior problems.

The T-CRS 2.1 should be completed by the child's teacher or another professional who has had four to six weeks of ongoing contact with the child at school. School personnel rate each item according to how much he/she agrees that the item describes the child. All items are rated on a five-point Likert scale, ranging from 1 = Strongly Disagree to 5 = Strongly Agree.

Administration

The T-CRS 2.1 takes no more than five minutes to complete.

Scoring

Explicit instructions for hand scoring are provided in the T-CRS 2.1 manual. Total raw scores for each domain scale can be converted to percentile ranks, with higher percentile scores indicating greater child well-being and lower percentile scores suggesting higher incidence of problem behaviors. The T-CRS 2.1 also can be computer scored by the Children's Institute.

Psychometric Properties

Norms: The normative sample consisted of 700 children (391 boys, 309 girls) from 21 states. The children ranged from prekindergarten to the eighth grade with most coming from first through 6th grade. Normative tables were established according to gender (male, female) and locale (Urban, Suburban, Rural).

Reliability: Two types of reliability were assessed for the T-CRS 2.1; Internal Consistency and Stability. Internal Consistency coefficient alphas for the four domain scales were .87 or higher. For the secondary scales, coefficient alphas were .75 or higher. Stability of the T-CRS 2.1 was assessed using pre- and post-test scores taken approximately 7 months apart. Correlations for all domains were significant at the $p < .001$ level.

Validity: Content validity for the T-CRS 2.1 was established concurrently with the revision and addition of items. During the revision, feedback on items was obtained from teachers, psychologists, measurement specialists, and other users of this instrument to ensure that items covered the content of interest. To examine the T-CRS 2.1 construct validity, Confirmatory Factor Analysis was used to test the replicability of the 32-item, four-scale structure. Goodness-of-fit statistics supported the four-scale structure with item loadings for each scale at .69 or higher. Additional support for the validity of the T-CRS 2.1 was obtained by comparing children's scores on this measure to scores on the Child Behavior Checklist-Teacher Report Form. High correlations were found on scales purporting to measure the same constructs, with low correlations among scales measuring different constricts. Criterion-related validity was assessed by comparing demographically matched children from an "at risk" or random sample. The two groups differed significantly on all T-CRS 2.1 scale scores with the random sample scoring higher on all scales. Taken as a whole, results from the validity analyses offer evidence of the validity of the T-CRS 2.1.

Clinical Utility

Limited. The authors state that the T-CRS 2.1 can be used as a diagnostic tool. However, the subscales do not correspond with DSM diagnoses. Additionally, this scale provides no information about the child's behavior outside of the school environment. For these reasons, the T-CRS 2.1 may best be used as a screening tool for school behavior. Other assessment methods should be used to attain a comprehensive evaluation of the child's overall functioning.

Strengths/Limitations

The T-CRS is a standardized tool that can be completed in 3–5 minutes. It identifies a child's classroom and peer related strengths and weaknesses as compared to the sample population, as well as within him/herself. Comparisons among the scales can help to identify intervention goals. This measure can be administered over time to assess the child's progress for target behaviors. One major limitation of the T-CRS 2.1 is that the technical manual does not provide cut-off scores or any information regarding what subscale scores should be considered normal versus clinically significant for a child.

Authors: Pamela Perkins & A. Dirk Hightower.

Publication Year: 2001 (most recent version).

Source: Children's Institute, Inc.

Fee: Yes.

TENNESSEE SELF-CONCEPT SCALE: SECOND EDITION ADULT FORM, CHILD FORM

Reviewed by: Rebecca Currier

Purpose

To assist clinicians in measuring multidimensional self-concept.

Population

Individuals ages 7 to 90.

Description

The TSCS: 2 is comprised of two Summary Scales, Total Self-Concept and Conflict, and six Self-Concept Scales: Physical, Moral, Personal, Family, Social, and Academic/Work. It contains four Validity Scores: Inconsistent Responding, Self-Criticism, Faking Good, and Response Distribution and three Supplementary Scores: Identity, Satisfaction, and Behavior. The TSCS: 2 has both a Child (ages 7–14; 76 items) and Adult (ages 13–90; 82 items) Form. A short form of the scale can also be administered and consists of the first 20 items of each form. Items are self-descriptive statements that an individual rates as "Always False", "Mostly False", "Partly False and Partly True", "Mostly True", or "Always True". Responses are weighted from 1–5 points.

The instrument was developed to consolidate materials that had not been available together previously. Items were derived from other self-concept measures and written self-descriptions of patients and nonpatients. Items were then classified by seven clinical psychologists using an intuitive procedure that has been found useful in personality inventory construction according to the authors. For the TSCS: 2 the measure was shortened, the Child Form created, and a new scale, the Academic/Work Self-Concept scale, was added. The retained scores are psychometrically equivalent to the earlier edition.

Administration

The TSCS: 2 can be administered individually or in groups and can be completed in 10–20 minutes.

Scoring

The TSCS: 2 can be scored by hand or computer and yields the two Summary Scores, six Self-Concept Scales, four Validity Scores, and three Supplementary Scores. Items for each scale are scored from 1–5. The measure also contains critical items, which are items for which certain responses should be investigated to determine if immediate intervention is necessary.

Psychometric Properties

Norms: The Adult Form was normed on 1944 ages 13–90. The Child Form was normed on 1784 ages 7–14. Both forms were standardized on ethnically diverse individuals from a wide range of settings throughout the U.S.

Reliability: Internal consistency was adequate to good and for the Adult Form ranged from .73 to .95. For the Child Form internal consistencies ranged from .66 to .92. Test-retest reliability ranged from .47 to .82 on the Adult Form and .55 to .83 for the Child Form.

Validity: Due to the strong equivalence of the 1988 edition of the TSCS and the TSCS: 2 much of the validity data supportive of the second edition is based on previous data collected. The TSCS has been found to be valid when distinguishing among groups as well as when it is compared to other accepted instruments. In addition, outcome studies have found changes in TSCS scores in the expected direction following intervention. The TSCS: 2 has been found to preserve this validity.

Clinical Utility

High. The TSCS: 2 manual contains descriptions of interventions that may be useful in targeting issues related to poor self-concept. This may provide helpful information to clinicians working with such individuals.

Strengths/Limitations

The TSCS: 2 appears to be a reliable and valid instrument to measure self-concept. Another strength of the TSCS: 2 is the low reading level which would allow the measure to be utilized with a wide variety of educational levels. Scoring the measure by hand appears to be time consuming and the authors do not include the cost of the various computerized scoring options.

Authors: W.H. Fitts and W.L. Warren.

Publication Year: 1996.

Source: Western Psychological Services, 12031 Wilshire Blvd., Los Angeles, California 90025-1251.

Fee: Yes.

TRANSITION BEHAVIOR SCALE

Reviewed by: Shannon Self-Brown & Mary Lou Kelley

Purpose

To assess junior and senior high school students' interpersonal skills and behaviors in order to provide a measure of readiness for transition to employment and independent living.

Population

High school students in grades 11th and 12th.

Description

The Transition Behavior Scale (TBS) includes 62 items representing behavioral characteristics which are rated as either 0 = does not perform the behavior, 1 = performs the behavior inconsistently, or 2 = performs the behavior consistently. It is recommended that the TBS be completed by at least three persons (teachers/supervisors) for each student in order to provide the most objective representation of student behavior. The TBS contains three subscales: Work Related, Interpersonal Relations, Social/Community Expectations. Ratings on these subscales can be used to identify weaknesses, problem areas, or deficits in the behavior necessary for success in the employment and independent living of students. Identification of such problems provides information for areas where the students need additional training, preparation, and support in order to reduce the likelihood of failure in employment and independent living. A Transition Behavior Scale IEP and Intervention manual is provided with the TBS specimen kit and contains detailed interventions specifically keyed to the TBS items.

Administration

Approximately 15 minutes by a teacher or employer.

Scoring

The scores for each subscale on the TBS are calculated by summing the ratings given to each item in the subscale. Using tables provided in the technical manual, the raw scores can be transformed into percentile ranks and standard scores. The total score of the TBS is calculated by summing the standard scores on the subscales which is then transformed to a percentile rank. From these scores, areas of intervention are identified.

Psychometric Properties

The TBS was normed on 2665 students from 23 states representing the four major geographical regions of the United States. The sample approximately represents the U.S. population in terms of sex, race, urban-rural residence, and parental occupation. Separate standardizations were developed for males and females based on significant differences in scores between the sexes on all three subscales and the total scale.

Reliability: Internal consistency between the subscales range between .84 and .87. Test-retest reliability ranged from .87 to .92 for the subscales and was .89 for the total scale. Inter-rater reliability was assessed using two different groups. The first group consisted of 311 students who were rated by two educators with the scale. Inter-rater reliability for this group was .90. The second group was made up of 200 students who were rated by both educators and employers/supervisors. The inter-rater reliability for this group was .79 indicating a strong degree of reliability across environments.

Validity: To assure the integrity of the content validity of the TBS, an item pool was developed based on a literature review and the input from diagnosticians, guidance counselors, educational personnel, and employers. Sixty-two items were chosen as the most relevant indicators of student behavior likely to predict success in employment and societal transition. Criterion validity for the TBS was established by correlating scores with the Behavior Evaluation Scale (McCarney, Leigh, Conrbleet, 1983) which is a commonly used measure of behavior problems of students in school systems in the nation. Significant correlations were found between all three subscales on these two measures. Construct validity was evidenced by the significantly lower scores demonstrated by students identified as having behavior/adjustment problems compared to students selected at random from a normative sample.

Clinical Utility

High. The TBS is a behaviorally worded scale which is unique in that it can be used to rate adolescents in both the school and work environment. The TBS can be especially useful to students who have had behavioral difficulties in the school environment by identifying their problem areas and providing interventions that can assist them in becoming successful in the adult realm.

Strength/Limitations

The TBS can be completed by a variety of informants in various environments. An intervention book that corresponds to the items of the scale is a helpful addition to this scale. The TBS is limited in some aspects by the technical manual. Scoring guidelines provided are confusing and incomplete and some other areas of the manual are poorly written.

Author: Stephen B. McCarney.

Publication Year: 1989.

Source: Hawthorne Educational Services, Inc., 800 Gray Oak Drive Columbia, Missouri 65201, 800-542-1673.

Fee: Yes.

ADDITIONAL INFORMATION/REFERENCES

Blackwell, M. (1995). Review of the Transition Behavior Scale. In: *Mental Measurement Yearbook: Volume 12*, pp. 1073–1074.

Herman, D. O. (1995). Review of the Transition Behavior Scale. In: *Mental Measurement Yearbook: Volume 12*, pp. 1074–1075.

Appendix
Glossary

Sharon L. Foster and Arthur M. Nezu

Concurrent validity
The extent to which scores on a target measure can be used to predict an individual's score on a measure of performance collected at the same time as the target measure.

Construct validity
The extent to which scores on a measure enter into relationships in ways predicted by theory or by previous investigations. Examinations of construct validity address the meaning of scores on a measure, and are relevant to the issue of whether the instrument assesses what it purports to assess. Construct validity has several specific subtypes; other investigations that speak to construct validity, but do not fall into any of the specific subtypes, are generally called "investigations of construct validity."

Content validity
Whether the measure appropriately samples or represents the domain being assessed. Substantiation of content validity requires systematic, replicable development of the assessment device, often with formal review by clients or experts to ensure appropriate material is included and excluded.

Convergent validity
The extent to which scores on the target measure correlate with scores on measures of the same construct.

Criterion-related validity
The extent to which test scores can be used to predict an individual's performance on some important task or behavior. Examinations of criterion-related validity speak to the utility of scores on a measure rather than to their meaning. Often one ideally would like a perfect match between scores on that target measure and those on the criterion measure. There are two subtypes of criterion-related validity—concurrent validity and predictive validity.

Discriminant validity
The extent to which scores on a measure are unrelated to scores on measures assessing other, theoretically unrelated constructs.

Discriminative validity
The extent to which scores on a measure distinguish between groups known or suspected to differ on the construct assessed by the target measure.

Internal consistency

A form of reliability indicating the extent to which different item groupings produce consistent scores on a measure, usually measured by (Cronbach's) coefficient alpha or KR-20

Interrater reliability

The extent to which two individuals who rate (score, or observe) the same person (or stimulus material) score the person (person's behavior, or stimulus material) consistently; usually established by having two independent observers or raters evaluate the same stimulus material at approximately the same time.

Predictive validity

The extent to which scores on a target measure can be used to predict an individual's score on a measure of performance collected some time after the target measure (i.e., in the future).

Sensitivity

The level at which a measure accurately identifies individuals who have a given characteristic in question using a given criterion or cutoff score (e.g., the proportion of people with major depression who are correctly identified as depressed by their score on a given measure of depression).

Specificity

The degree to which a measure accurately identifies people who do *not* have a characteristic that is being measured (e.g., the proportion of people who do *not* have a diagnosis of major depression and who are correctly identified as *not* depressed by their score on a given measure of depression).

Test–retest reliability

The extent to which scores on a measure are consistent over a specified period of time, established by administering the same instrument on two separate occasions.

Treatment sensitivity

Whether the measure is sensitive to changes produced by treatment that have been documented or corroborated by other measures. Note that a measure can have good content and construct validity, but still not be sensitive to treatment effects.

Index